AQUAPAPIER schwimmt!
W0249100

Vorwort

Sind Sie auch von Schiffen und Booten fasziniert?

Als Kind eines Schiffers haben mich Wasser und Boote immer schon angezogen. Meine Eltern waren Kapitäne. Als Kind bin ich einfach mitgefahren. Es war eine wundervolle Zeit. Mit den Booten im Konvoi über das IJsselmeer, die Eisbrecher voraus, weil das Meer eisbedeckt war. Nachtfahrten, weil die Ladung unbedingt pünktlich ausgeliefert werden musste. Im Nebel war immer das Nebelhorn angeschaltet. Woher mein Vater immer wusste wohin er musste, bleibt mir bis heute ein Rätsel.
Als ich gefragt wurde, ein Origamibuch über Boote zu schreiben, musste ich schon lächeln: Ein Schifferkind macht ein Bootebuch. Das ist schon was Besonderes!
Das Hobby Origami begleitet mich schon viele Jahre. Ich habe viel aus einem Buch von Aart van Breda sowie von meinen Eltern und meiner Tante gelernt. In dem vorliegenden Bootebuch habe ich traditionelle Modelle, meine eigenen Modelle und Modelle von Mark Botilho und Paula Versnick , denen ich beiden herzlich danke, aufgenommen. Die einfachen Boote mit verschiedenen Schwierigkeitsgraden sind dabei nicht nur zum Spielen gedacht, sondern eignen sich auch für Segelwettstreite oder zur Beförderung von Lasten. Fahrende Boote, die mit AQUAPAPIER gefertigt wurden, weisen darüber hinaus noch eine Besonderheit auf. Die Boote werden bei der Verwendung von AQUAPAPIER wasserfest, unsinkbar und fallen nicht zusammen. Denkbar sind aber auch flache, nicht schwimmbare Boote etwa für Urlaubsgrüße oder andere Gelegenheiten.

Ich wünsche Ihnen viel Vergnügen beim Falten und „Action“ mit den Booten.

Jannie van Schuylenburg

Foreword

Are you fascinated of ships and boats?

I am a child of a shipman and I was attracted by water and boats throughout my childhood. My parents were captains. As a child I accompanied my parents on their ship. It was a wonderful time. With the boats in convoys over the Sea of IJssel, the ice-breaker ahead, whilst the sea was full of ice. Journeys during the night, because the loading had to be delivered punctually. In fog the nebula horn was turned on. It is a mystery for me how my father always knew where to go on the sea.
When I was asked to write an Origami book on boats, I almost had to smile: the child of a shipman makes a book on boats. That's something very special!
The hobby Origami accompanies me for years. I have learned a lot of a book by Aart van Breda as well as of my parents and my aunt. In the available book on boats I have chosen traditional models as well as own models and models by Mark Botilho and Paula Versnick (my sincere thanks to both). The simple boats with different degrees of difficulty are not meant only for playing but also for sail contests and transports of loads. Sailing boats made of AQUAPAPIER exhibit a characteristic. The boats made of AQUAPAPIER are water resistant, unsinkable and do not collapse. Also flat and not swimmable boats are conceivable i.e. for holiday greetings or other opportunities.

I wish you much fun with folding and “action” with the boats.

Jannie van Schuylenburg

Inhaltsverzeichnis Table of contents

Schwierigkeitsgrad — Level of difficulty

- einfach / very easy ★
- mittel / easy ★★
- intensiv / intermediate ★★★

Fröbelboote und Geschichte / Fröbel boats and history

Seite 8-9

Seite 10-11

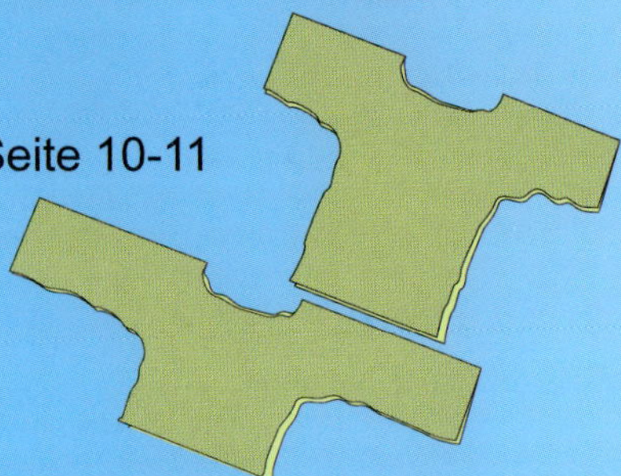

Freizeit Boote / Boats for leisure time

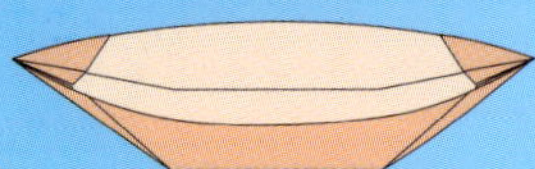

Seite 14

Seite 15-17

Seite 24-25

Freizeit Boote / Boats for leisure time

Seite 22

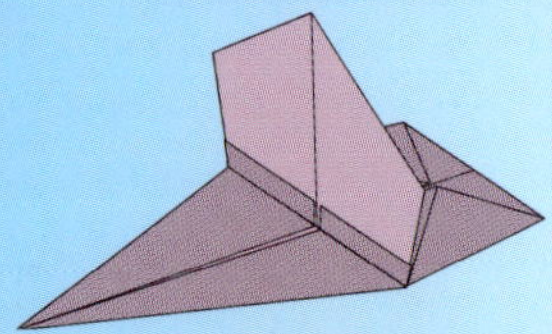

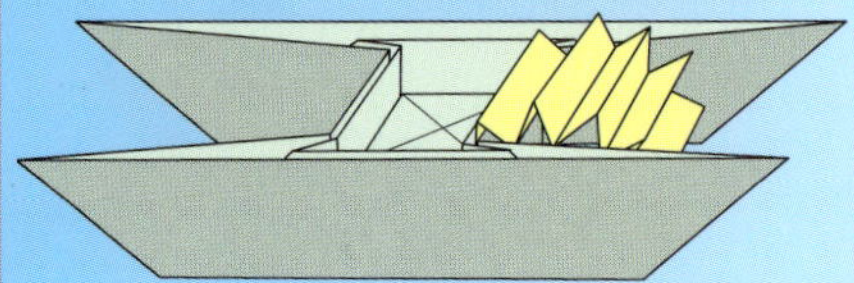

Seite 24-25

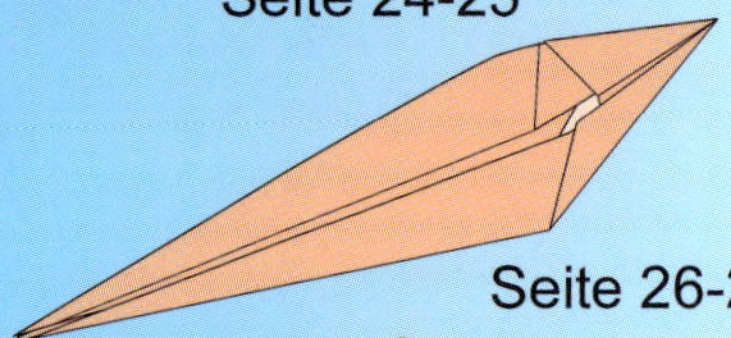

Seite 26-27

Seite 27

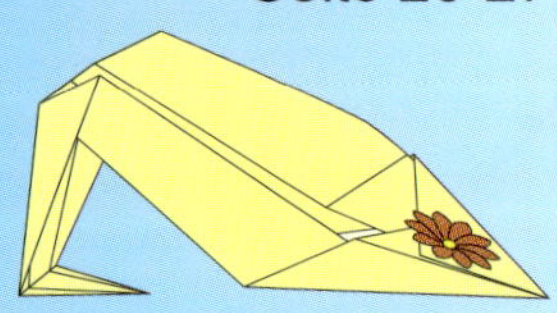

Seite 28

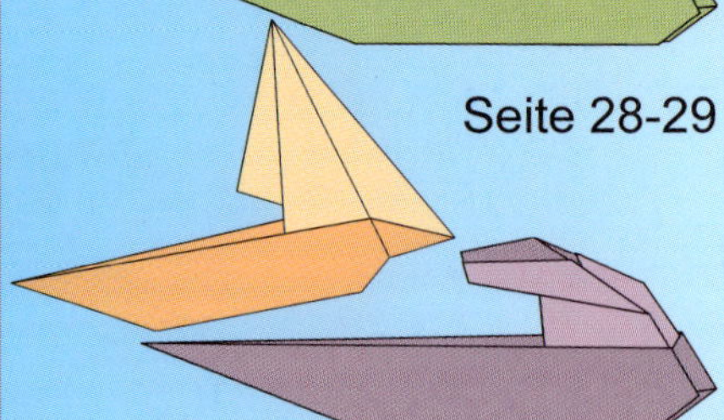

Seite 28-29

Jachten und Segelboote / Yachts and sailing boats

Seite 32-33

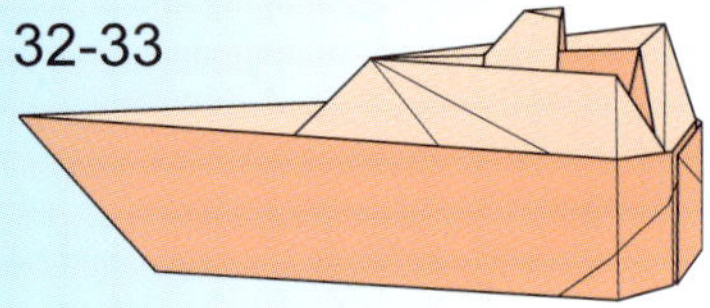

Seite 34-35

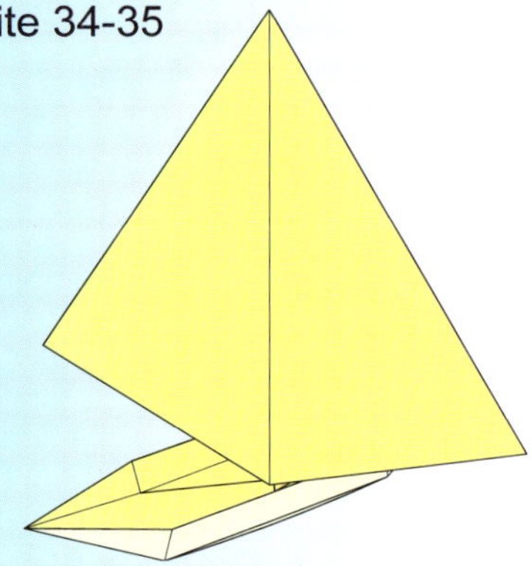

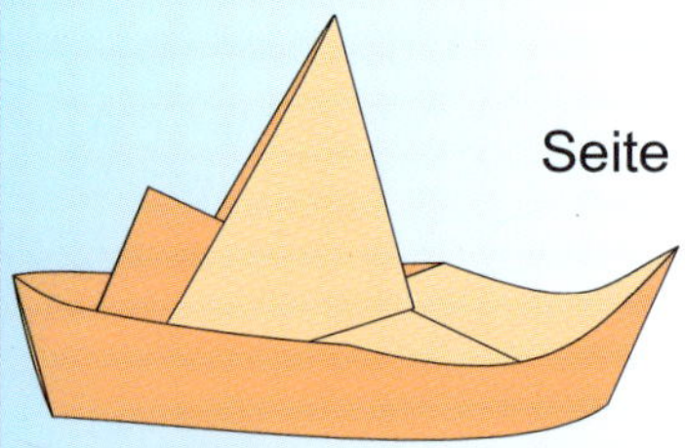

Seite 36-37

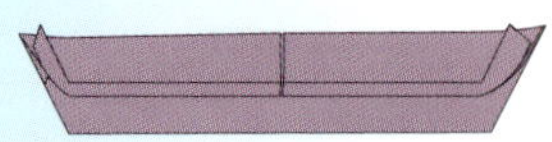

Seite 38

Historische Boote

Historical boats

Seite 40-41

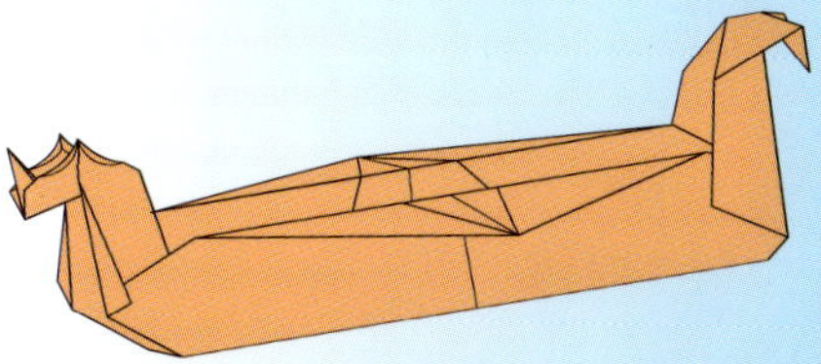

Seite 42-43

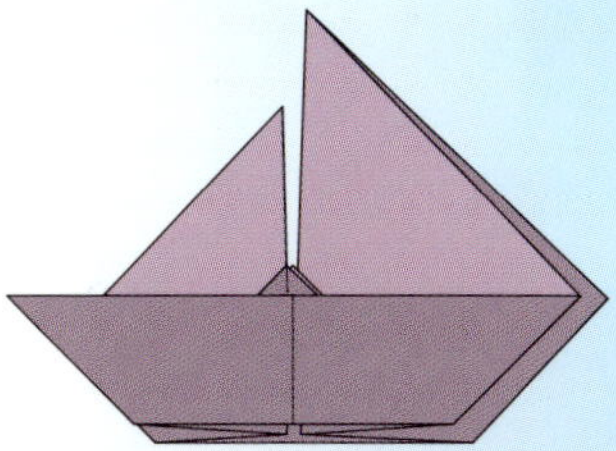

Seite 44

Seite 46-47

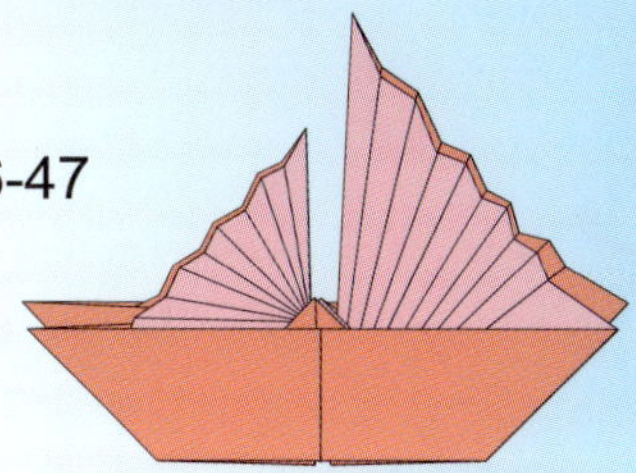

Hochsee-Schifffahrt

High navigation shipping

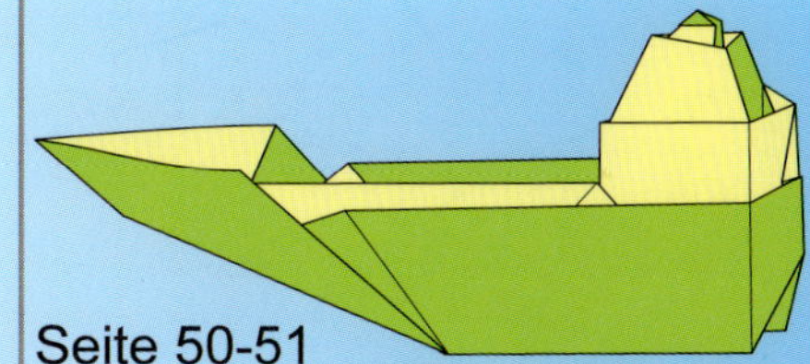

Seite 50-51

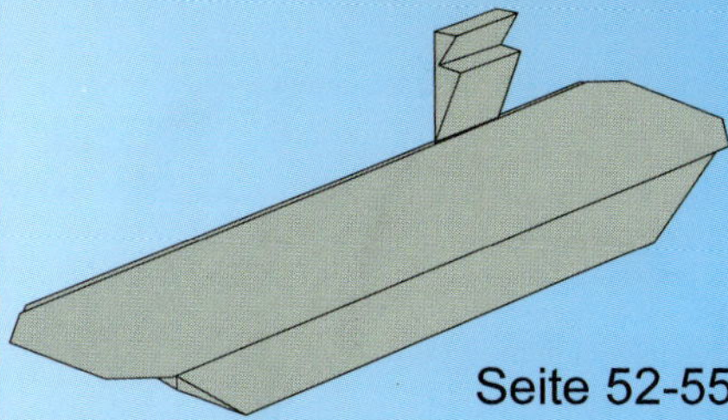

Seite 52-55

Seite 58-61

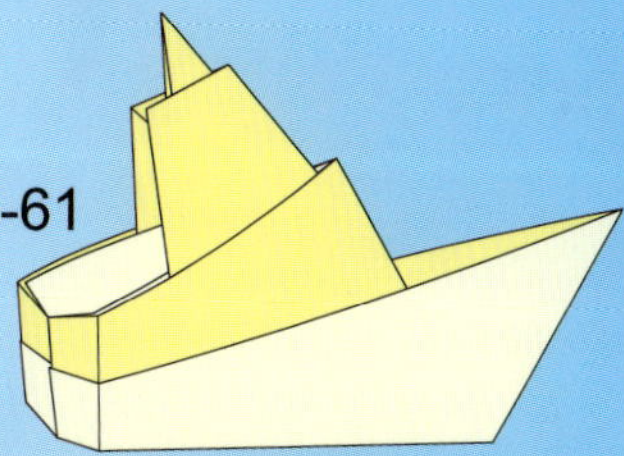

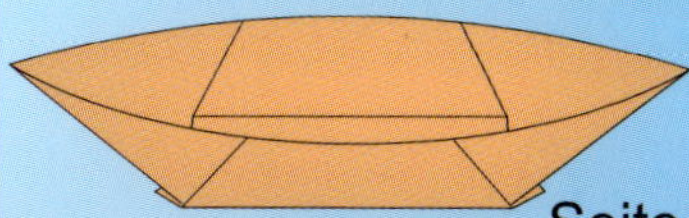

Seite 62-63

Seite 64-67

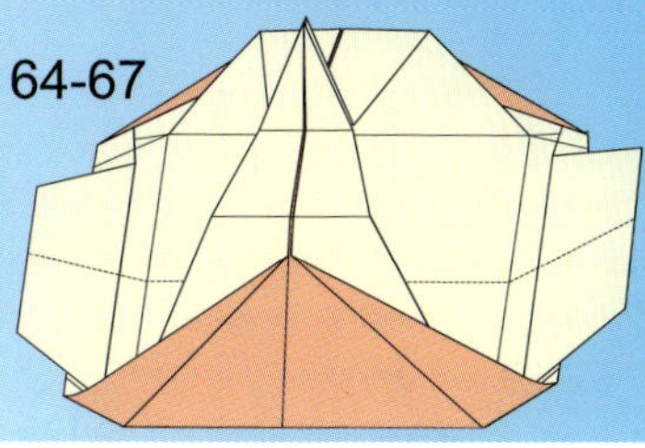

Zubehör

Accessories

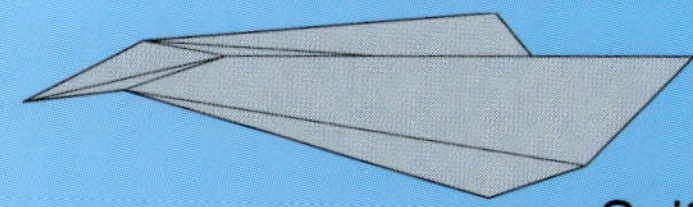

Seite 56

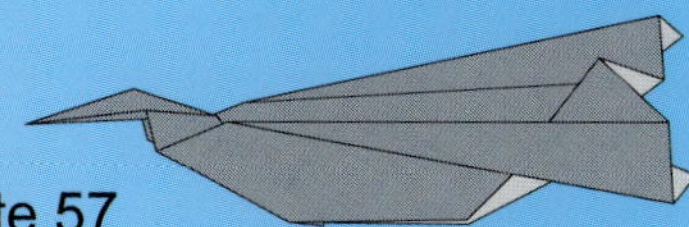

Seite 57

Urlaubsgrüße

Holiday greetings

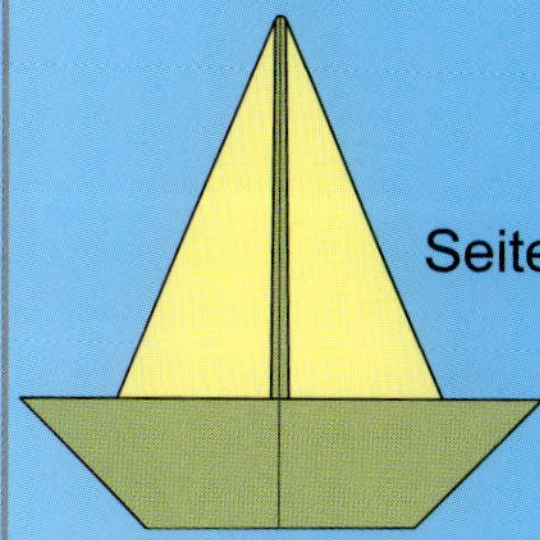

Seite 68

Seite 68

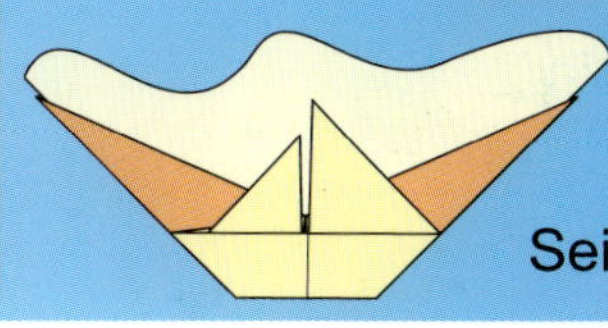

Seite 69

Die in diesem Buch abgebildeten Schiffe wurden, wegen der Schwimmfähigkeit, alle mit AQUAPAPIER hergestellt.
Boote und Schiffe können noch mit wasserfester Farbe bemalt werden.
Origamiarbeiten benötigen grundsätzlich kein Werkzeug.

Bei Faltungen, wo das Papier in mehreren Lagen liegt, ist es sehr angenehm mit einem Falzbein zu arbeiten.

All ships shown on this book are folded with AQUAPAPIER, because of the ability to swim. Boats and ships can be painted with water proofed color.

For Origami you fundamentally don‘t need any tools. If the paper lies in several layers, it is pleasant to work with a bonefolder.

Bonefolder

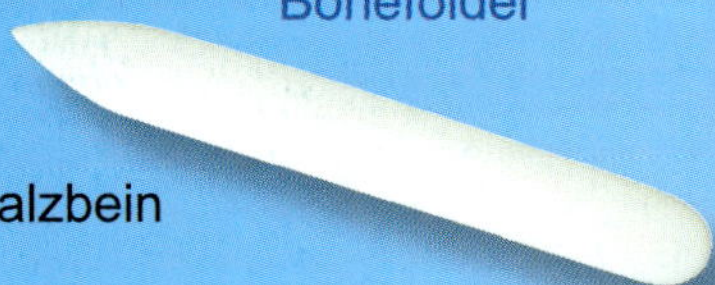

Falzbein

Origami Zeichnungen

Alle Zeichnungen sind mit Symbolen versehen. Aktuell wird immer die rote Linie gearbeitet. Zur besseren Darstellung von Vorder- und Rückseite wurden bei allen Zeichnungen verschiedene Farben verwendet, wie auch bei der Symbolerklärung. Gleichzeitig ist noch ausreichend Text angegeben worden, so dass das Gelingen der Arbeit auch gewährleistet ist.
Auf der Seite Nr.7 sind die internationalen Origami Zeichen abgebildet.

Origami charts

All charts have symbols. Actual you work the red line only. For a better representation of front and back side of the paper, we did use different colours for all charts, as you can see on this explanation of symbols. All charts have symbols and enough text, so that you will come safely to success.
The international Origami symbols are shown on page No 7.

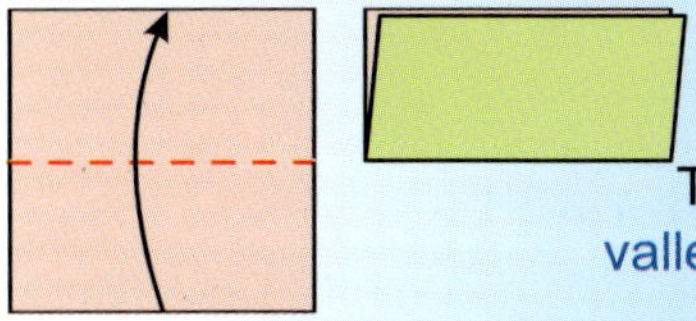

Talfalte
valley-fold

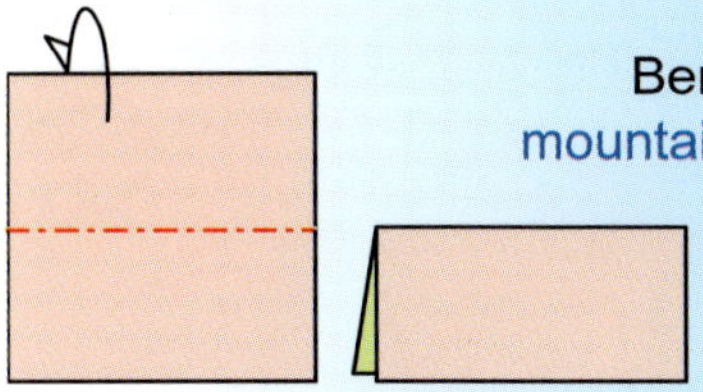

Bergfalte
mountain-fold

Falten, wieder öffnen.
Fold and open again.

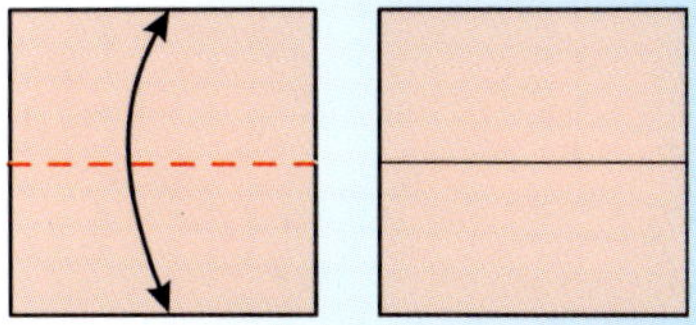

Zickzackfaltung
zigzag folding

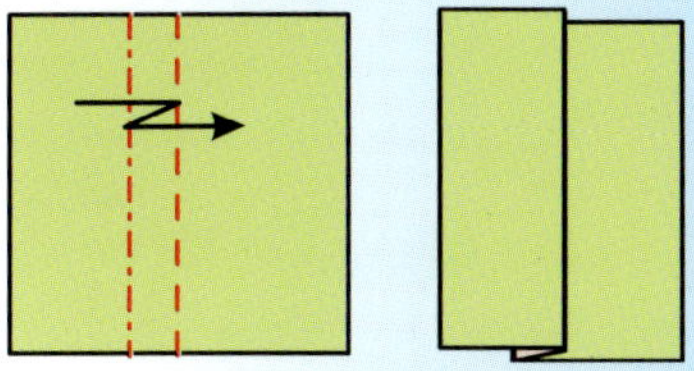

Gegenbruch nach innen
inside reverse fold

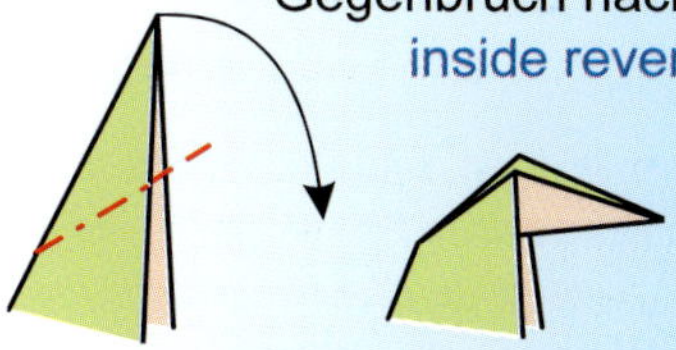

Gegenbruch nach außen
outside reverse fold

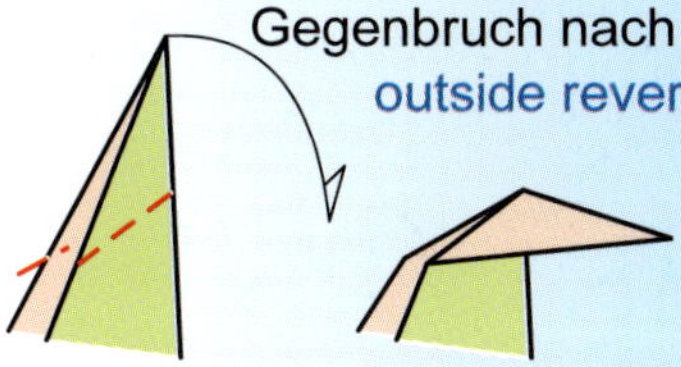

Mitte versenken
Sink in the middle

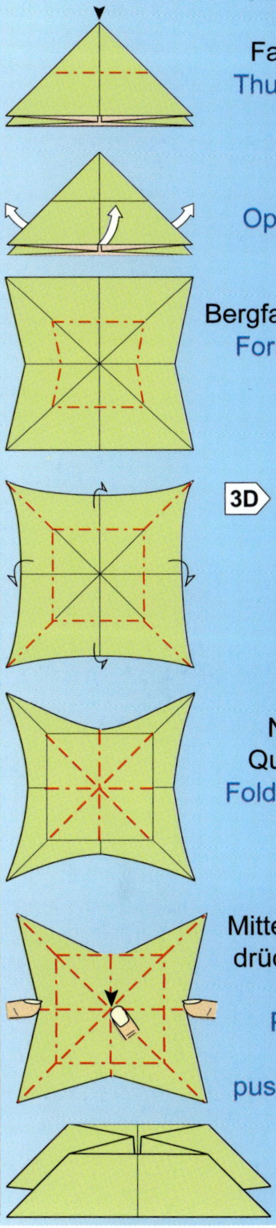

So sieht der Faltschritt aus.
Thus the folding step looks.

Nach außen öffnen.
Open outwards

Bergfalten formen.
Form mountain-folds

Seiten nach unten falten.
Fold sides upwards.

Nur Linien im Quadrat falten.
Fold only lines in the square.

Mitte nach unten drücken, seitlich eindrücken.
Press middle downwards, push in laterally.

Fertig.
Ready.

Symbole Symbols

Gefaltetes Teil nach außen ziehen, siehe nächste Zeichnung.
Pull the folded part outwards, see next chart.

Um 90° drehen.
Turn model 90 degrees around.

Arbeitsschritte auf der Rückseite wiederholen.
Repeat working steps on the back.

Rückseite nach oben legen.
Put back upwards.

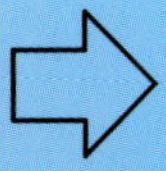

Ansicht der Zeichnung wurde vergrößert.
The sight of the chart has been enlarged.

Eindrücken und glatt falten.
Push in and fold flatly.

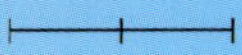

Papier in gleiche Teile einteilen.
Divide paper into equal parts.

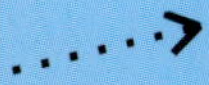

Papier nach innen falten.
Fold paper inwards.

3D

Nächste Zeichnung 3D.
Next chart 3D.

Einschneiden oder abschneiden.
Cut in or cut off.

Aufblasen.
Inflate.

Fröbel-Boote

Fröbel-boats

Modell bekannt seit 1734

3 Variationsmöglichkeiten

Model known since 1734

3 variation options

MATERIAL

1 Bogen 20x20 cm AQUAPAPIER

1 sheet 20x20 cm AQUAPAPIER

1. Papier an der senkrechten Linie durchschneiden.
Cut paper on vertical line.

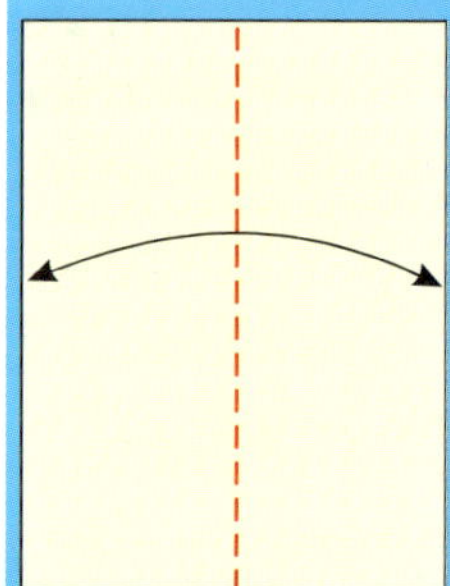

2. Senkrechte Linie falten, wieder öffnen.
Fold vertical line and open again.

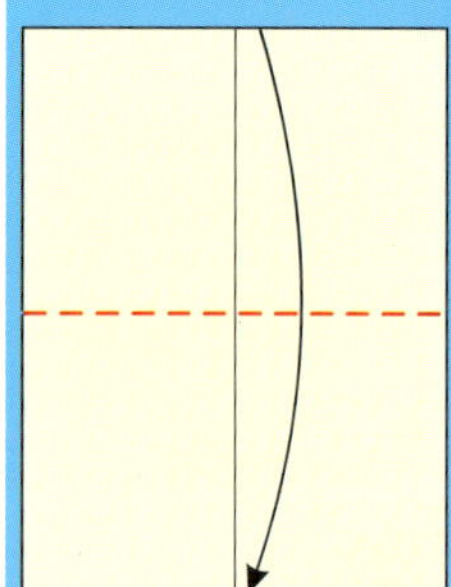

3. Waagerechte Linie falten, liegen lassen.
Fold horizontal line and leave.

4. Schräge Linien falten, siehe Pfeile, liegen lassen.
Fold diagonal line, see arrows, and leave.

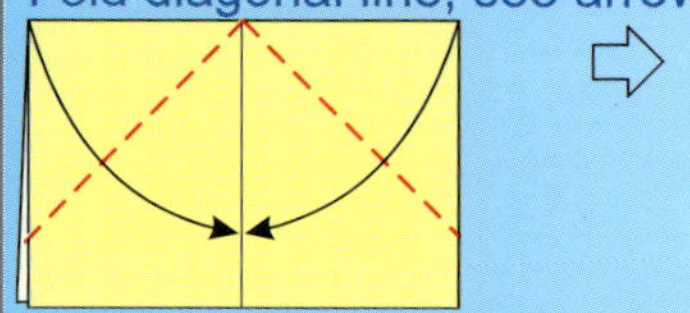

5. Waagerechte Linie falten, liegen lassen. Auf der Rückseite wiederholen.
Fold horizontal line and leave. Repeat on the back.

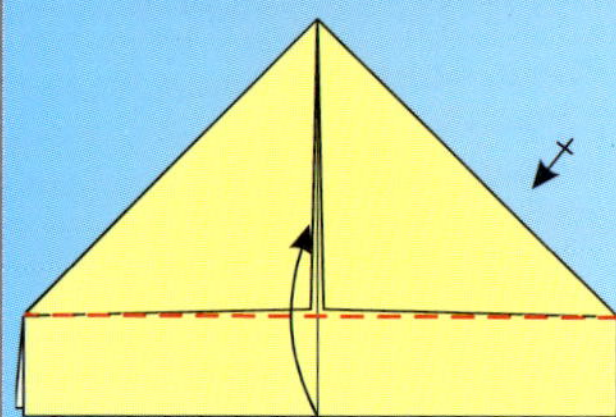

6. Fertiges Hut Modell.
Finished hat model.

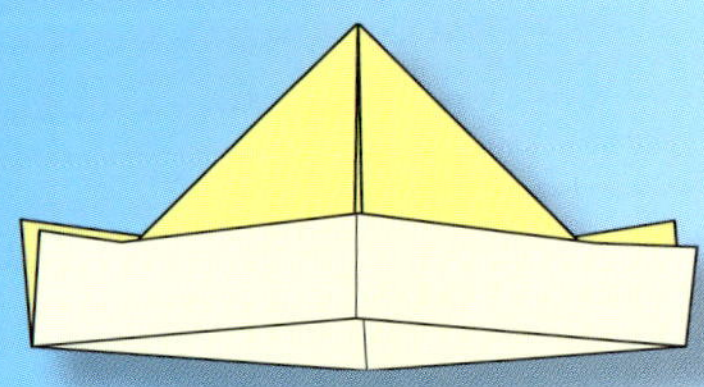

7. Gefaltetes Teil nach außen ziehen, siehe nächste Zeichnung.
Pull the folded part outwards, see next chart.

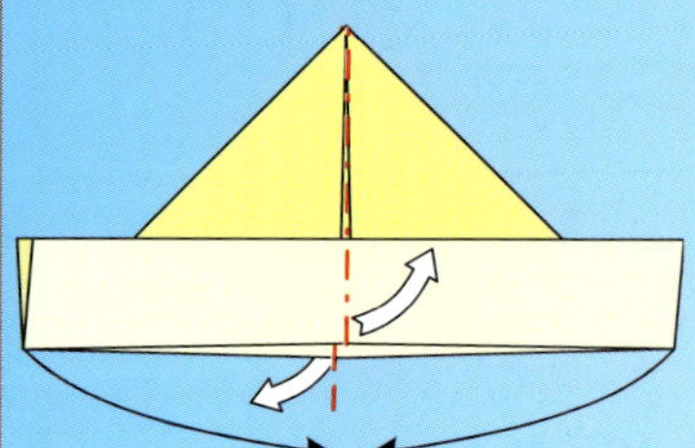

8. Waagerechte Linie falten, liegen lassen. Auf der Rückseite wiederholen.
Fold horizontal line and leave. Reapat the back.

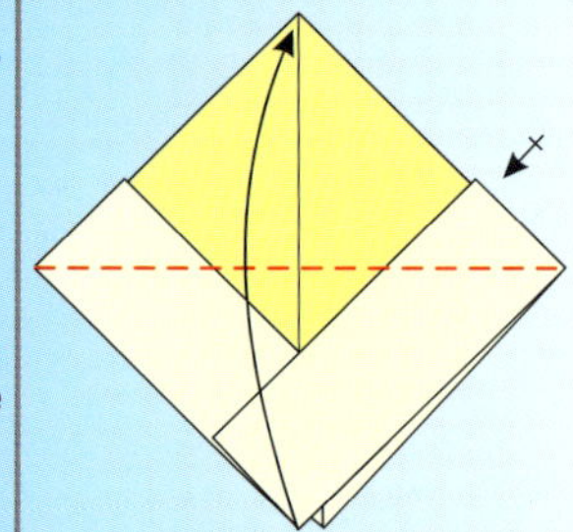

9. Gefaltetes Teil nach außen ziehen, siehe nächste Zeichnung.
Pull the folded part outwards, see next chart.

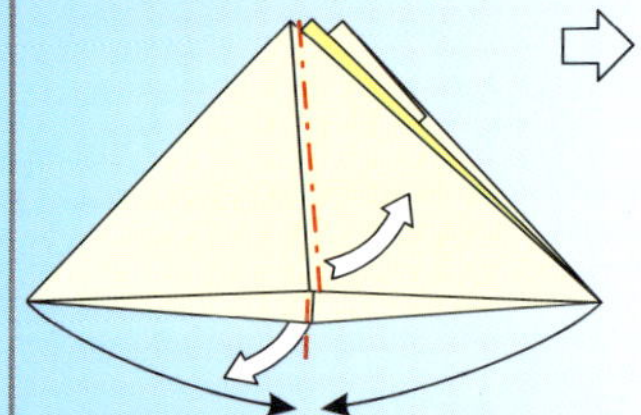

10. Rechts und links nach außen ziehen, fertig.
Pull the folded parts outwards, ready.

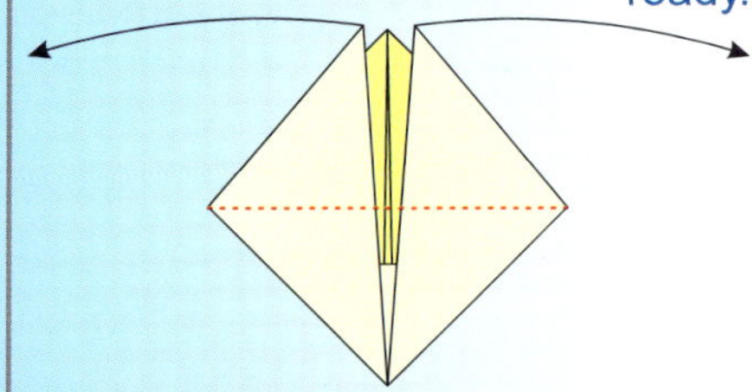

11. Fertiges Boot Modell.
Finished boat model.

Variation 1

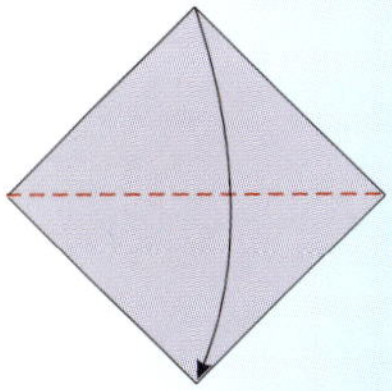

1. Waagerechte Linie falten, liegen lassen.
Fold horizontal line and leave.

2. Linke Spitze zur Vorderseite falten, siehe Pfeil, liegen lassen. Rechte Spitze zur Rückseite falten, siehe Pfeil, liegen lassen.
Fold left point to the front, see arrow, and leave. Fold right point to the back, see arrow, and leave.

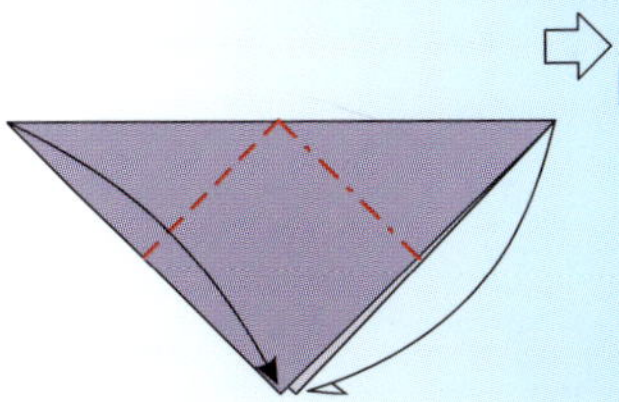

3. Waagerechte Linie falten, wieder öffnen. Auf der Rückseite wiederholen.
Fold horizontal line and leave. Repeat on the back.

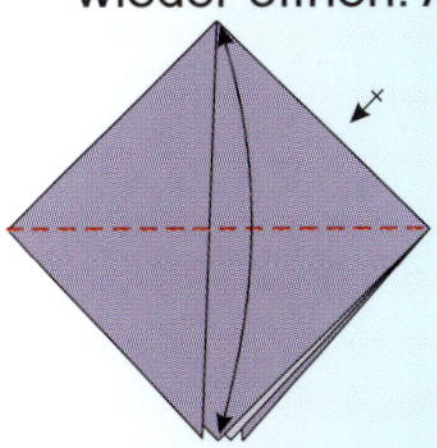

4. Waagerechte Linie falten, liegen lassen. Auf der Rückseite wiederholen.
Fold horizontal line and leave. Repeat on the back.

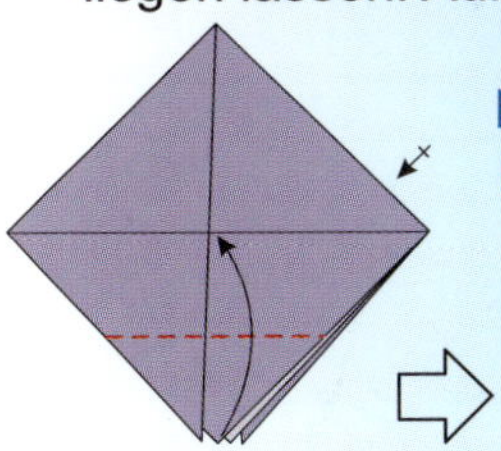

5. Waagerechte Linie falten, liegen lassen. Auf der Rückseite wiederholen.
Fold horizontal line and leave. Repeat on the back.

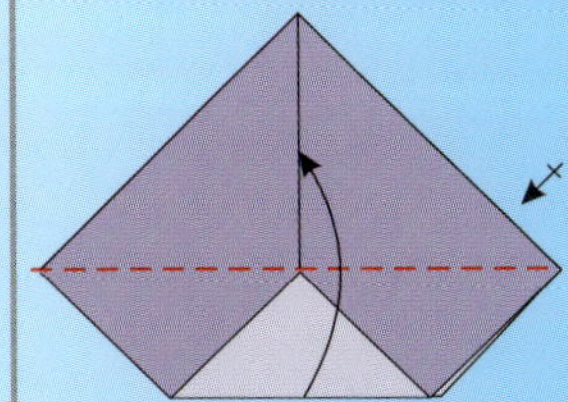

6. Gefaltetes Teil nach außen ziehen, siehe nächste Zeichnung.
Pull the folded part outwards, see next chart.

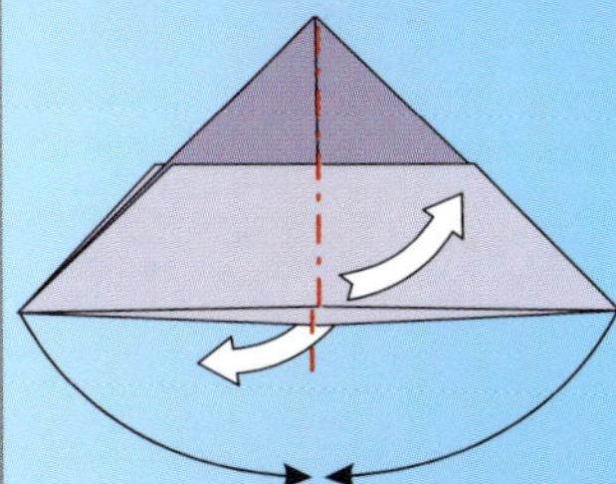

7. Waagerechte Linie falten, liegen lassen. Auf der Rückseite wiederholen.
Fold horizontal line and leave. Repeat on the back.

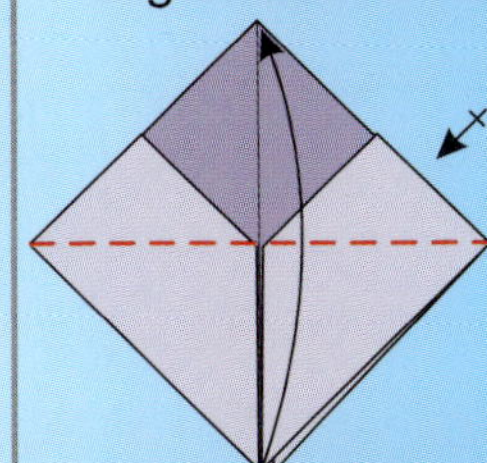

8. Gefaltetes Teil nach außen ziehen, siehe nächste Zeichnung.
Pull the folded part outwards, see next chart.

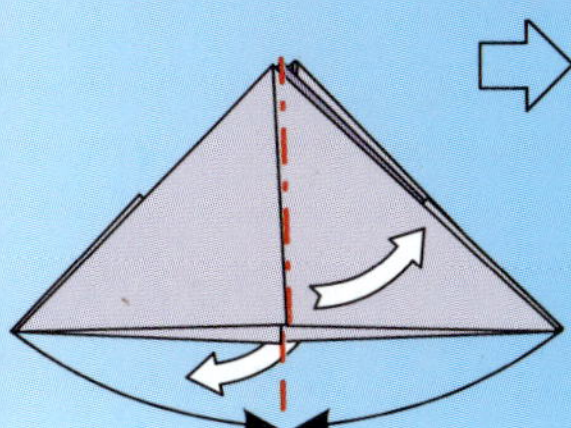

9. Rechts und links nach außen ziehen, fertig.
Pull the right and the left outwards, ready.

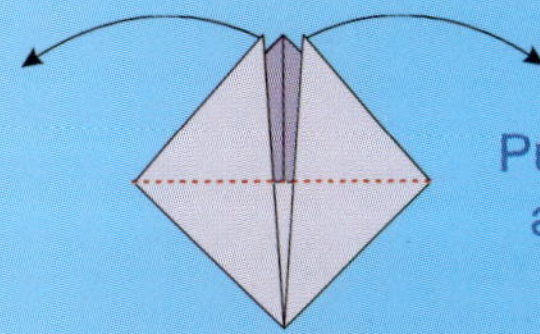

10. Fertiges Modell.
Finished model.

Variation 2

1. Beginn bis Nr.3.
Beginning until no. 3.

2. Waagerechte Linien falten, liegen lassen. Auf der Rückseite wiederholen.
Fold horizontal lines and leave. Repeat on the back.

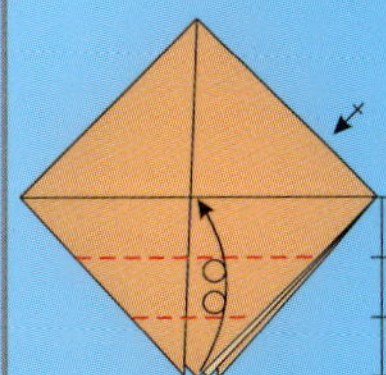

3. Weiter mit Nr.5 - 8.
Go on with no. 5 - 8.

4. Rechts und links nach außen ziehen, fertig.
Pull the right and the left outwards, ready.

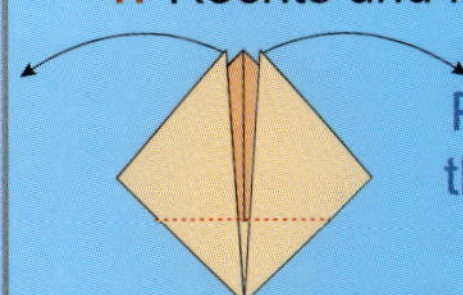

5. Fertiges Modell.
Finished model.

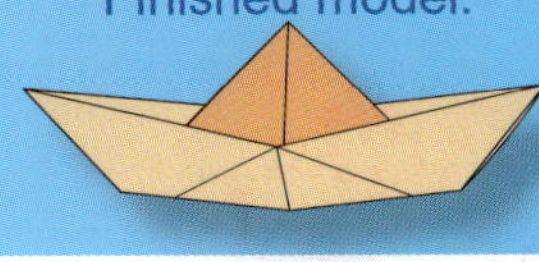

Schifflein vor und nach dem Sturm

1. Jetzt soll das Schifflein eine Reise auf stürmischer See antreten. Das ist sehr gefährlich, weil man nie weiß, was einem auf hoher See passieren kann.

A journey on the stormy sea begins. It is very dangerous since you never know what can happen on high sea.

2. Schließlich hält auch das Ruder dem Sturm und den hohen Wellen nicht mehr stand. Oje, was die Mannschaft für Angst aussteht.

Finally also the rudder does not withstand the storm and the high waves. Oh, which fear the crew stands.

3. Das Unwetter ist so heftig, dass das Vorderteil des Schiffes, der Bug, abbricht. Das Schiff ist jetzt in allergrößter Gefahr.

The tempest is so violent that the front part of the ship, the nose, breaks off. The ship now is in all-largest danger.

4. Dann verschwindet sogar der Mast in den Wellen. Das Unwetter hat ganze Arbeit geleistet.

Finally even the mast in the waves disappears. The tempest carried whole work out.

5. Das Schifflein ist rettungslos verloren, es geht mit Mann und Maus unter.
The small boat is rescueless lost, it goes down with man and mouse.

6. Was mag wohl von dem einst so stolzen Schiff übrig geblieben sein?
What can probably have remained by the once so proud ship?

7. Taucher holen die Reste des Schiffes hoch. Wir können daran erkennen, ob das Schiff im Sommer oder im Winter gesunken ist.
Divers save the remainders of the ship. We can recognize by the nightgown whether the ship sank in the summer or in the winter.

8. Wir brauchen nur die Reste auszulegen, es bleibt uns … das Nachthemd des Kapitäns.
We only need to lay out the remainders, it remains for us... the nightgown of the captain.

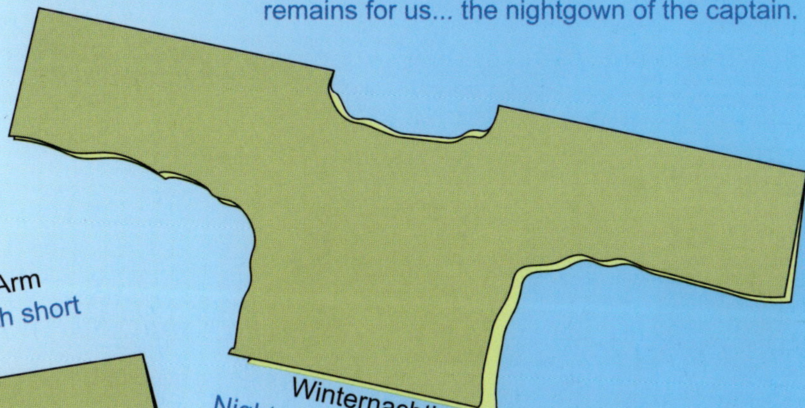

Winternachthemd mit langem Arm
Nightgown worn in wintertime with long sleeves

Sommernachthemd mit kurzem Arm
Nightgown worn in summertime with short sleeves

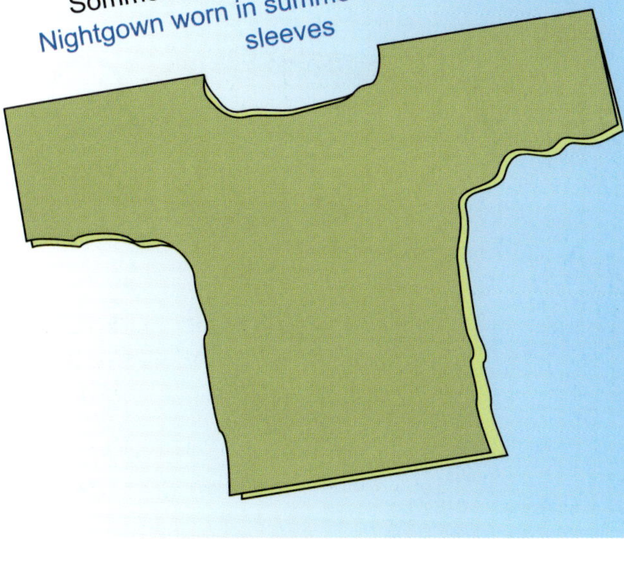

Am Strand

At the beach

MATERIAL
1 Bogen 20x20 cm AQUAPAPIER
1 sheet 20x20 cm AQUAPAPIER

1. Papier an der waagerechten Linie durchschneiden.
Cut paper on the horizontal line.

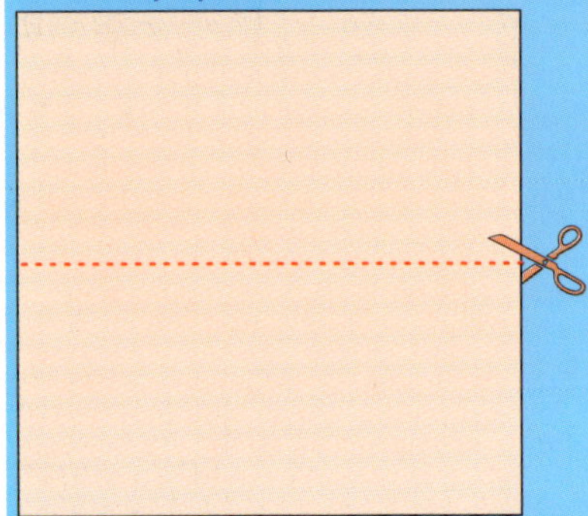

2. Waagerechte Linie falten, wieder öffnen.
Fold horizontal line and open again.

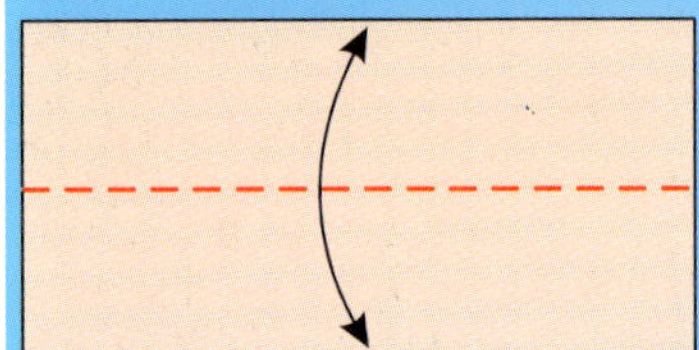

3. Waagerechte Linien falten, liegen lassen.
Fold horizontal lines and leave.

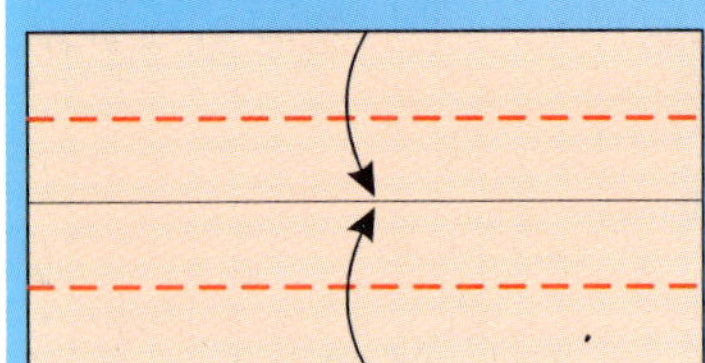

4. Alle vier Ecken falten, siehe Pfeile, liegen lassen.
Fold all four corners, see arrows, and leave.

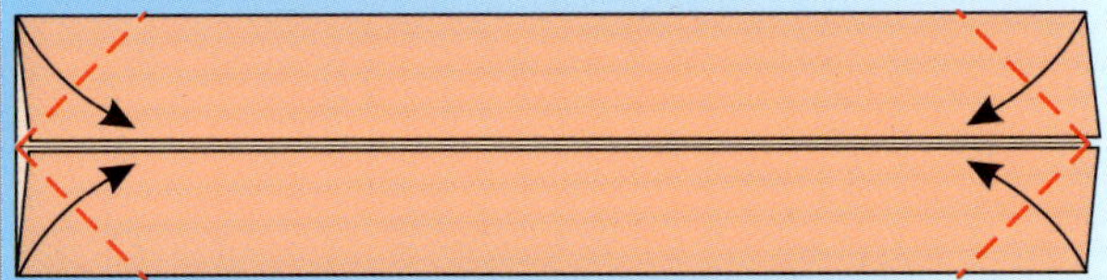

5. Alle vier schrägen Linien falten, siehe Pfeile, wieder öffnen.
Fold all four diagonal lines, see arrows, and open again.

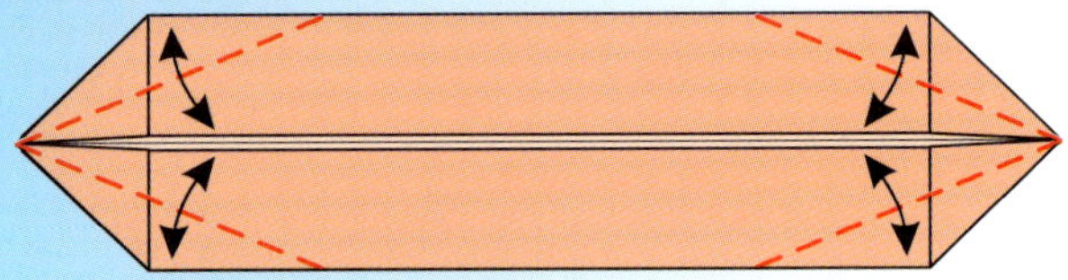

6. Nur mit der oberen Papierlage, siehe Pfeile, schräge Linien falten, liegen lassen.
Using only the top layer of paper, see arrows, fold diagonal lines and leave.

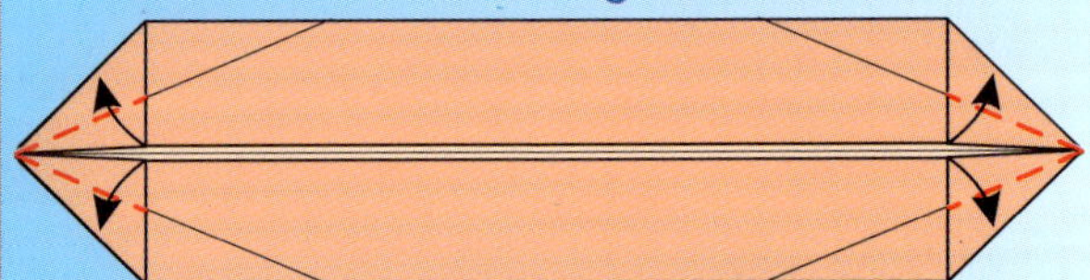

7. Gefaltetes Teil von innen nach außen öffnen, dabei an beiden Spitzen die oberen Papierlagen nach innen legen, siehe Pfeile.
Pull the folded part outwards by laying the top layer of paper at both points inwards, see arrows.

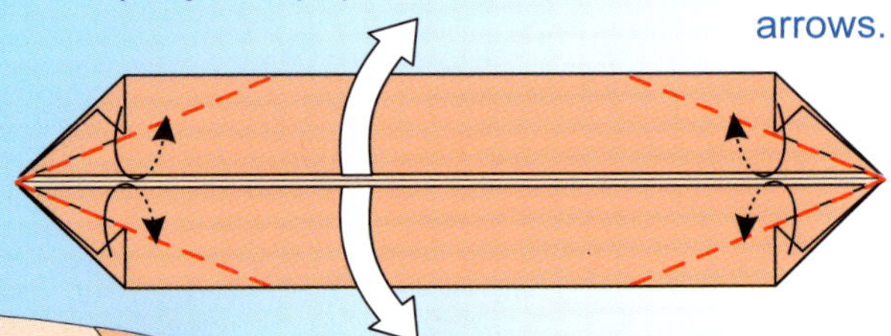

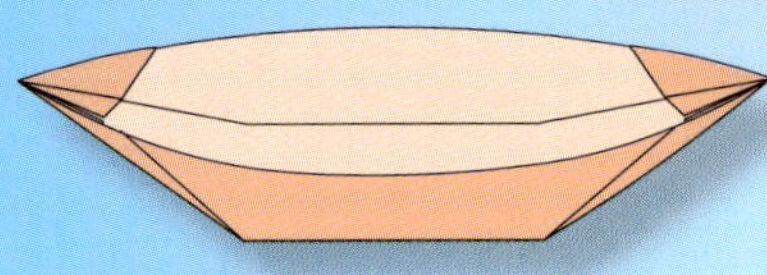

8. Fertiges Modell.
Finished model.

Ruderboot mit Segel ⟡ Rowboat with sail

MATERIAL
1 Bogen 20x20 cm AQUAPAPIER
1 sheet 20x20 cm AQUAPAPIER

1. Waagerechte Linie falten, wieder öffnen.
Fold horizontal line and open again.

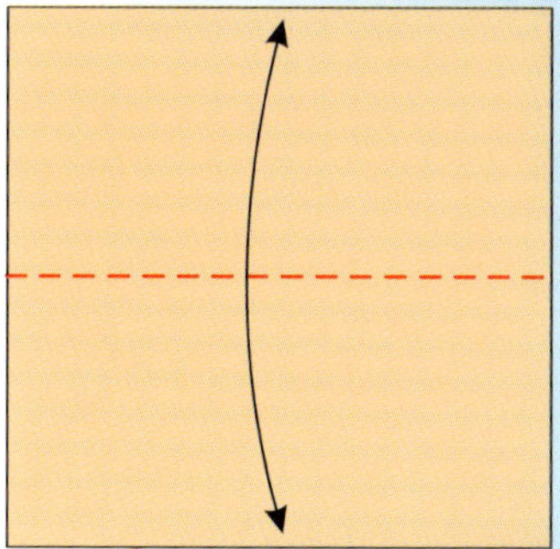

2. Waagerechte Linien falten, liegen lassen.
Fold horizontal lines and leave.

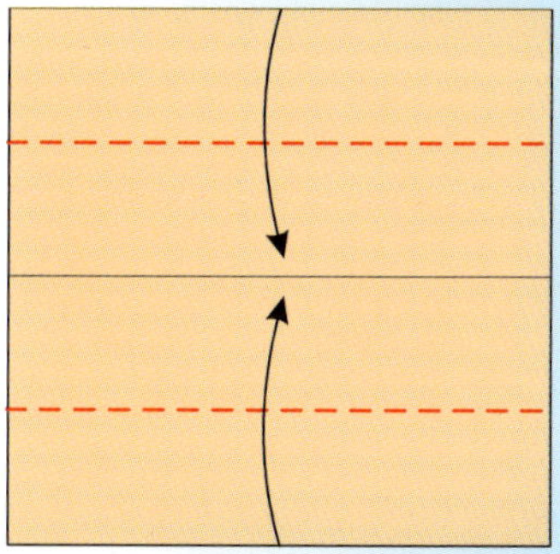

3. Waagerechte Linien falten, liegen lassen.
Fold horizontal lines and leave.

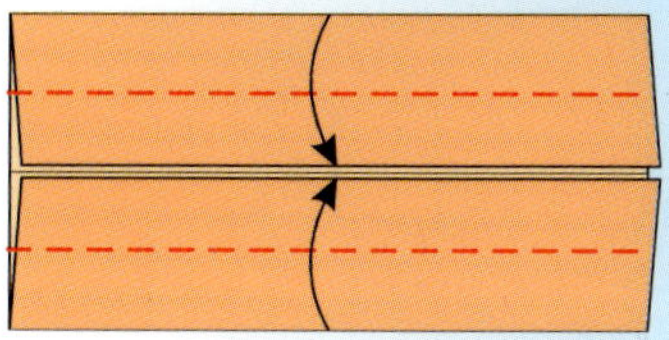

4. Alle vier Ecken falten, siehe Pfeile, liegen lassen.
Fold all four corners, see arrows, and leave.

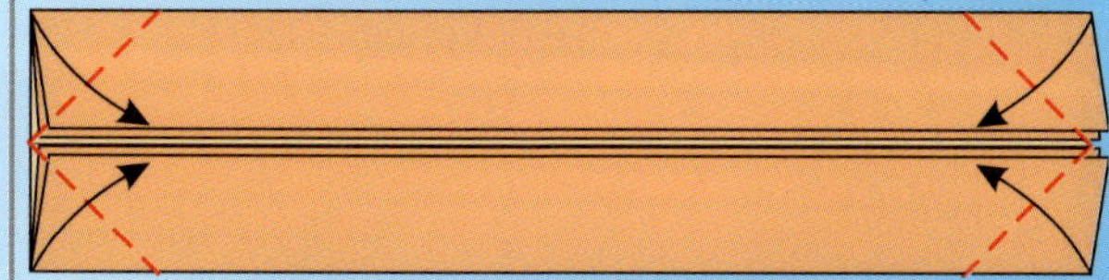

5. Alle vier schrägen Linien falten, siehe Pfeile, wieder öffnen.
Fold all four diagonal lines, see arrows, and open again.

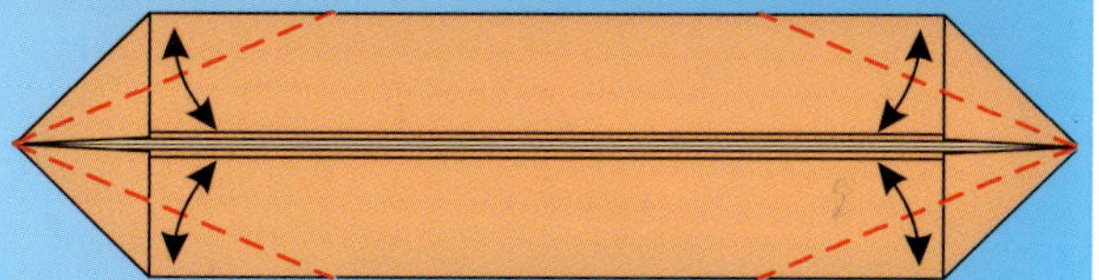

6. Gefaltetes Teil von innen nach außen öffnen, dabei an beiden Spitzen die oberen Papierlagen nach innen legen, siehe Pfeile.
Open the folded part outwards by laying the top layer of paper at both points inwards, see arrows.

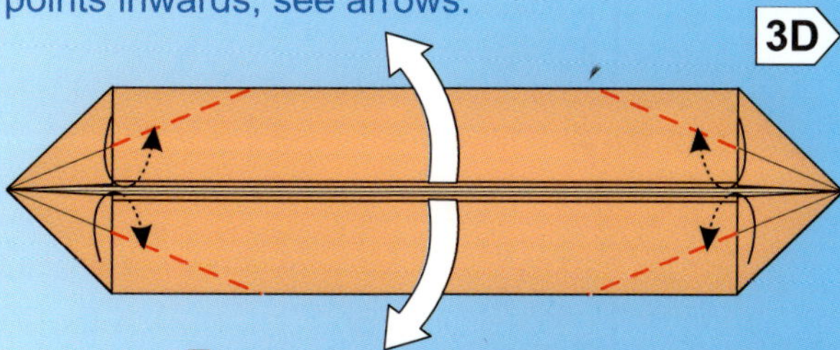

7. Die oberen Papierlagen an den Spitzen, siehe Pfeile, nach innen legen, liegen lassen. Auf der Rückseite wiederholen.
Pull the top layers of paper inwards on the points, see arrows, and leave. Repeat on the back.

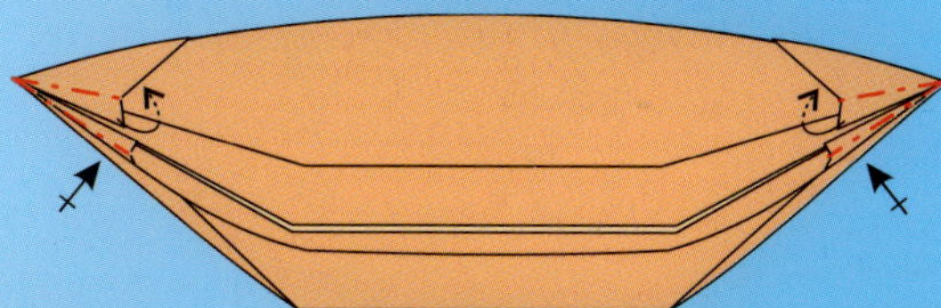

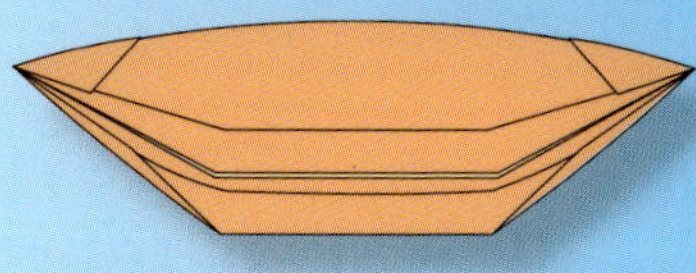

8. Fertiges Modell.
Finished model.

MATERIAL
1 Bogen 20x20 cm AQUAPAPIER
1 sheet 20x20 cm AQUAPAPIER

1. Senkrechte Linie falten, wieder öffnen.
Fold vertical line and open again.

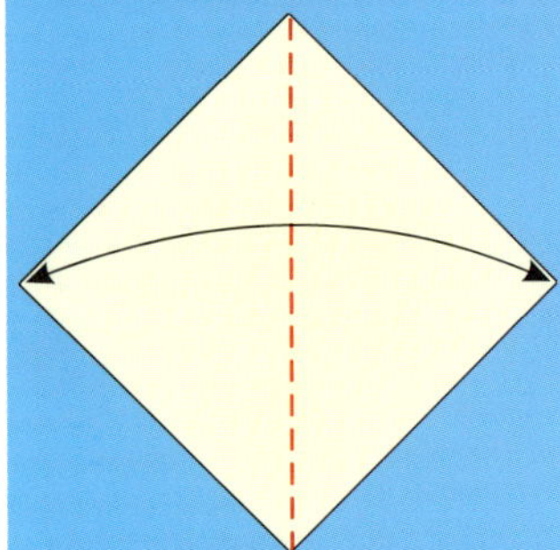

2. Schräge Linie falten, liegen lassen.
Fold diagonal line and leave.

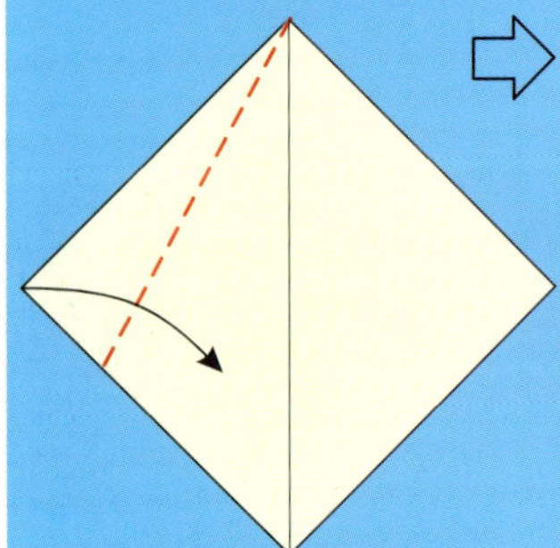

3. Senkrechte Mitte falten, liegen lassen.
Fold vertical middle and leave.

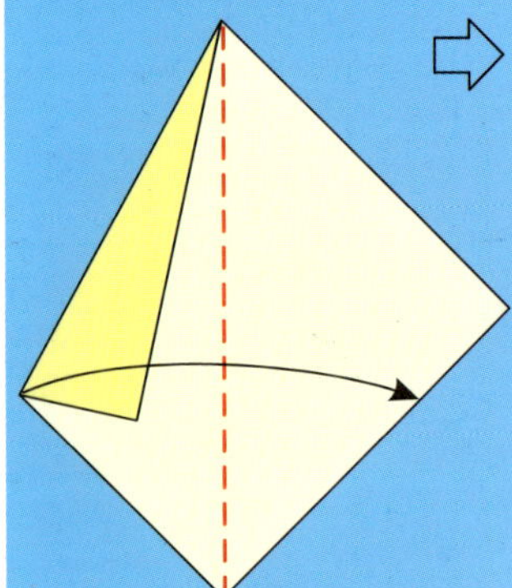

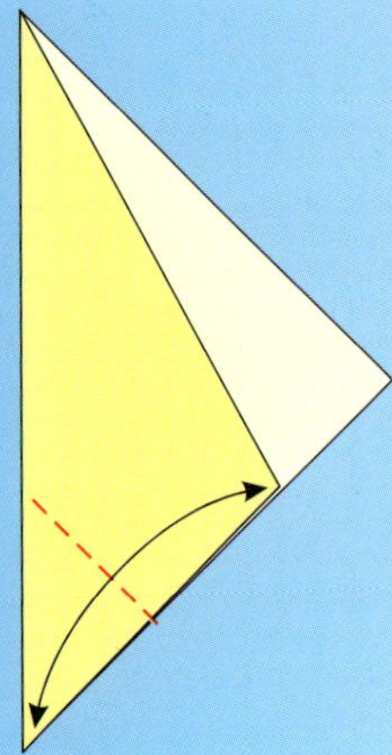

4. Schräge Linie falten, wieder öffnen.
Fold vertical line and open again.

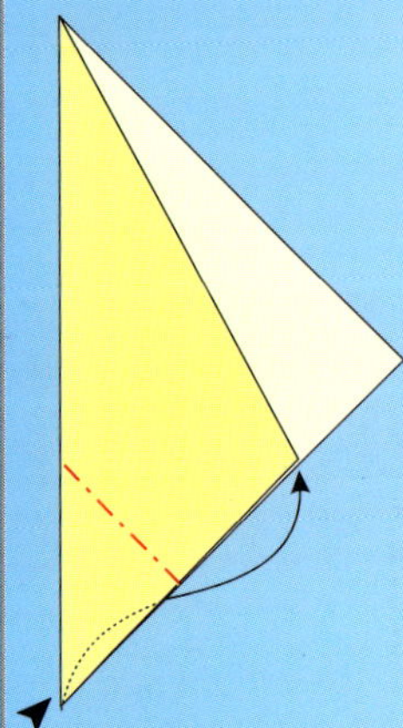

5. Linie zur Bergfalte formen, Spitze nach innen legen.
Fold line to mountain-fold, put points inwards.

6. Rückseite nach oben legen.
Put back upwards.

7. Senkrechte Linie falten, liegen lassen.
Fold vertical line and leave.

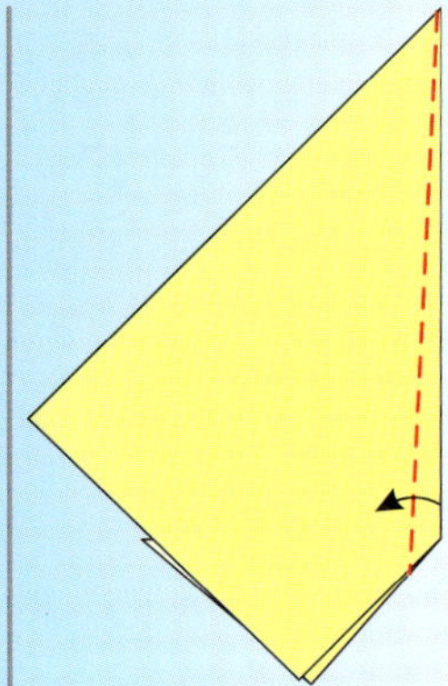

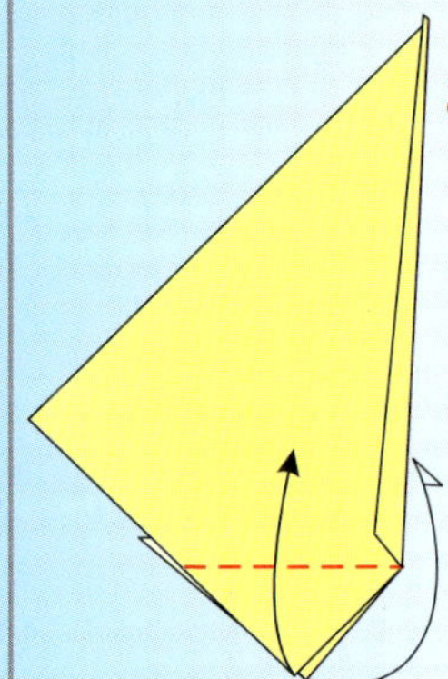

8. Waagerechte Linie falten, liegen lassen. Rückseite wiederholen.
Fold horizontal line and leave. Repeat the back.

9. Waagerechte Linie falten, liegen lassen. Rückseite nach oben legen.
Fold horizontal line and leave. Put back upwards.

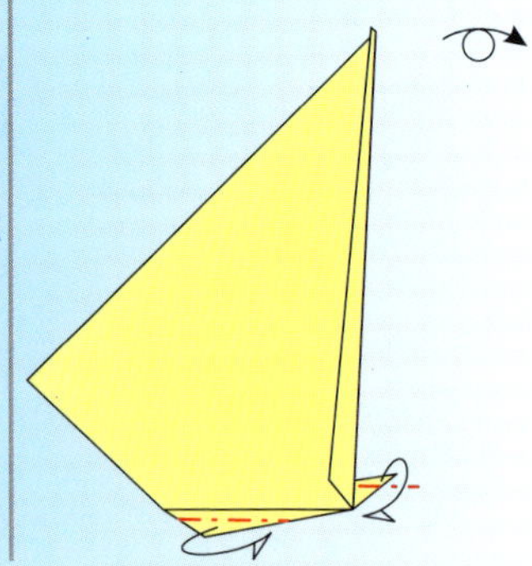

10. Segel, siehe Pfeile, im Boot unter die innere Papierlage schieben, fertig.
Push sails, see arrows, below the inside layer of paper, ready.

11. Fertiges Modell seitlich gesehen.
Finished model seen from the side.

Segel Variation

Variation of sail

1. Beginn Seite 16 bis Nr.9.
Beginning on page 16 until no. 9.

2. Schräge Linie falten, liegen lassen.
Fold diagonal line and leave.

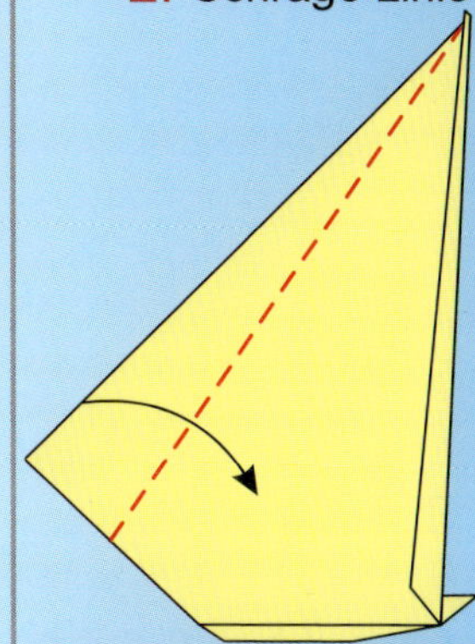

3. Fertige Segel Variation.
Finished sail variation.

Katamaran mit Segel

Modell bekannt seit 1823
Model known since 1823

MATERIAL
1 Bogen 20x20 cm AQUAPAPIER
1 sheet 20x20 cm AQUAPAPIER

1. Zweimal diagonal die Mitte falten, wieder öffnen.
Fold twice the middle diagonally and open again.

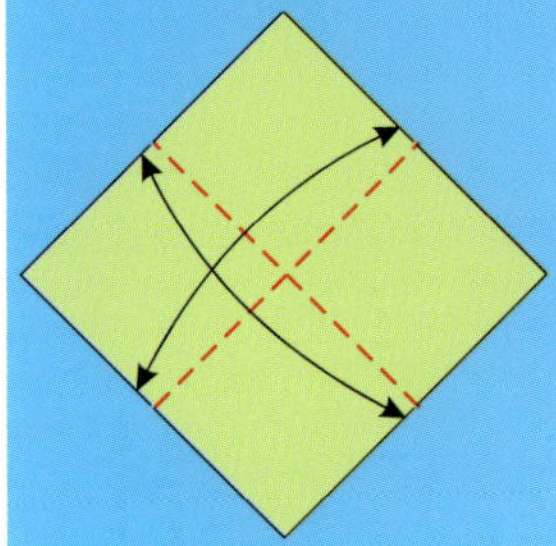

2. Zweimal waagerecht die Mitte falten, wieder öffnen.
Fold twice the middle horizontally and open again.

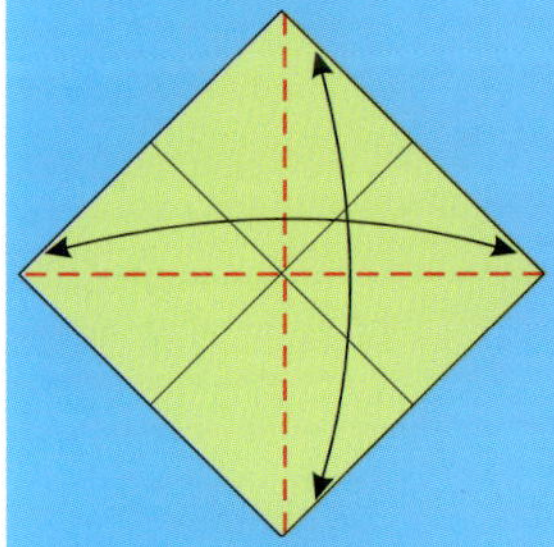

3. Alle vier Ecken zur Mitte falten, liegen lassen.
Fold all four corners to the middle and leave.

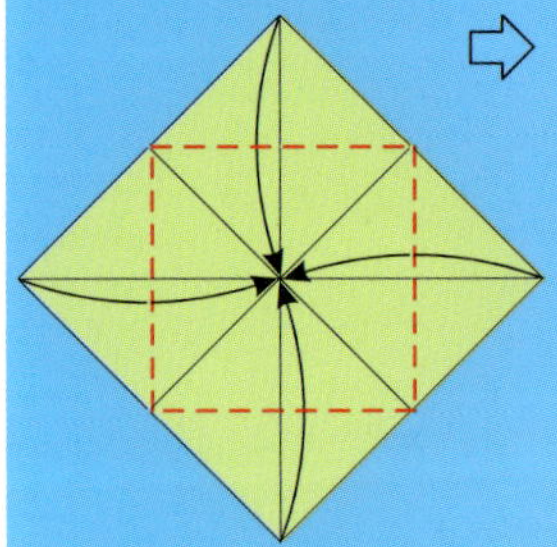

4. Rückseite nach oben legen.
Put back upwards.

5. Alle vier Ecken zur Mitte falten, wieder öffnen. Rückseite nach oben legen.
Fold all four corners to the middle and open again. Put back upwards.

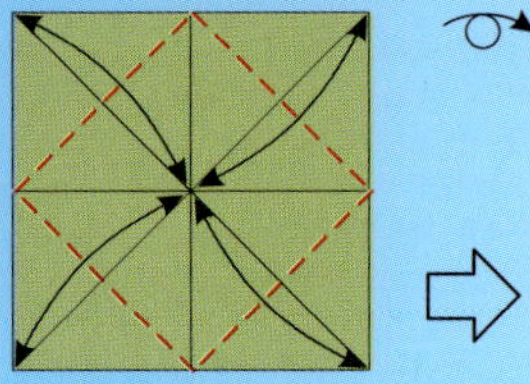

6. Waagerechte Linien falten, wieder öffnen.
Fold horizontal lines and open again.

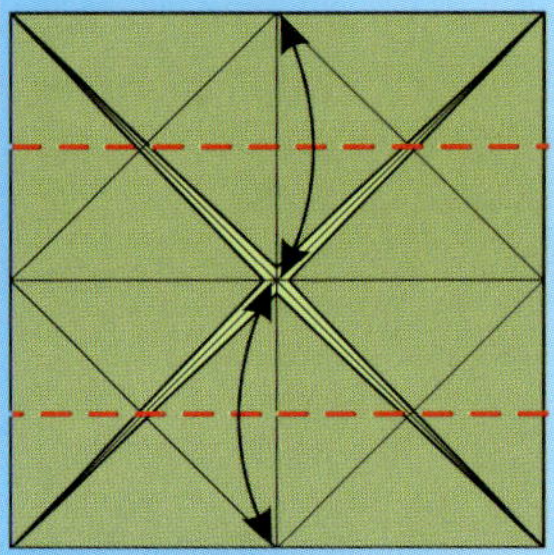

7. Senkrechte Linien falten, liegen lassen.
Fold horizontal lines and leave.

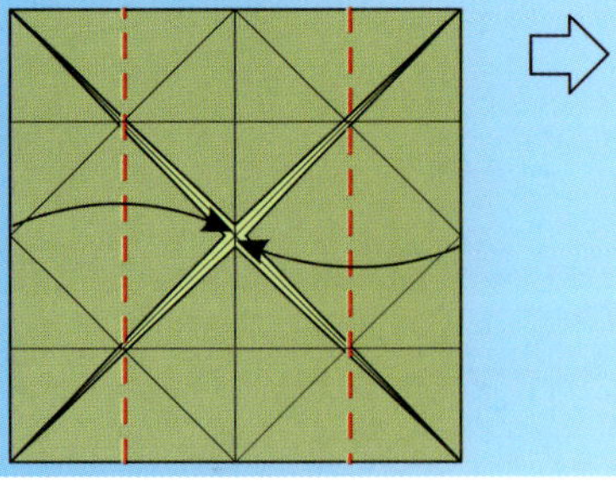

8. Zweimal schräge Linien in der Mitte falten, wieder öffnen. Danach oben und unten die untere Papierlage zur Mitte drücken.
Fold twice the middle diagonally and open again.
Press the lower layer of paper upwards and downwards to the center.

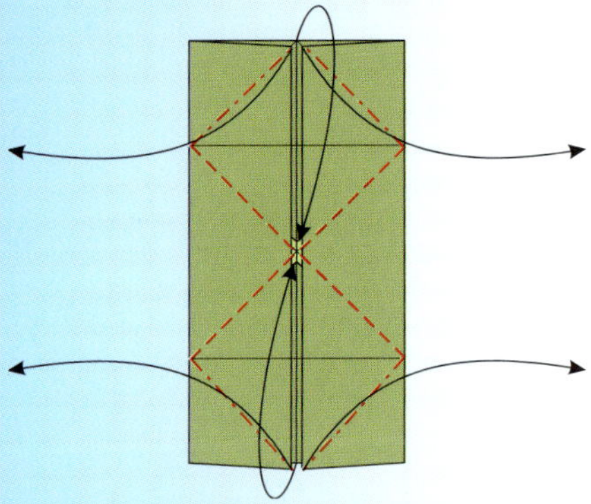

9. Waagerechte Linie zur Rückseite falten, liegen lassen.
Fold horizontal line to the back and leave.

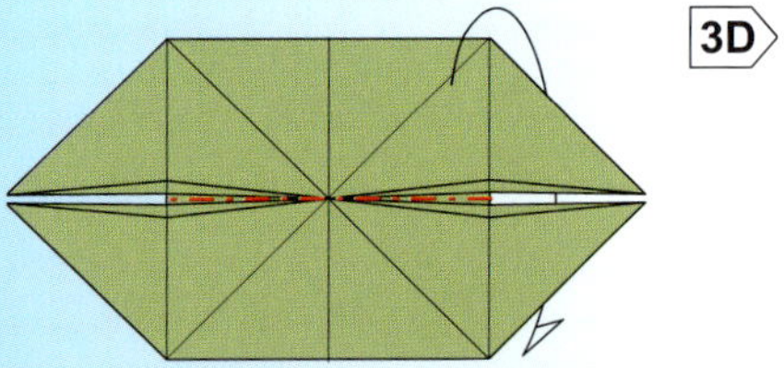

10. Fertiges Modell Boot.
Finished model.

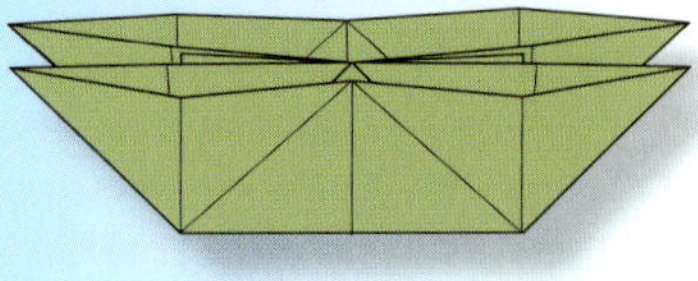

Catamaran with sail

MATERIAL
1 Bogen 20x20 cm AQUAPAPIER
1 sheet 20x20 cm AQUAPAPIER

1. Senkrechte Linie falten, wieder öffnen. Rückseite nach oben legen.
Fold vertical lines and open again. Put back upwards.

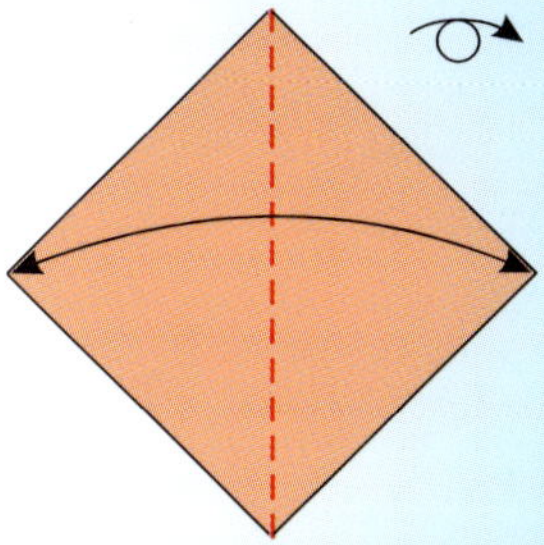

2. Markierung auf 1/3 anbringen.
Attach marking on 1/3.

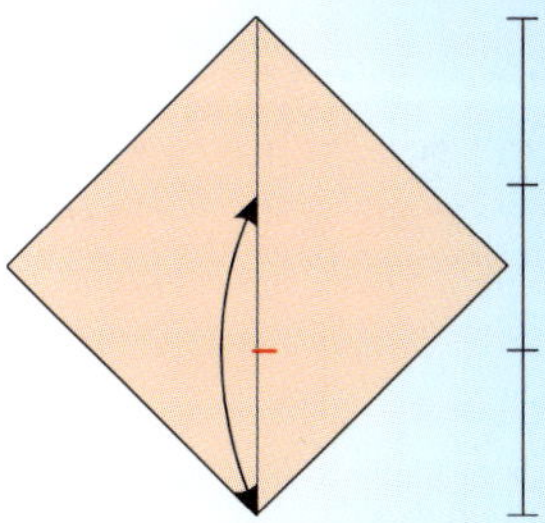

3. Schräge Linie falten, liegen lassen.
Fold diagonal line and leave.

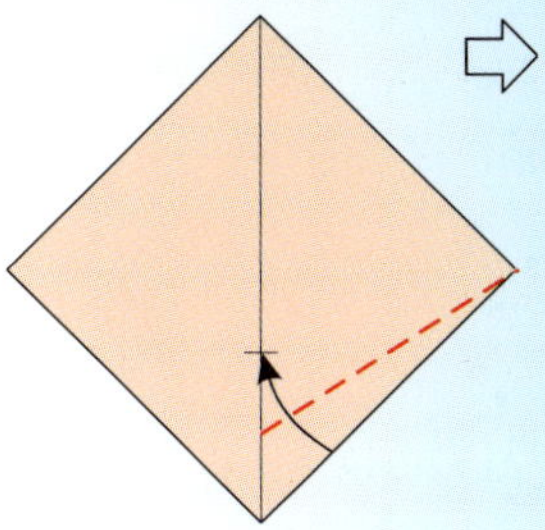

4. Schräge Linie falten, alles wieder öffnen.
Fold diagonal line and open again.

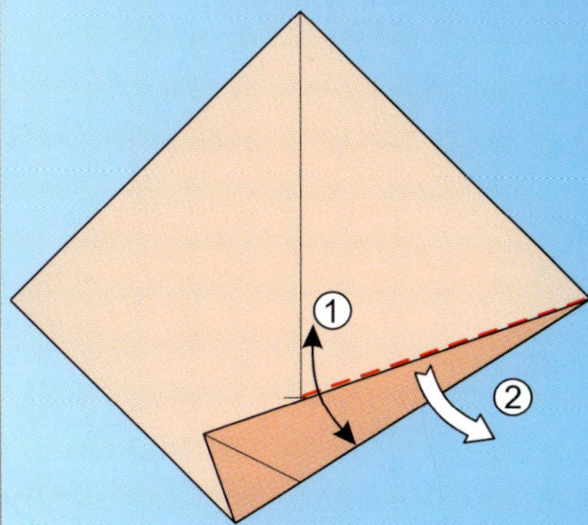

5. Schritt Nr.3 + 4 an der linken Seite wiederholen.
Repeat step no. 3 and 4 on the left side.

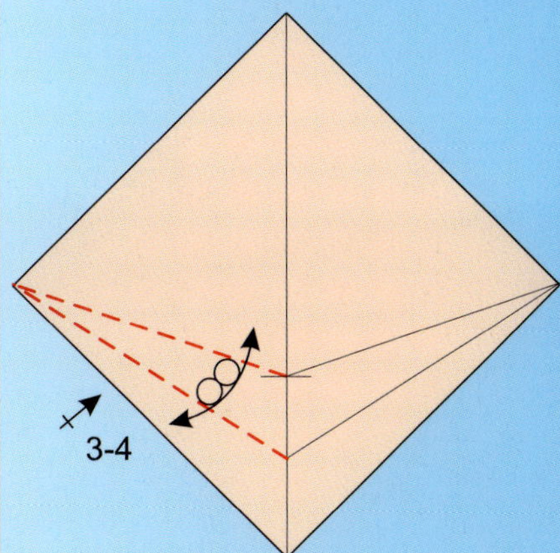

6. Linien, siehe Pfeile, nach oben legen, liegen lassen.
Put lines, see arrows, upwards and leave.

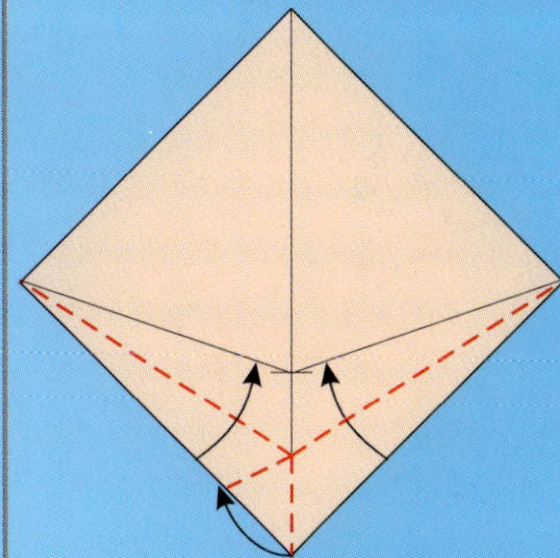

7. Waagerechte Linie zur Rückseite falten, wieder öffnen.
Fold horizontal line to the back and open again.

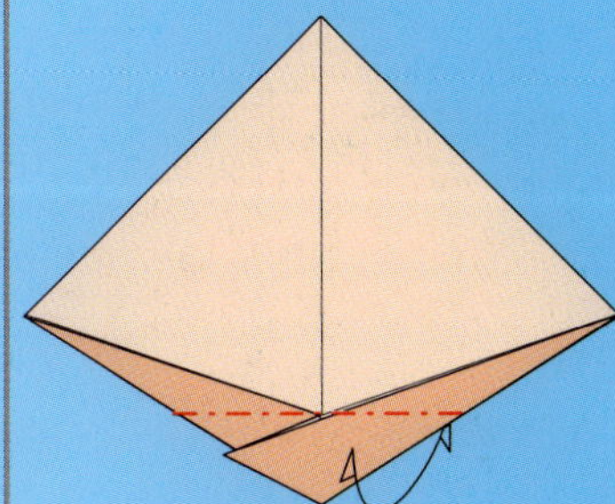

8. Senkrechte Linie zur Rückseite falten, liegen lassen.
Fold vertical line to the back and leave.

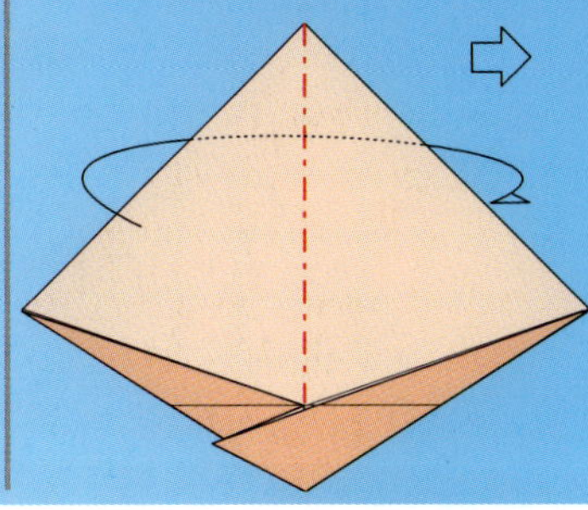

Katamaran mit Segel

9. Schräge Linie wieder nach oben falten, Rückseite auch, dabei die linke Spitze nach unten formen, siehe Pfeile.
Fold vertical line upwards, the back as well, by forming the left point downwards, see arrows.

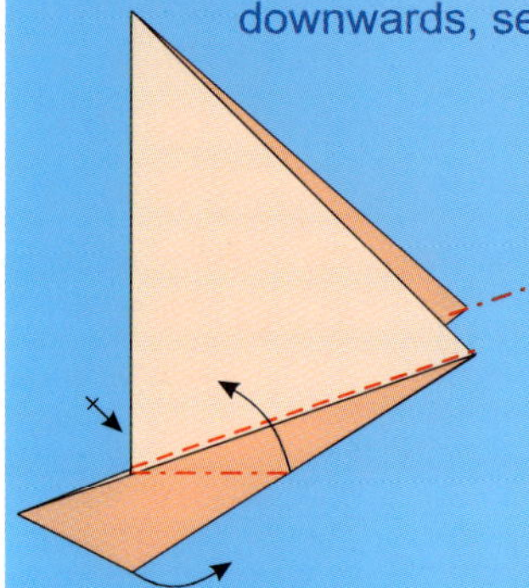

10. Schräge Linie falten, siehe Pfeil, wieder öffnen.
Fold diagonal line, see arrow, and open again.

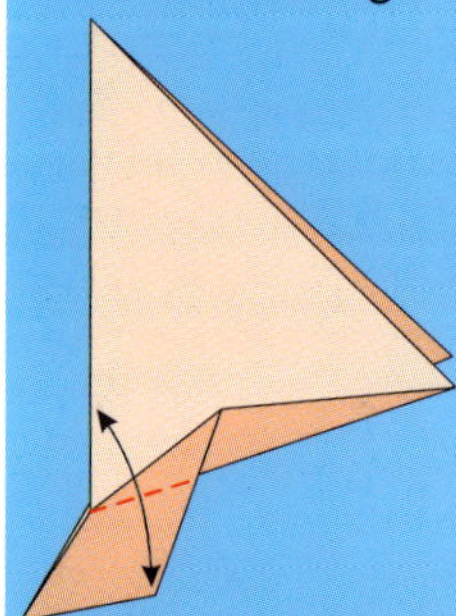

11. Schräge Linie falten, siehe Pfeil, wieder öffnen.
Fold diagonal line, see arrow, and open again.

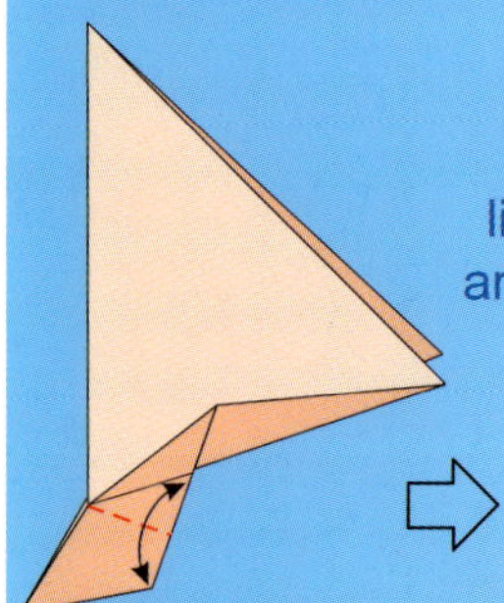

12. Die gefaltete Linie Nr.11 zur Bergfalte formen, siehe Pfeil, und nach oben legen.
Form the folded line no.11 to mountain-fold, see arrow, and put upwards.

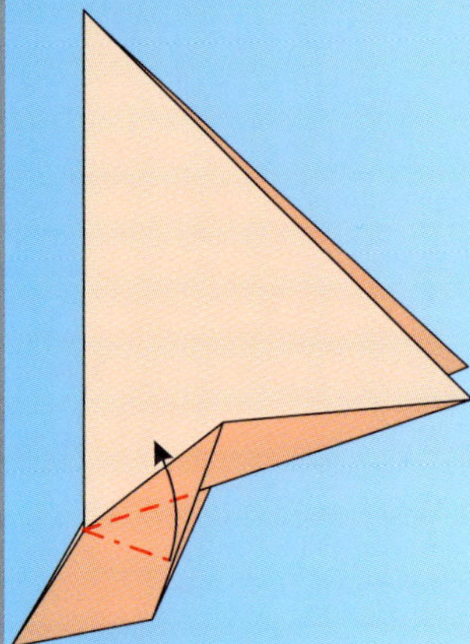

13. Spitze eindrücken, dabei die Bergfalte formen, siehe Pfeil, und nach oben legen.
Press the point by forming a mountain-fold, see arrow, and put upwards.

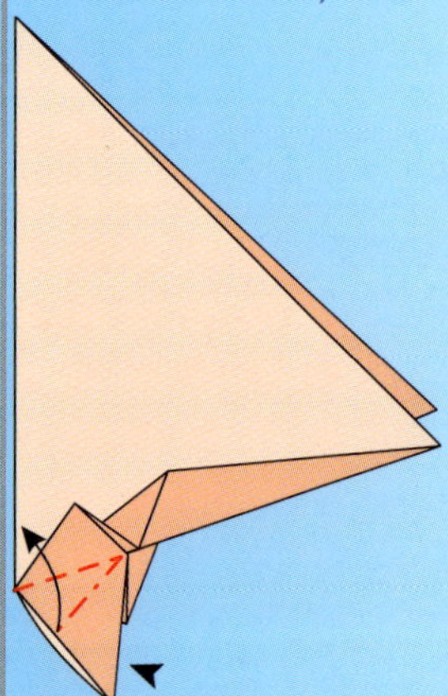

14. Senkrechte Linie nach links falten, Rückseite wiederholen. Untere Spitze waagerecht legen, siehe Pfeil.
Fold vertical line to the left, repeat the back. Put the below point horizontally, see arrow.

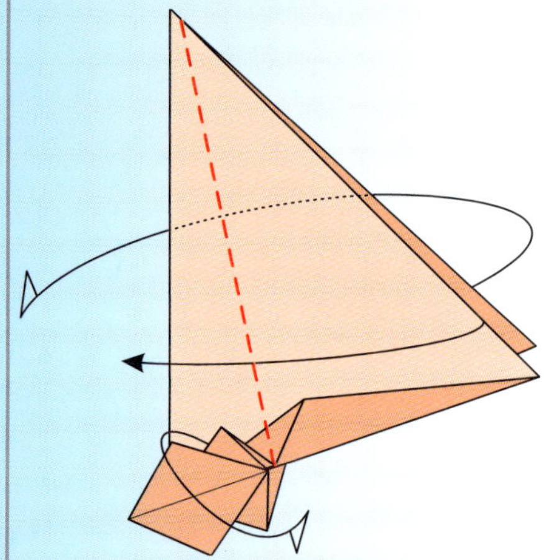

15. Fertiges Segel.
Finished sail.

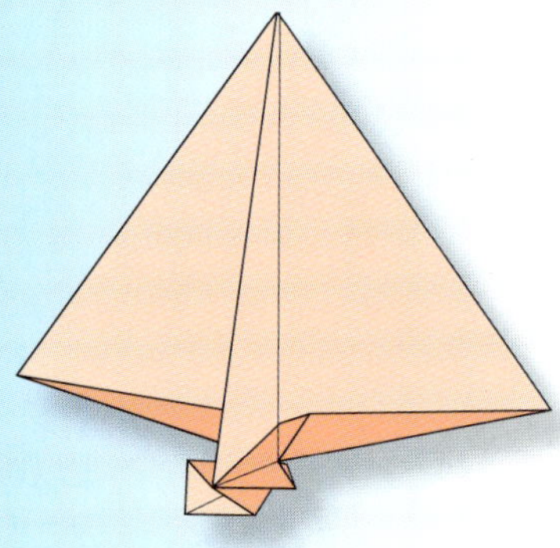

Catamaran with sail

16. Gefaltetes Boot nach außen ziehen, siehe nächste Zeichnung.
Pull the folded boat outwards, see next chart.

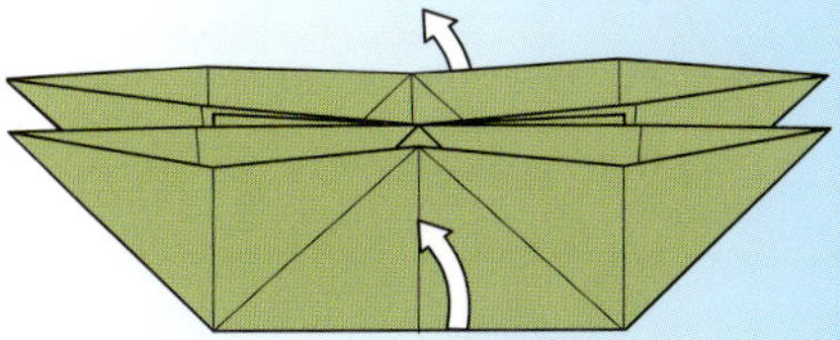

17. Segel, siehe Pfeile, im Boot unter die inneren Papierlagen schieben, fertig.
Push the sails in the boat below the inside layers of paper, see arrows, and ready.

18. Mittige waagerechte Linie wieder zur Bergfalte formen, fertig.
Form the central horizontal line to a mountain-fold, ready.

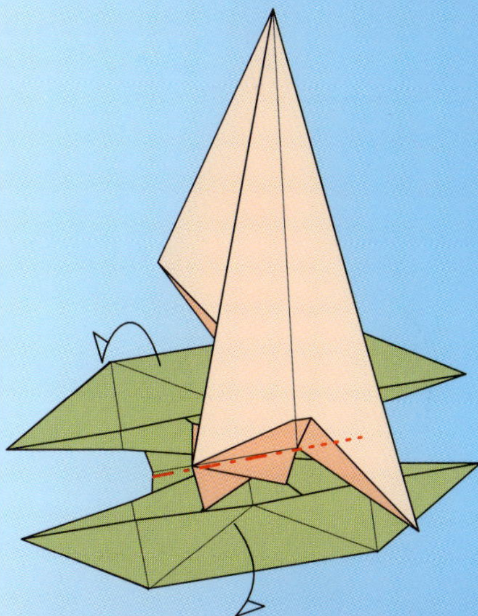

19. Fertiges Modell seitlich gesehen.
Finished model seen from the side.

Windsurfer

Windsurfer

Sehr einfach und optimal zum Treiben und Segeln

Very simple and optimal for driving and sailing

MATERIAL

1 Bogen 20x20 cm AQUAPAPIER

1 sheet 20x20 cm AQUAPAPIER

1. Senkrechte Linie falten, wieder öffnen.

Fold vertical line and open again.

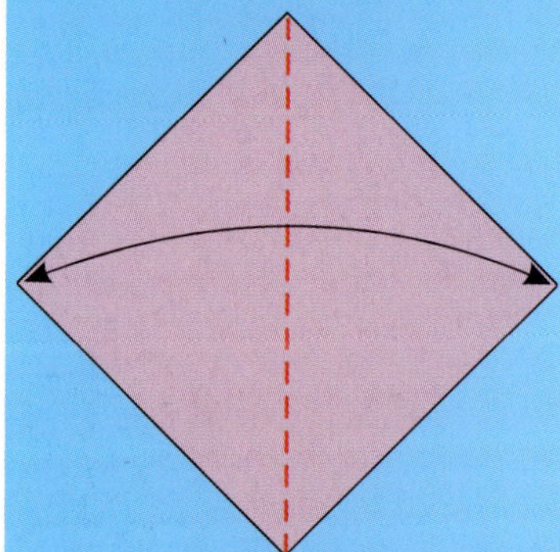

2. Schräge Linien falten, liegen lassen.

Fold diagonal lines and leave.

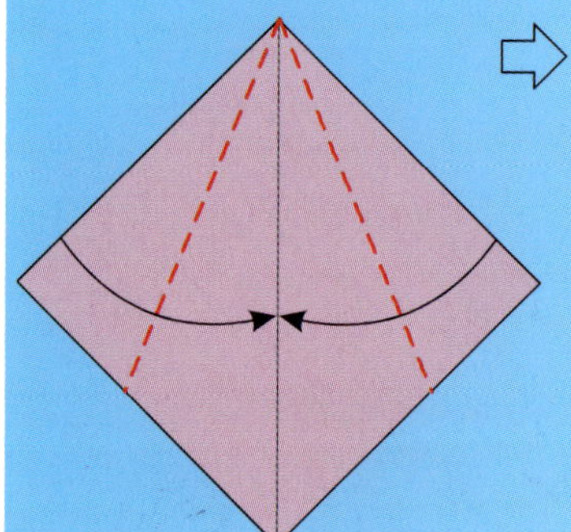

3. Waagerechte Linie falten, liegen lassen.

Fold horizontal line and leave.

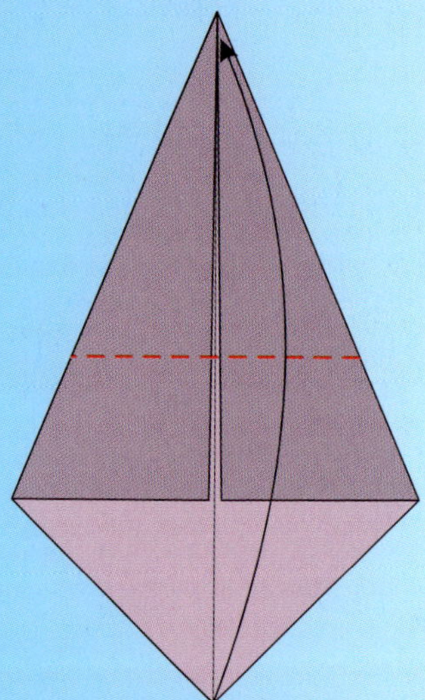

4. Senkrechte Linien falten, liegen lassen.

Fold vertical lines and leave.

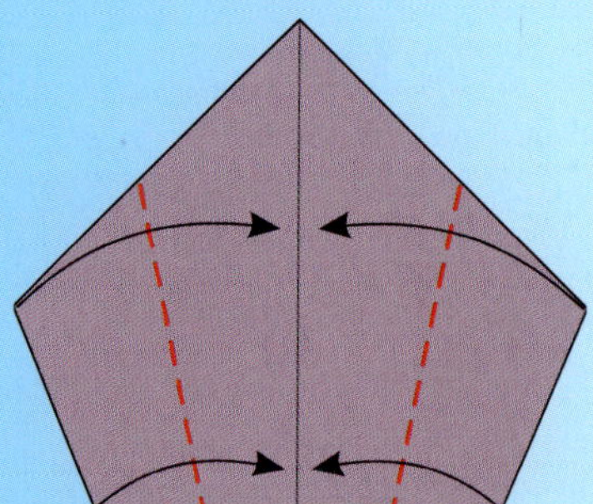

5. Spitze nach unten falten, liegen lassen. Modell drehen, fertig.

Fold point downwards and leave. Turn model, ready.

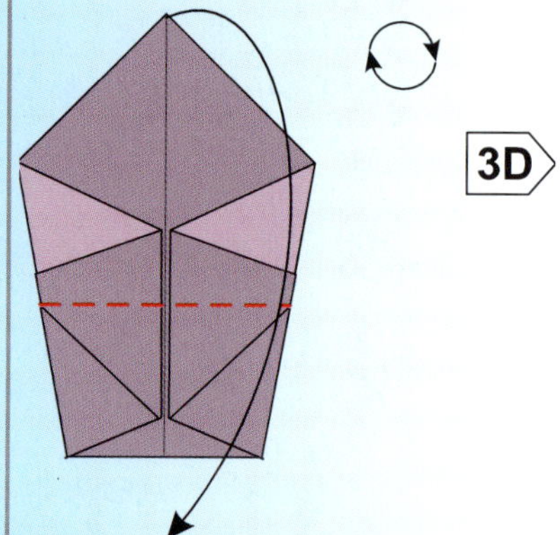

6. Fertiges Modell seitlich gesehen.

Finished model seen from the side.

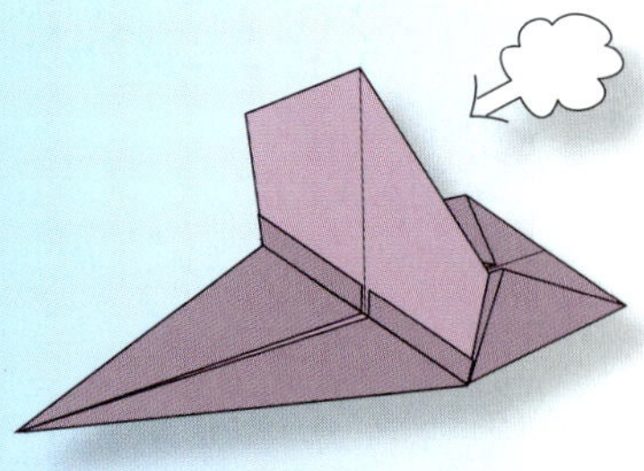

Tretboot

Pedal boat

MATERIAL

1 Bogen 20x20 cm AQUAPAPIER

1 sheet 20x20 cm AQUAPAPIER

1. Zweimal diagonal die Mitte falten, wieder öffnen. Rückseite nach oben legen.

Fold twice the middle diagonally and open again. Turn back upwards.

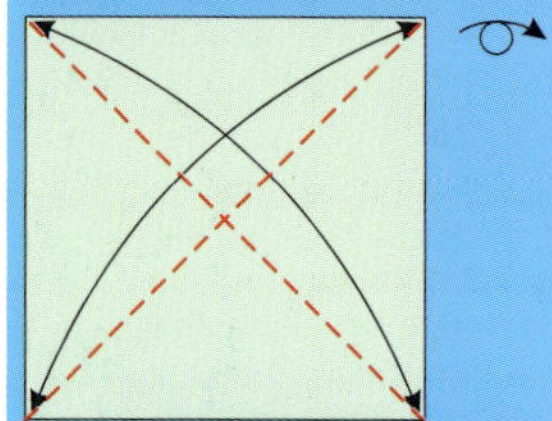

2. Zweimal waagerecht die Mitte falten, wieder öffnen. Rückseite nach oben legen.

Fold twice the middle horizontally and open again. Turn back upwards.

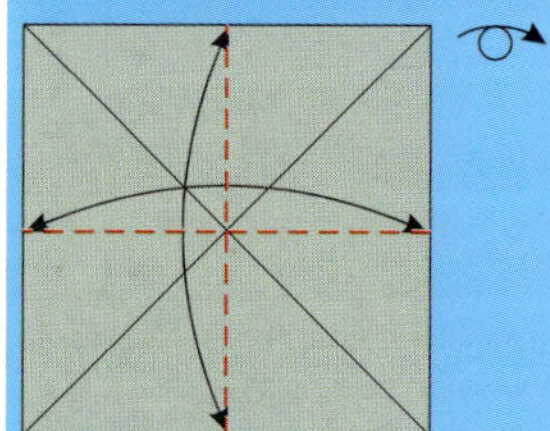

3. Von der waagerechten Mitte (Bergfalte), Papier seitlich zum oberen Mittelpunkt legen, siehe Pfeile. Es entsteht ein Dreieck.

From the horizontal middle (mountain-fold), put paper from the side to the upper center. A triangle arises.

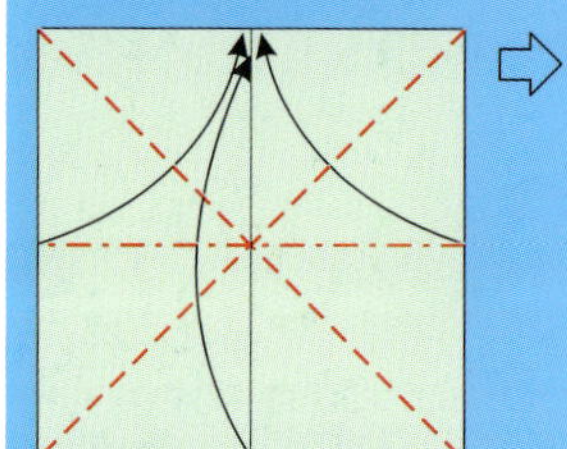

4. Waagerechte Linie falten, wieder öffnen.

Fold horizontal line and open again.

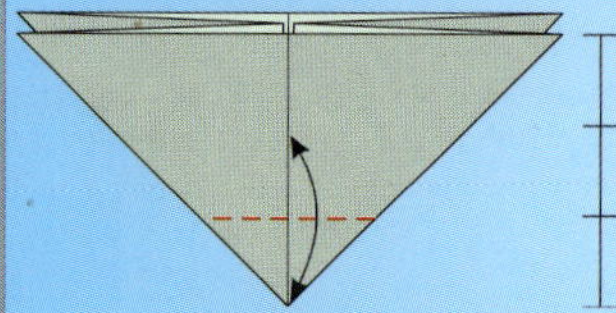

5. Waagerechte Linie falten, wieder öffnen.

Fold horizontal line and open again.

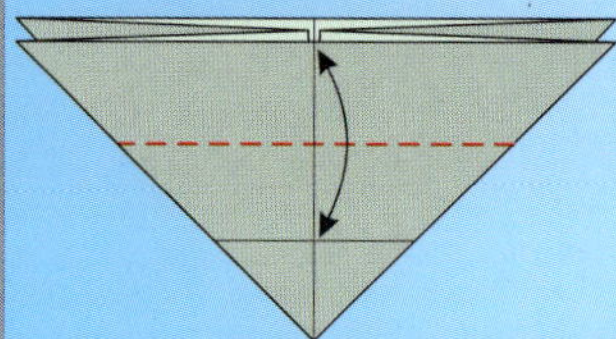

6. An der unteren Spitze die Linie falten, wieder öffnen. Danach komplett öffnen.

Fold the line on the lower point and open again. Open afterwards completely.

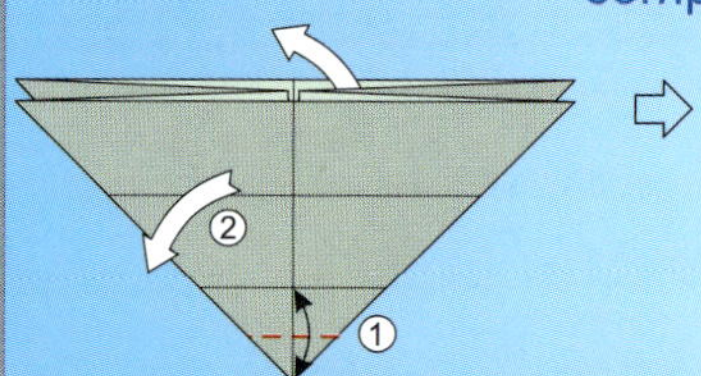

7. Beide waagerechte Linien falten, wieder öffnen.

Fold both horizontal lines and open again.

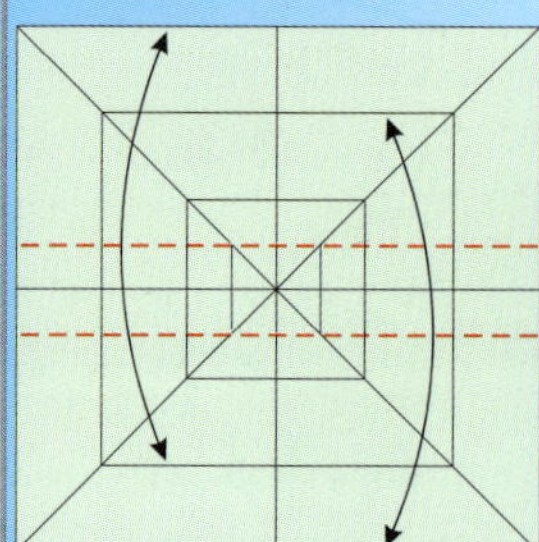

8. Rot gekennzeichnete Linien zu Berg- oder Talfalten formen.

Form red characterized lines to mountain and valley-folds.

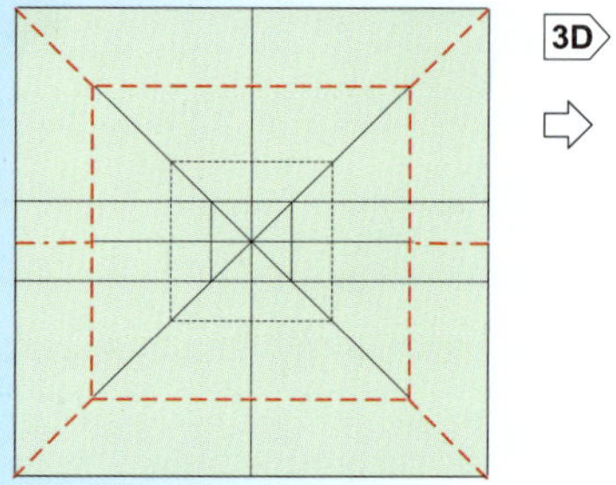

9. Nun die mittleren Linien zu Berg- oder Talfalten formen, rot gekennzeichnet.

Form the inside lines to mountain and valley-folds, red marked.

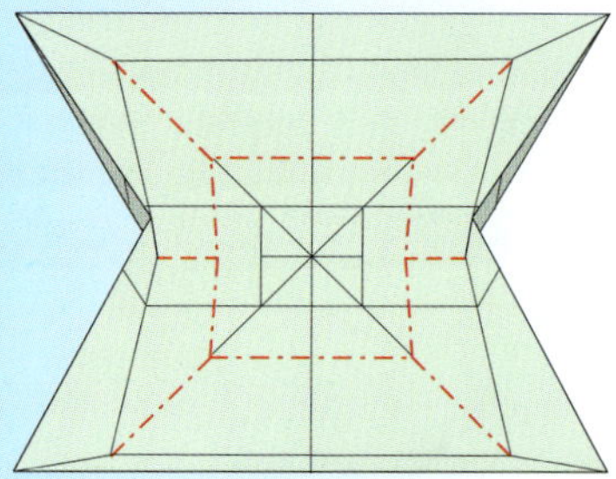

10. Jetzt die inneren Linien zu Talfalten formen, rot gekennzeichnet.

Form the inside lines to valley-folds, red marked.

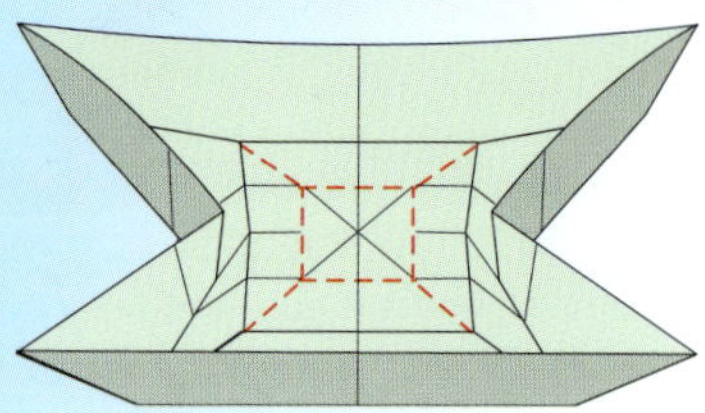

11. Senkrechte Linien falten, liegen lassen.
Fold vertical lines and leave.

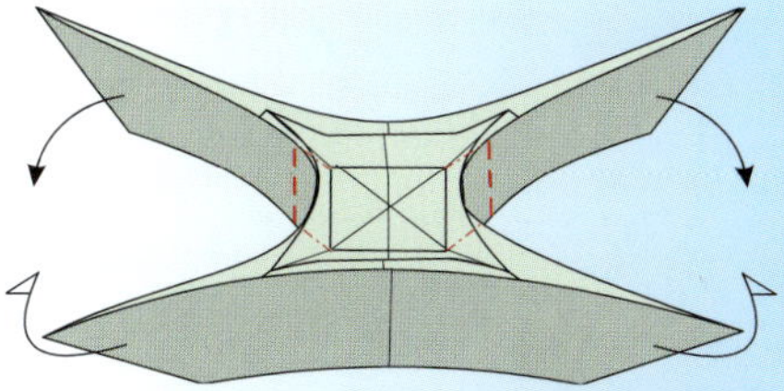

12. Fertiges Modell seitlich gesehen.
Finished model seen from the side.

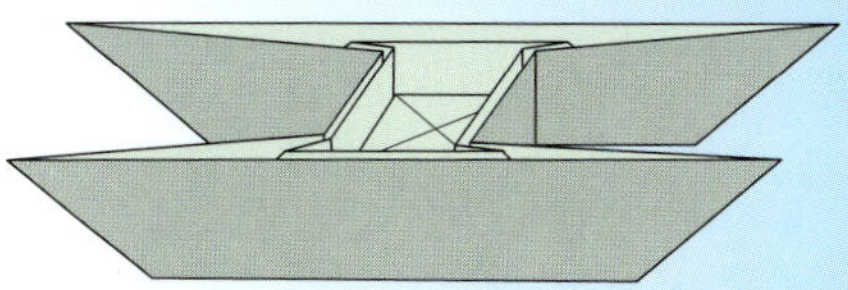

Rad für Tretboot
Wheel for pedal-boat

MATERIAL
1 Bogen 20x20 cm AQUAPAPIER
1 sheet 20x20 cm AQUAPAPIER

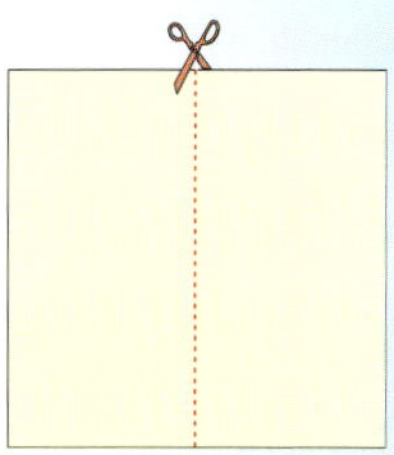

1. Papier an der senkrechten Linie durchschneiden.
Cut paper on the vertical line.

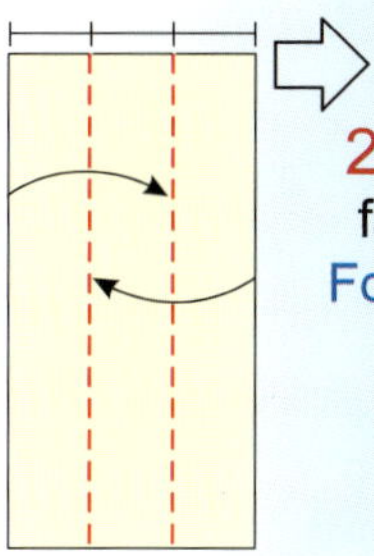

2. Senkrechte Linien falten, liegen lassen.
Fold vertical lines and leave.

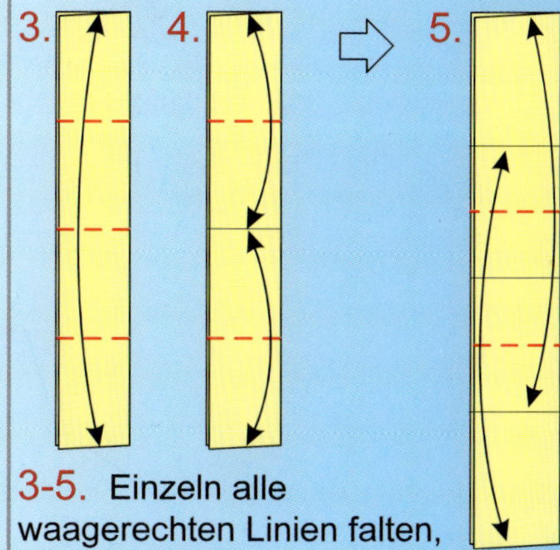

3-5. Einzeln alle waagerechten Linien falten, wieder öffnen.
Fold all horizontal lines separately and open again.

6. Waagerechte Linien falten, wieder öffnen. Rückseite nach oben legen.
Fold horizontal lines and open again.Put back upwards..

7. Zwischen den einzeln Linien nochmals waagerechte Linien falten, wieder öffnen.
Fold horizontal lines between the inidivual lines and open again.

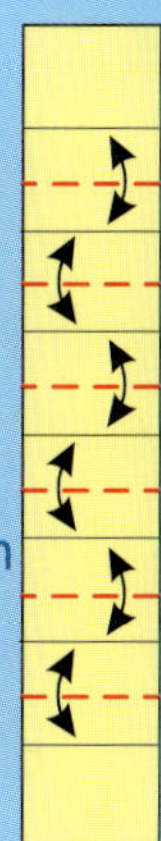

8. Jetzt wird zwischen den gefalteten Linien jeweils noch eine Zickzackfaltung durchgeführt.
Between the folded lines in each case a zigzag line is now accomplished.

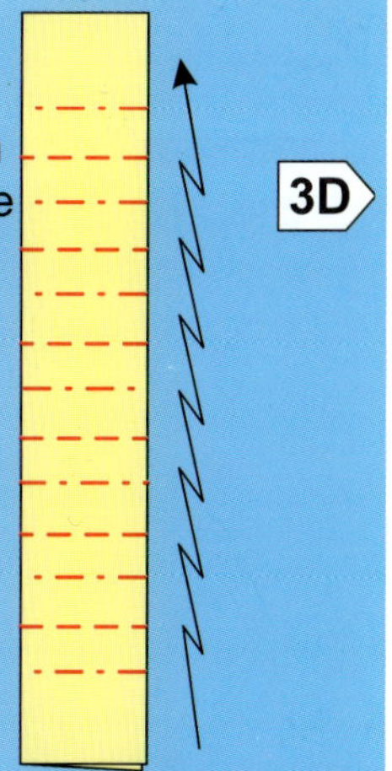

9. Rad, siehe Pfeile, im Boot unter die Papierlagen schieben, kleben, fertig.
Push wheel, see arrows, below the layers of paper, stick and ready.

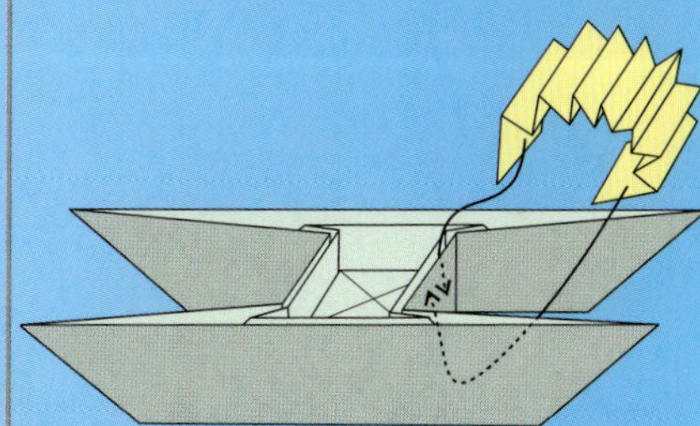

10. Fertiges komplett Modell seitlich gesehen.
Finished model seen from the side.

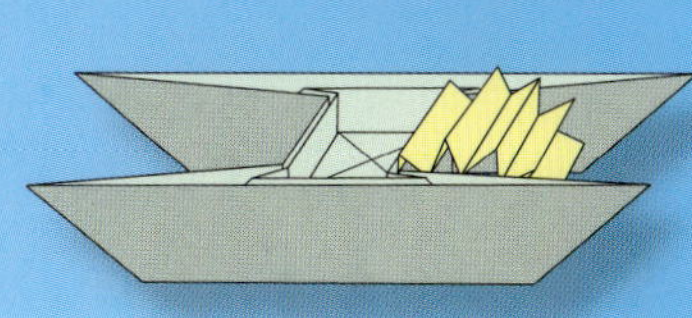

Schnellboot — Motor-torpedo boat

Boot für Wettfahrten
Boat für bet drivings

MATERIAL

1 Bogen 20x20 cm AQUAPAPIER
1 sheet 20x20 cm AQUAPAPIER

1. Senkrechte Linie falten, wieder öffnen.
Fold vertical line and open again.

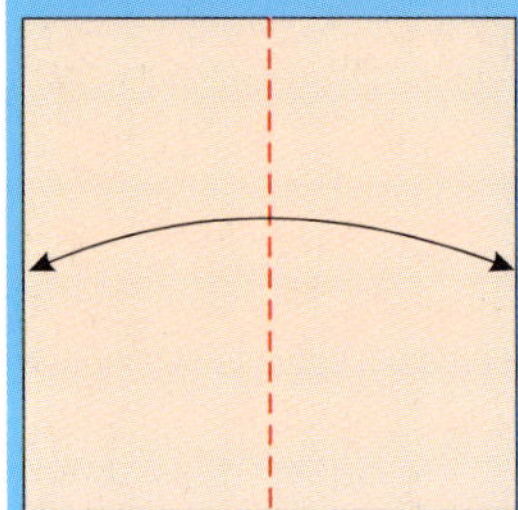

2. Schräge Linien falten, siehe Pfeile, liegen lassen.
Fold diagonal lines, see arrows, and leave.

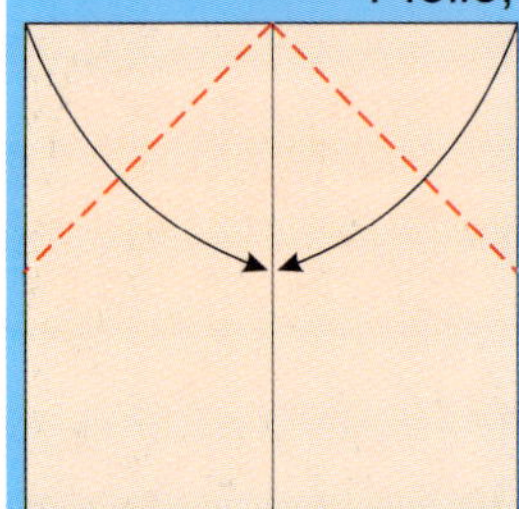

3. Schräge Linien falten, siehe Pfeile, liegen lassen.
Fold diagonal lines, see arrows, and leave.

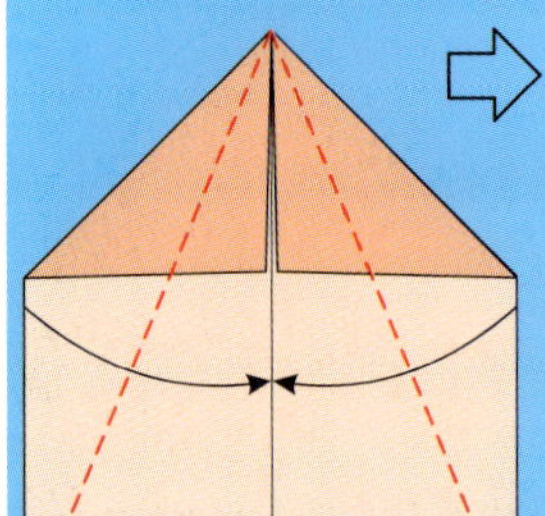

4. Senkrechte Linien falten, siehe Pfeile, liegen lassen.
Fold vertical lines, see arrows, and leave.

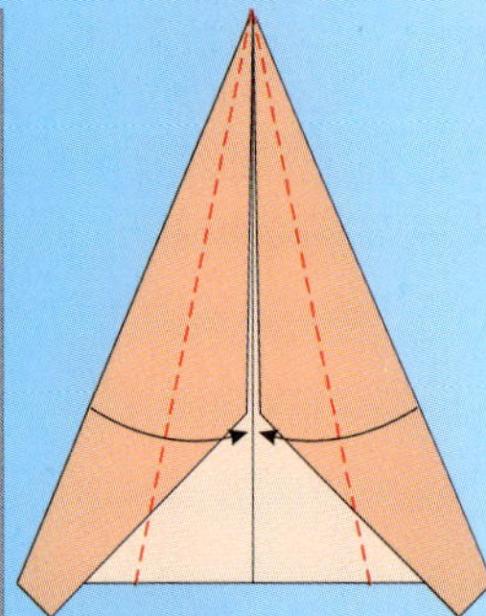

5. Waagerechte Linie falten, siehe Pfeile, liegen lassen.
Fold horizontal line, see arrows, and leave.

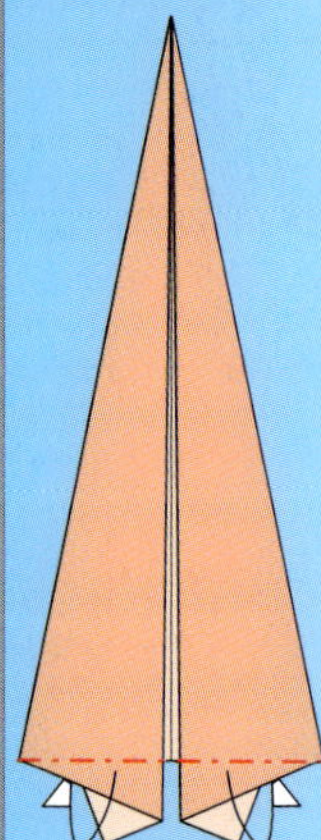

6. Schräge Linien falten, siehe Pfeile, liegen lassen.
Fold diagonal lines, see arrows, and leave.

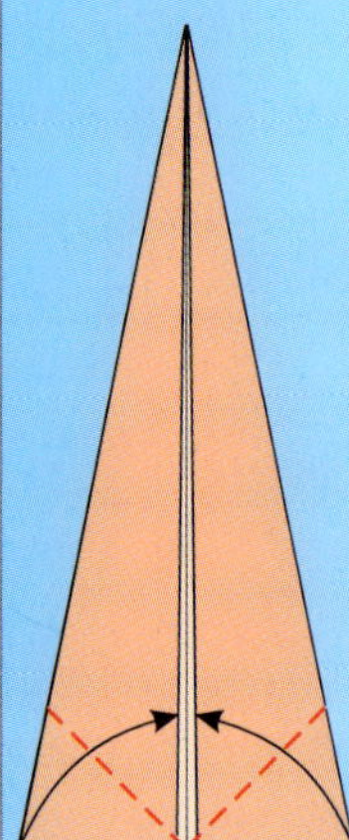

7. Schräge Linien falten, siehe Pfeile, liegen lassen.
Fold diagonal lines, see arrows, and leave.

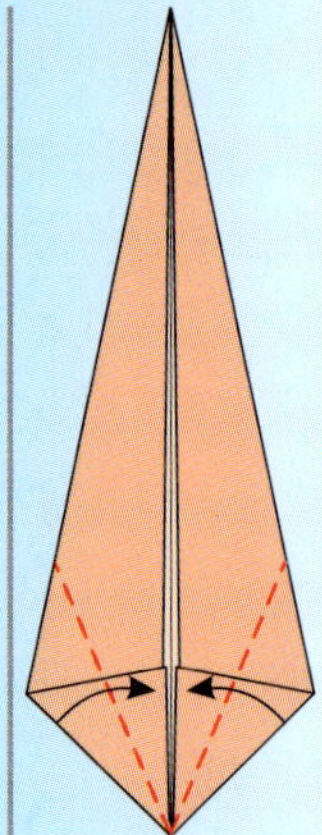

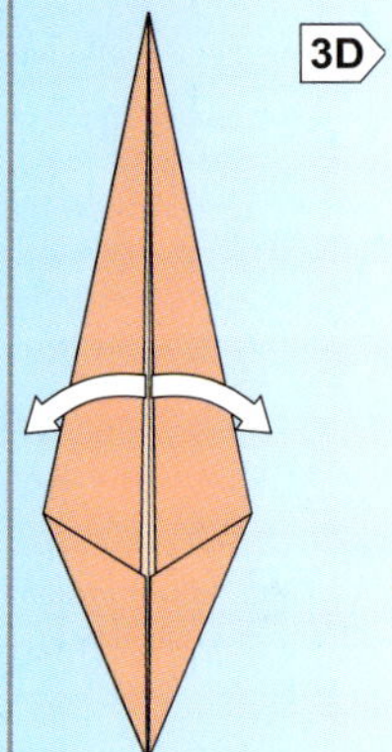

8. Gefaltetes Teil von innen nach außen öffnen, dabei die Schritte Nr. 6 + 7 wieder öffnen.
Pull the folded part outwards whilst opening steps no. 6 and 7.

9. An der unteren Spitze die oberen Papierlagen nach innen legen, siehe Pfeile.
Put the top layers of paper on the lower point inwards, see arrows.

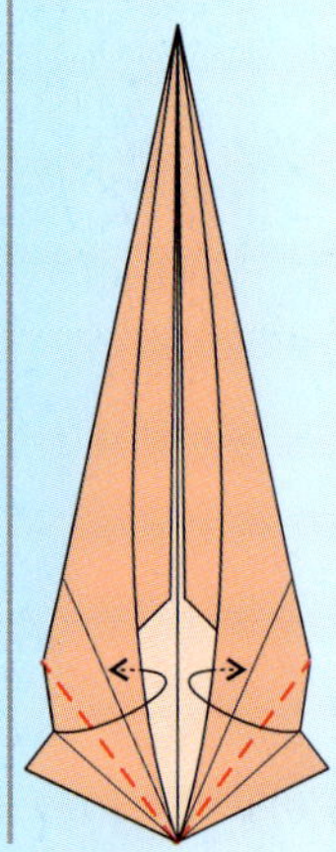

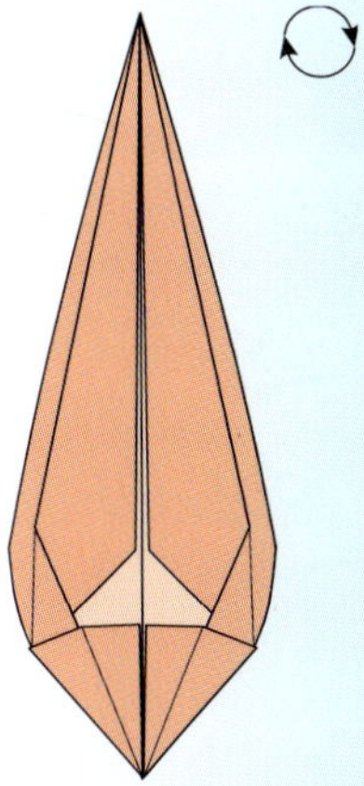

10. Modell um 90 Grad drehen, fertig.
Turn the model 90 degrees around, ready.

11. Fertiges Modell seitlich gesehen.
Finished model seen from the side.

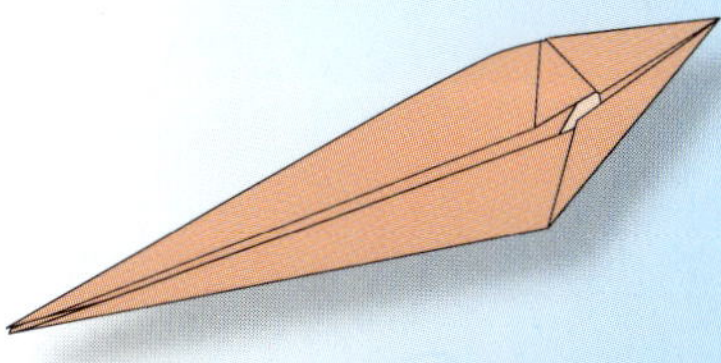

Start. Diagramme von Seite 26 bis Nr.6 falten.
Fold charts of page 26 until step no. 6.

1. Schräge Linien falten, siehe Pfeile, liegen lassen. Von der Mitte aus nach außen öffnen. An der unteren Spitze die oberen Papierlagen nach innen legen.
Fold the diagonal lines, see arrows, and leave. Open from the center outwards. Put the top layers of paper on the lower point inwards.

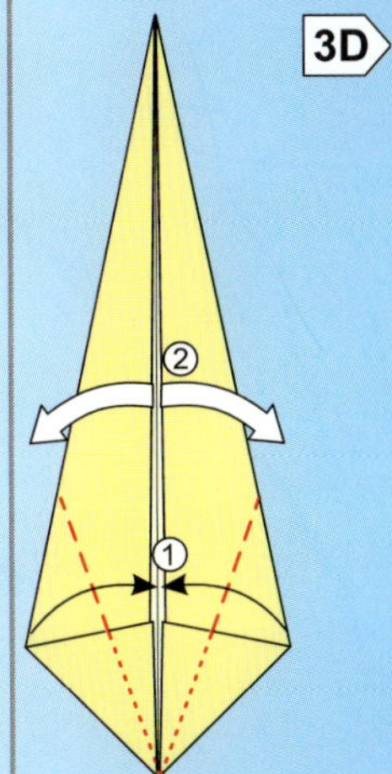

2. Waagerechte Linie zur Rückseite falten, Modell um 90 Grad drehen.
Fold horizontal line to back. Turn the model 90 degrees around.

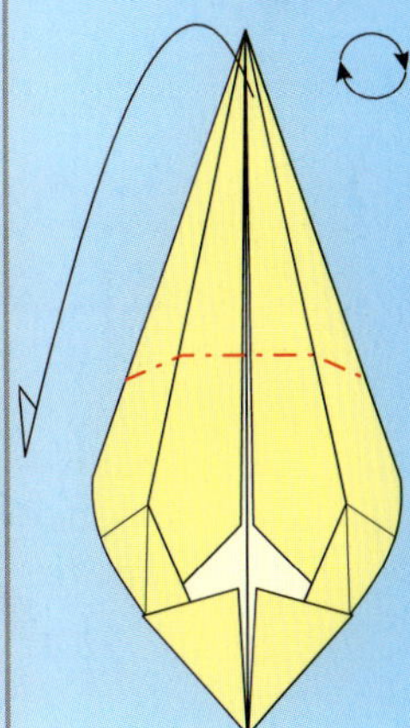

3. Papierlagen aufeinander kleben.
Stick layers of paper together.

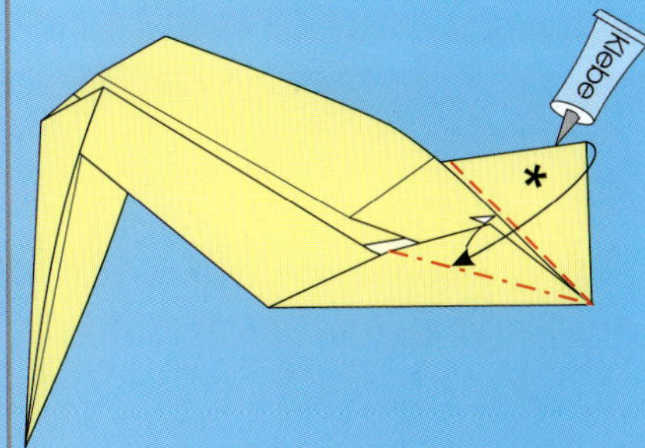

4. Linien falten wie gezeichnet, siehe Pfeile, liegen lassen.
Fold lines as indicated, see arrows, and leave.

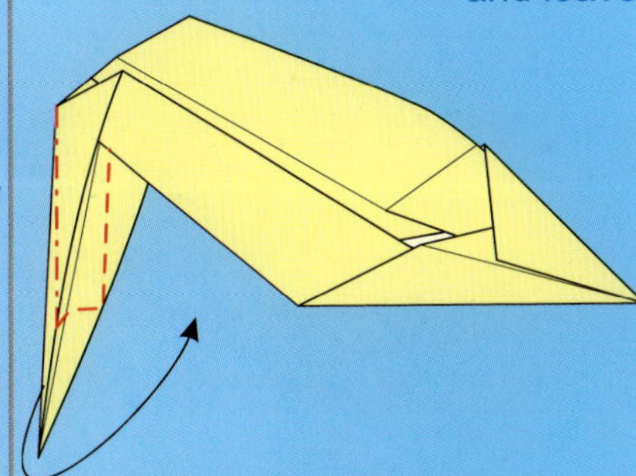

5. Fertiges Modell seitlich gesehen.
Finished model seen from the side.

Speedboote / Speed boats

Verschiedene Variationen möglich
Different variations are possible

MATERIAL
1 Bogen 20x20 cm AQUAPAPIER
1 sheet 20x20 cm AQUAPAPIER

1. Waagerechte Linie falten, wieder öffnen.
Fold horizontal line and open again.

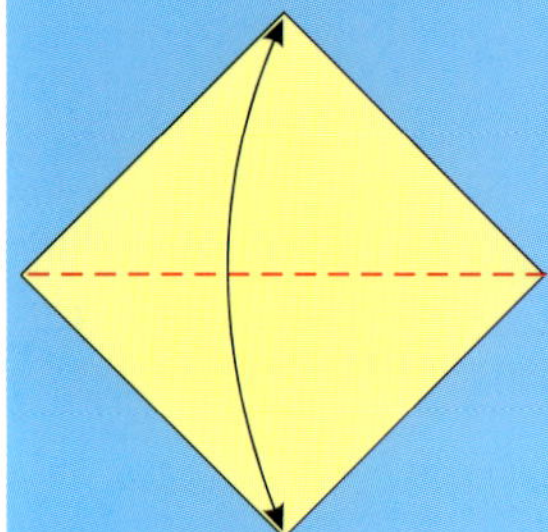

2. Schräge Linien falten, siehe Pfeile, wieder öffnen.
Fold diagonal lines, see arrows, and open again.

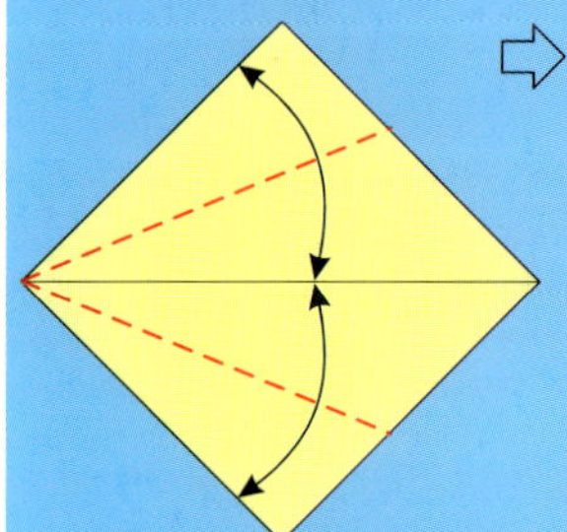

3. Schräge Linien falten, siehe Pfeile, liegen lassen.
Fold diagonal lines, see arrows, and leave.

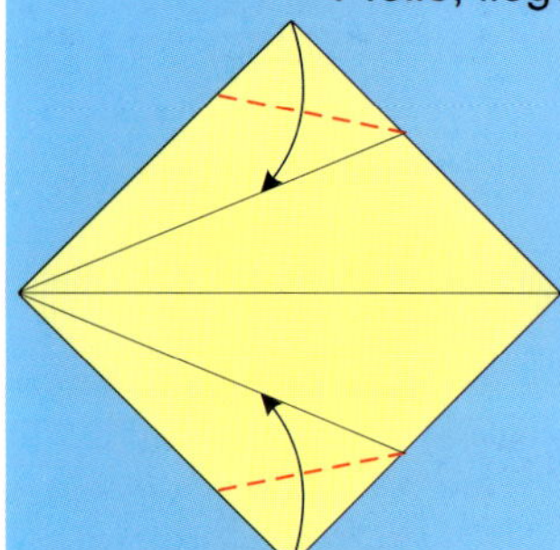

4. Schräge Linien falten, siehe Pfeile, liegen lassen.
Fold diagonal lines, see arrrows, and leave.

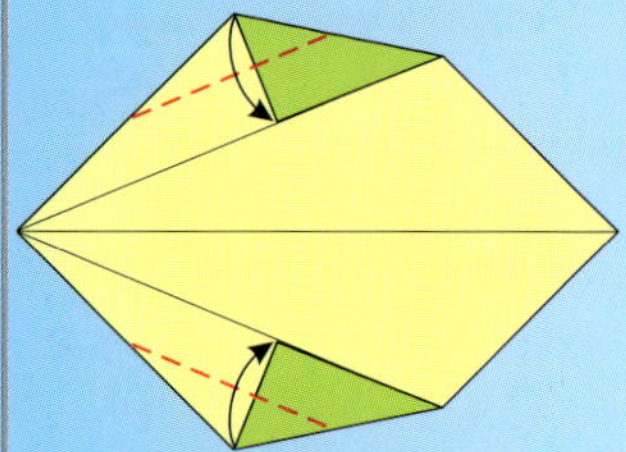

5. Schräge Linien falten, siehe Pfeile, liegen lassen.
Fold diagonal lines, see arrrows, and leave.

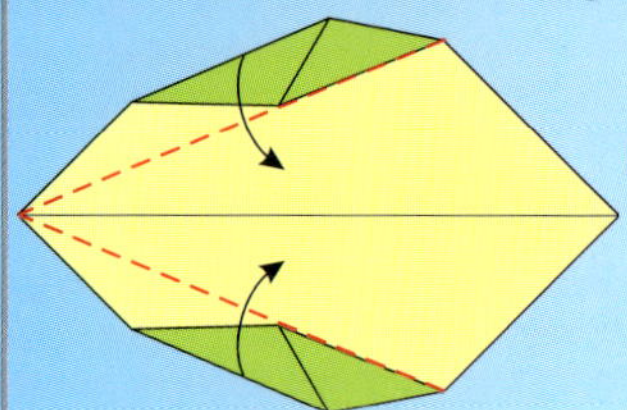

6. Waagerechte Linie falten, liegen lassen. Modell drehen.
Fold horizontal line and leave. Turn model.

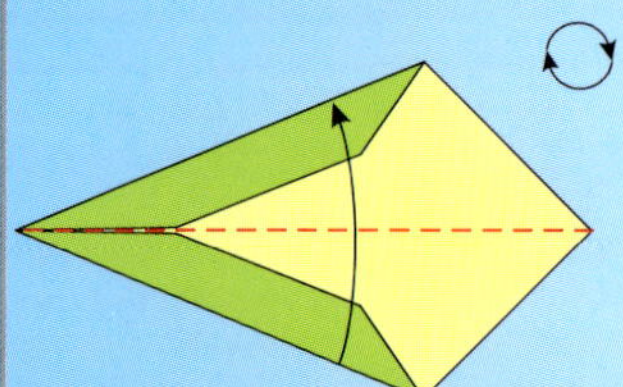

7. Schräge Linie falten, siehe Pfeil, wieder öffnen.
Fold diagonal line, see arrows, and open again.

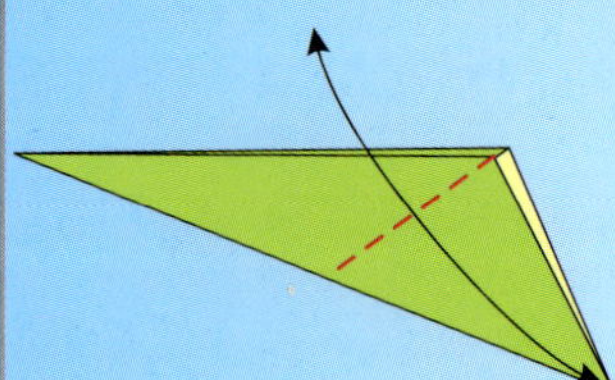

8. Schräge Linie im Gegenbruch nach innen legen, siehe Pfeil und nächste Zeichnung, liegen lassen.
Put diagonal line in inside reverse fold, see arrow and next chart, and leave.

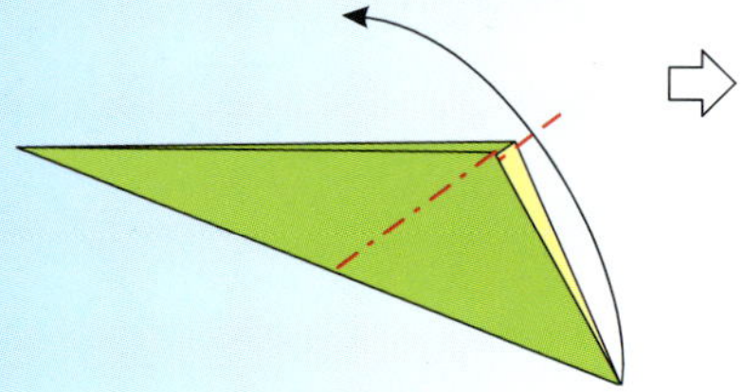

9. Waagerechte Linie falten, dann im Gegenbruch nach innen legen.
Fold horizontal line, put it then in inside reverse fold.

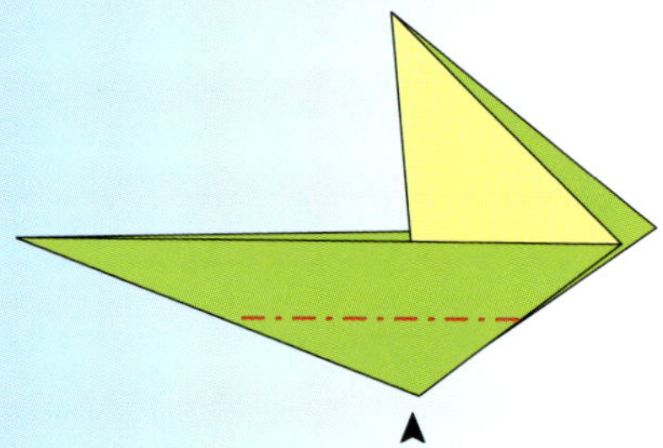

10. Fertiges Modell seitlich gesehen.
Finished model seen from the side.

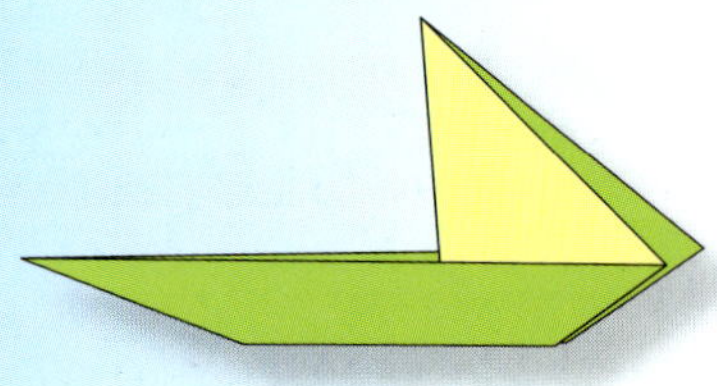

Variation 1

Start. Diagramme von Seite 28 bis Nr. 9 falten.
Fold charts of page 28 until no. 9.

1. Schräge Linie nach vorne falten, siehe Pfeil, Rückseite wiederholen.
Fold diagonal line forwards, see arrrow, repeat back.

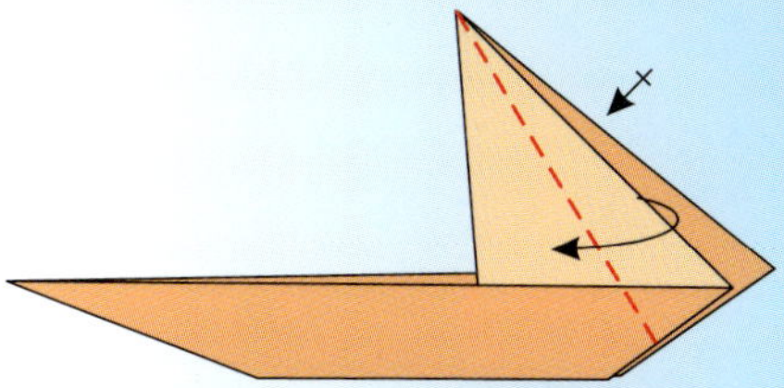

2. Fertiges Modell seitlich gesehen.
Finished model seen from the side.

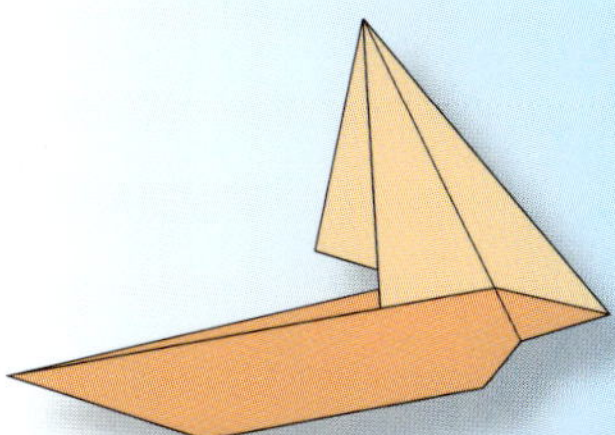

Variation 2

Start. Diagramme von Seite 28 bis Nr. 9 falten.
Fold charts of page 28 until no. 9.

1. Schräge Linie nach innen falten, siehe Pfeil, Rückseite wiederholen.
Fold diagonal line inwards, see arrow, repeat back.

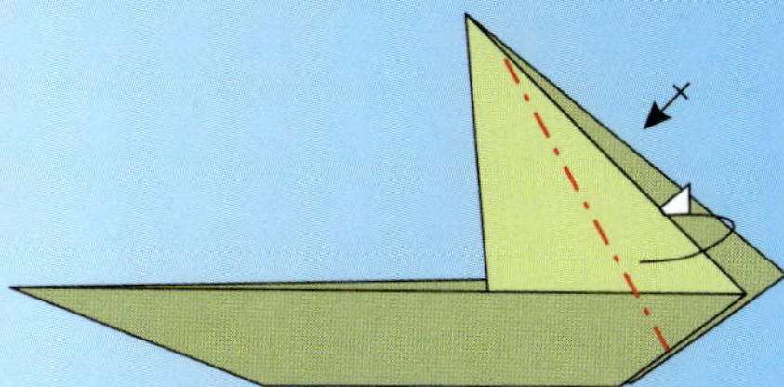

2. Fertiges Modell seitlich gesehen.
Finished model seen from the side.

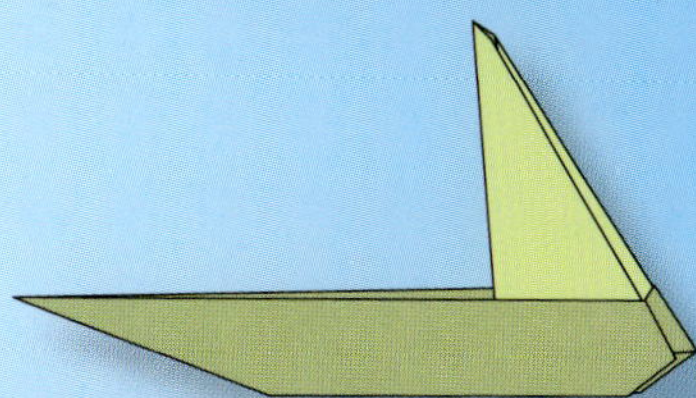

Variation 3

Start. Diagramme von Seite 28 bis Nr.9 falten. Dann Variation 2 bis Nr.2 falten.
Fold charts of page 28 until no. 9. Fold then the second variation until no. 2.

1. Waagerechte Linie falten, dann im Gegenbruch nach vorne legen.
Fold horizontal line, put it then forwards in reverse fold.

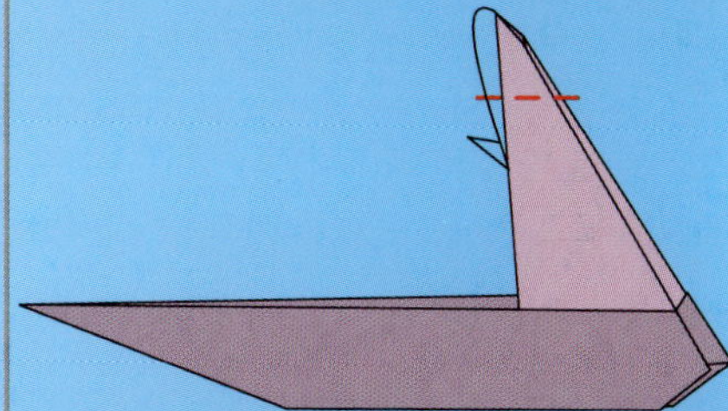

2. Schräge Linie falten, dann im Gegenbruch nach vorne legen.
Fold diagonal line, put it then forwards in reverse fold.

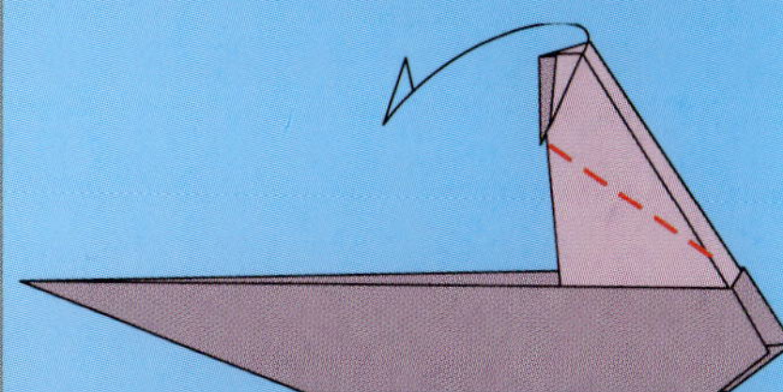

3. Fertiges Modell seitlich gesehen.
Finished model seen from the side.

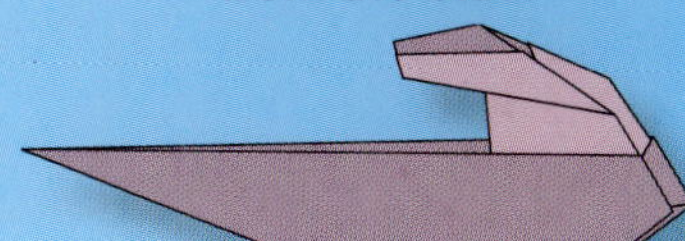

Auf hoher See

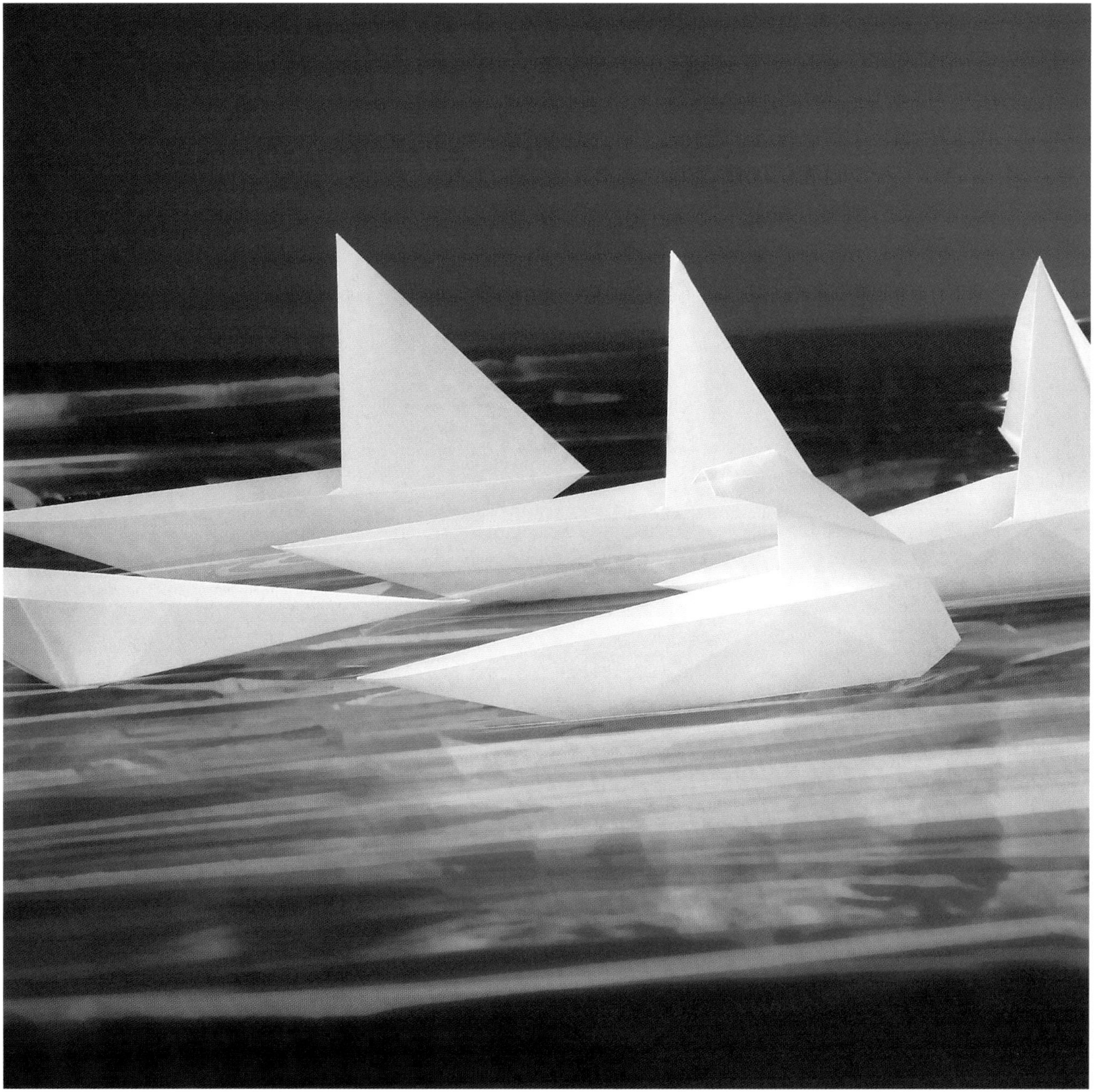

At sea

Motorjacht

Motor Yacht

MATERIAL
1 Bogen 20x20 cm AQUAPAPIER
1 sheet 20x20 cm AQUAPAPIER

1. Zweimal diagonal die Mitte falten, wieder öffnen.
Fold twice the middle diagonally and open again.

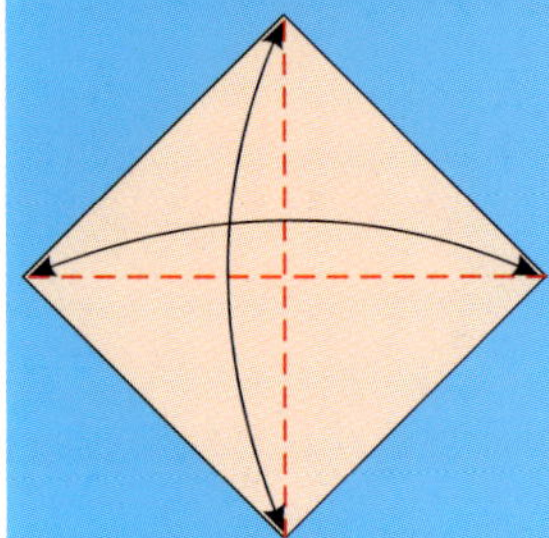

2. Senkrechte Linie falten, liegen lassen.
Fold vertical line and leave.

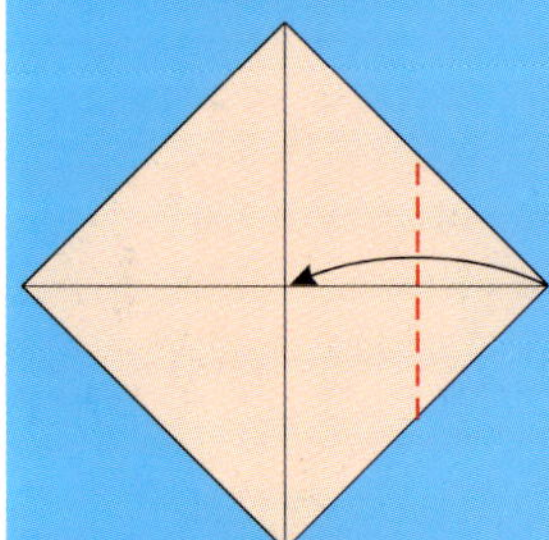

3. Waagerechte Linie zur Rückseite falten, liegen lassen.
Fold horizontal line to the back and leave.

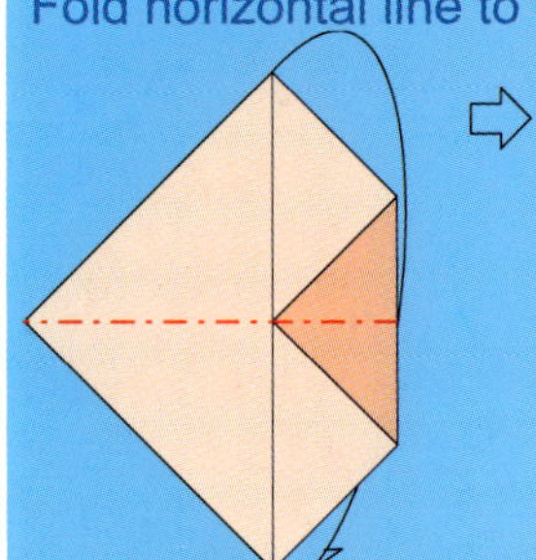

4. Senkrechte Linie falten, liegen lassen.
Fold vertical line and leave.

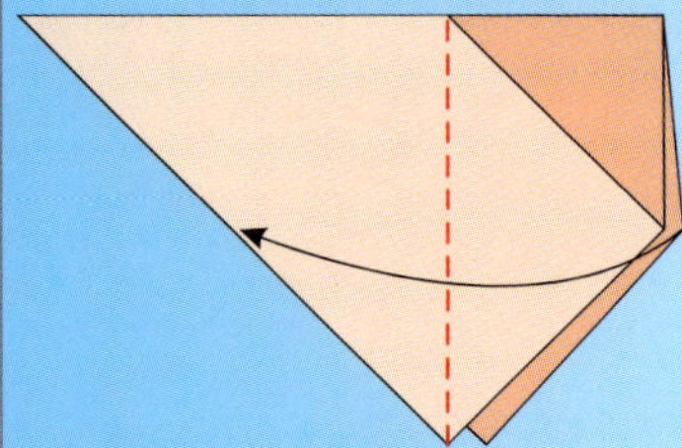

5. Linie zur Bergfalte formen und nach rechts legen, dabei die Ecke eindrücken.
Fold line to mountain-fold and put to the right. Push corner.

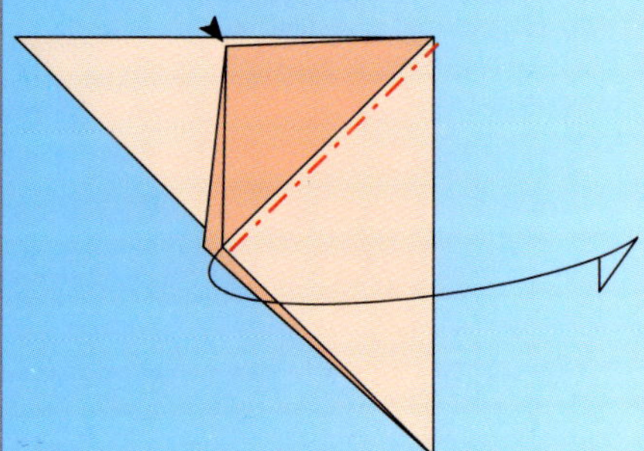

6. Nur mit der oberen Papierlage schräge Linie falten, liegen lassen.
Fold diagonal line with the top layer of paper only and leave.

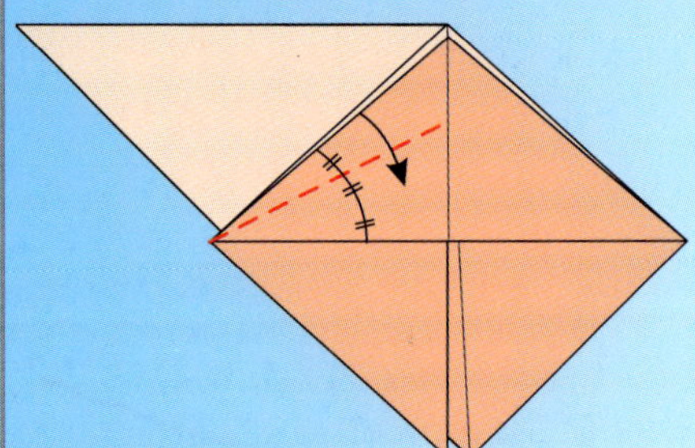

7. Nur mit der oberen Papierlage schräge Linie falten, liegen lassen.
Fold diagonal line with the top layer of paper only and leave.

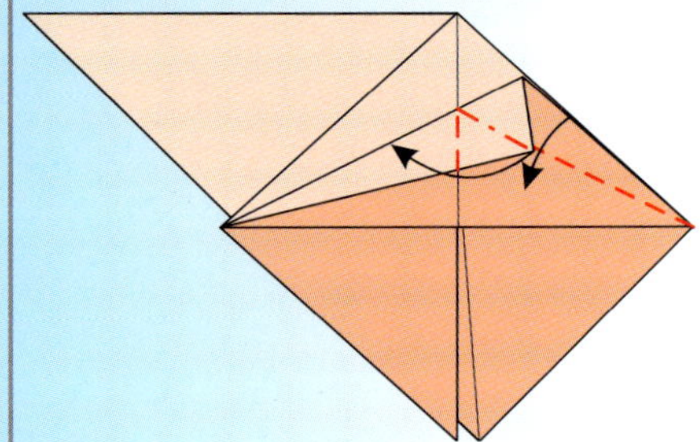

8. Beide schräge Linien falten, wieder öffnen.
Fold both diagonal lines and open again.

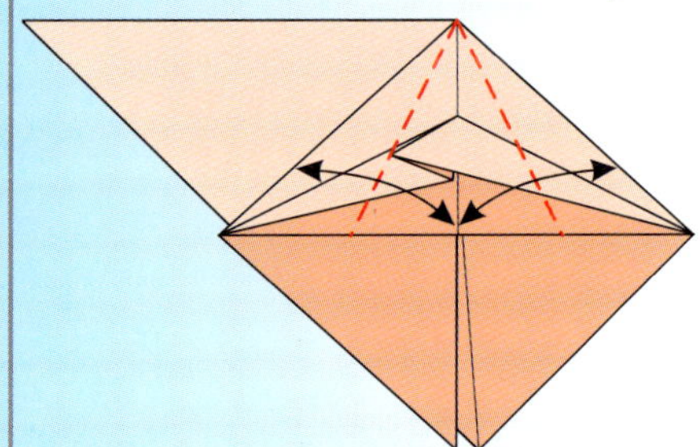

9. Beide schräge Linien falten, liegen lassen.
Fold both diagonal lines and leave.

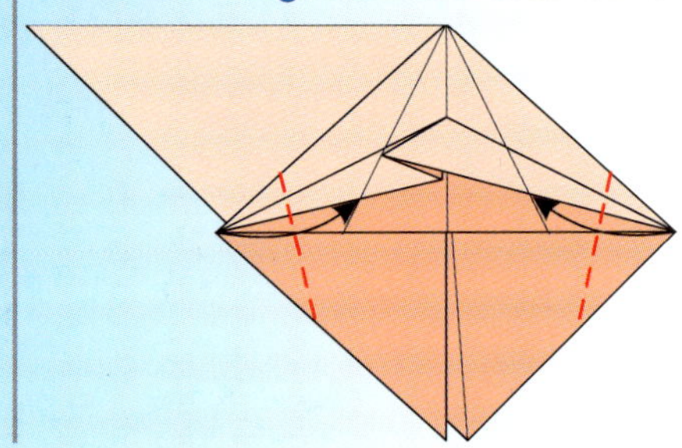

10. Senkrechte Mitte zur Bergfalte formen, siehe Pfeile, dann nach rechts legen.
Form vertical middle to mountain-fold, see arrows, and put to the right.

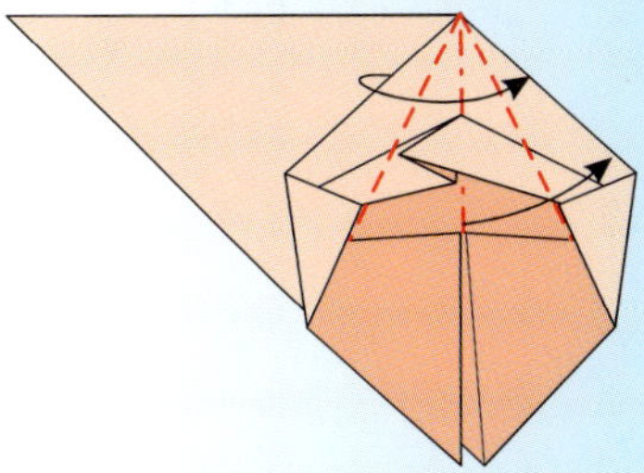

11. Siehe Pfeil, Papierlage nach rechts legen.
Put layer of paper to the right, see arrow.

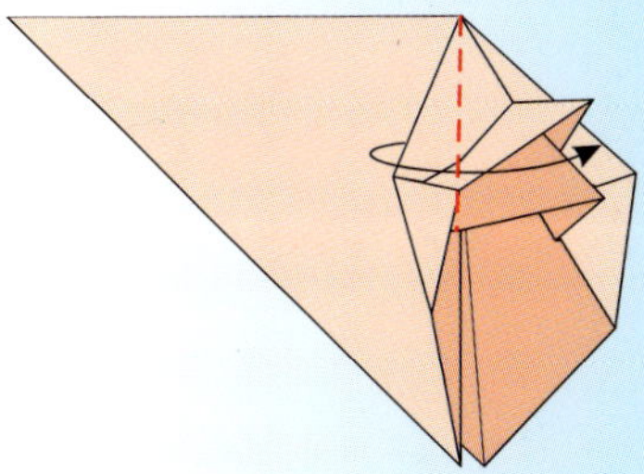

12. Schräge Linie falten, wieder öffnen. Siehe Pfeile, Papierlage nach oben wenden und drehen.
Fold diagonal line and open again. Turn layer of paper upwards., see arrows.

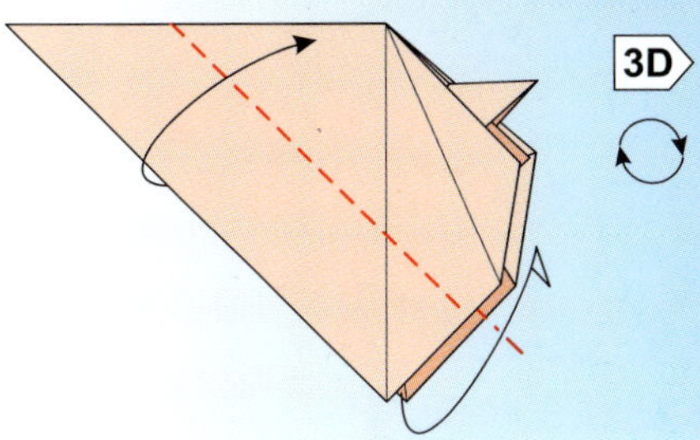

13. Schräge Linie an der Spitze nach innen falten. Senkrechte Linien falten, wieder öffnen. Die offenen Enden ineinanderschieben und kleben, fertig.
Fold diagonal line on the point inwards. Fold vertical lines and open again. Push the open ends together, stick them, ready.

14. Fertiges Modell seitlich gesehen.
Finished model seen from the side.

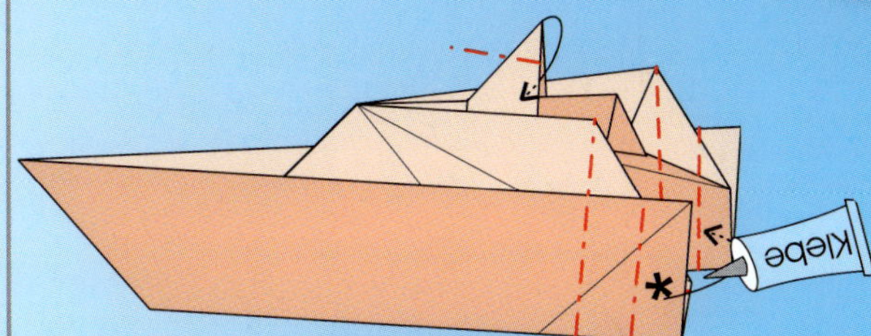

Segeljacht — Sailing Yacht

Boot und Segel ais einem Blatt
Boat and sail as one sheet

MATERIAL

1 Bogen 20x20 cm AQUAPAPIER
1 sheet 20x20 cm AQUAPAPIER

1. Waagerechte Linie falten, wieder öffnen.
Fold horizontal line and open again.

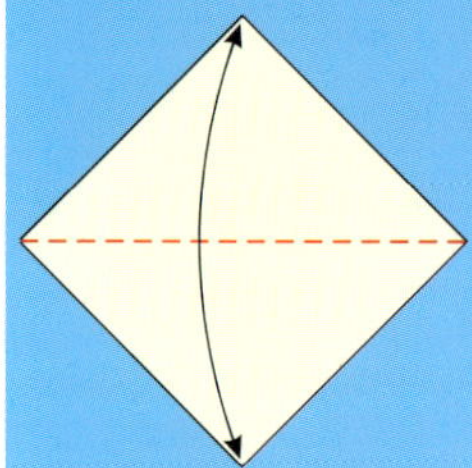

2. Schräge Linien falten, liegen lassen.
Fold diagonal lines and leave.

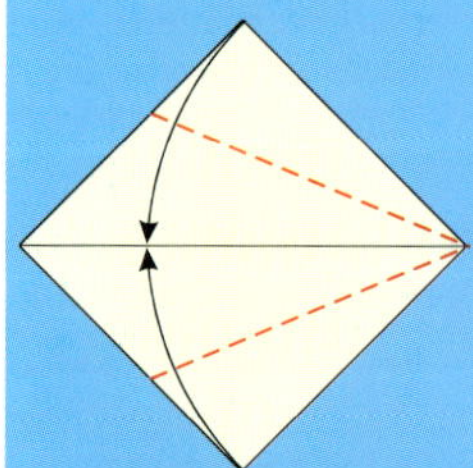

3. Senkrechte Linie falten, wieder öffnen.
Fold vertical line and open again.

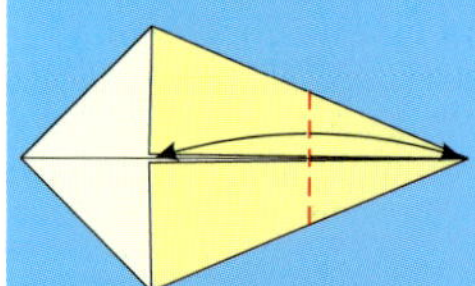

4. Modell komplett öffnen.
Open model completely.

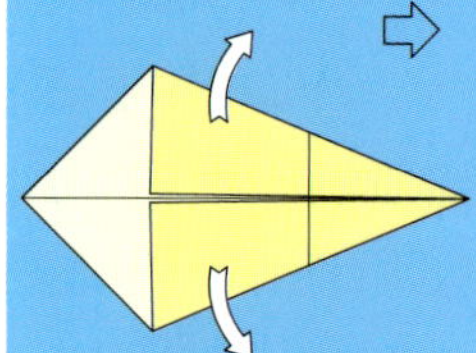

5. Schräge Linien falten, liegen lassen.
Fold diagonal lines and leave.

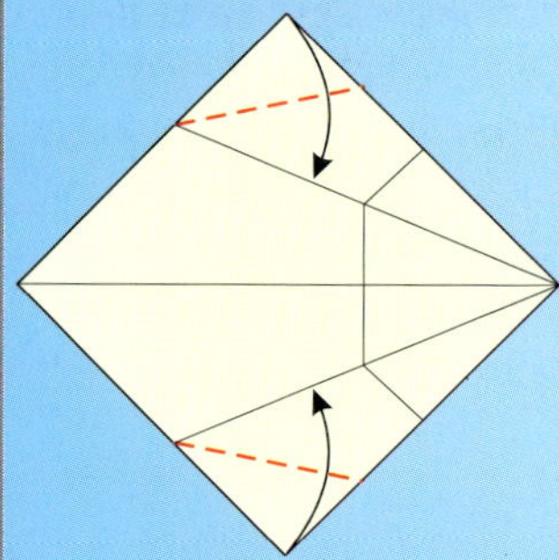

6. Schräge Linien falten, liegen lassen.
Fold diagonal lines and leave.

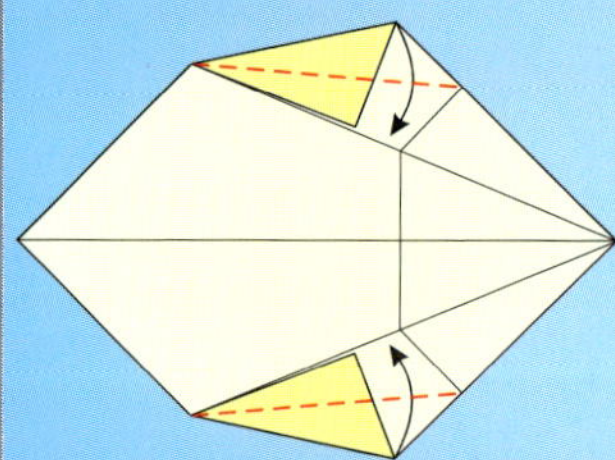

7. Schräge Linien falten, liegen lassen.
Fold diagonal lines and leave.

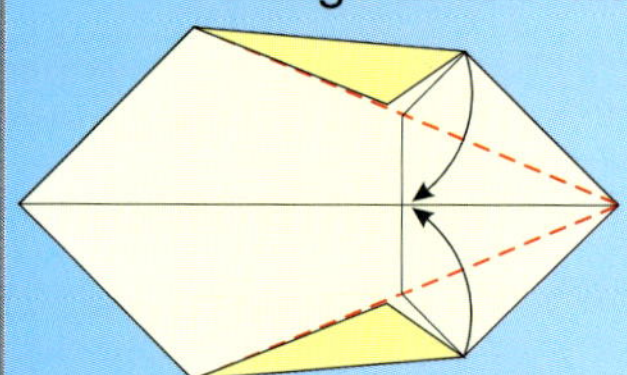

8. Waagerechte Linie zur Rückseite falten, liegen lassen.
Fold horizontal line to the back and leave.

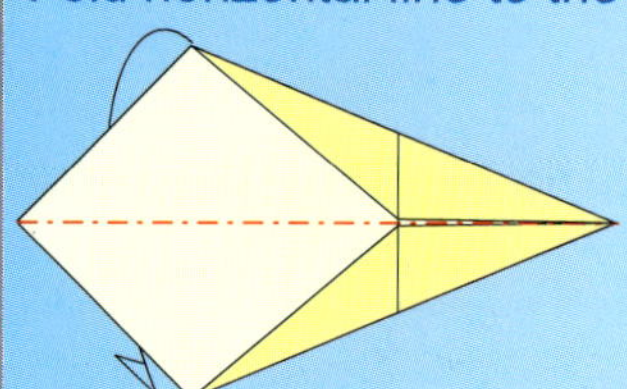

9. Linie zur Bergfalte formen, dann im Gegenbruch nach unten legen.
Form line to mountain-fold, put it then in reverse fold downwards.

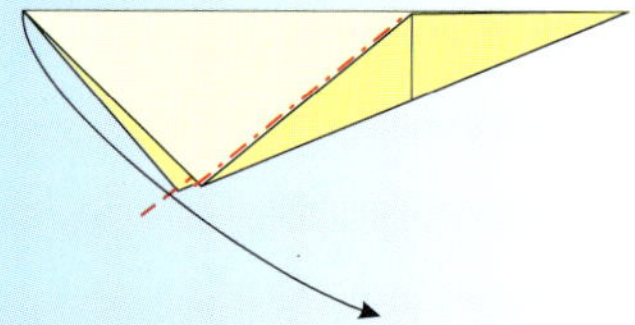

10. Linie zur Bergfalte formen, dann im Gegenbruch nach unten legen.
Form line to mountain-fold, put it then in reverse fold downwards.

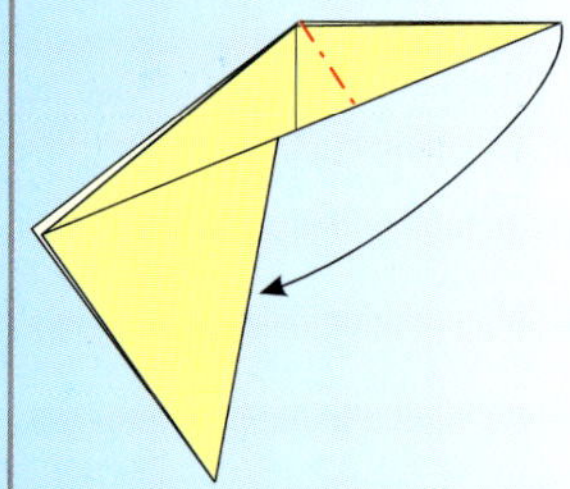

11. Linie zur Bergfalte formen, dann im Gegenbruch nach oben legen.
Form line to mountain-fold, put it then in reverse fold upwards.

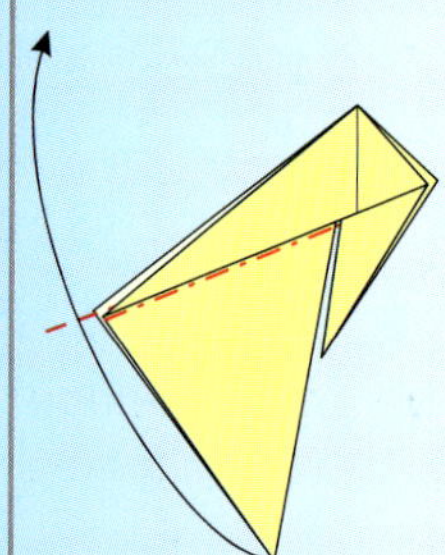

12. Modell um 90 Grad drehen, fertig.
Turn the model 90 degrees around, ready.

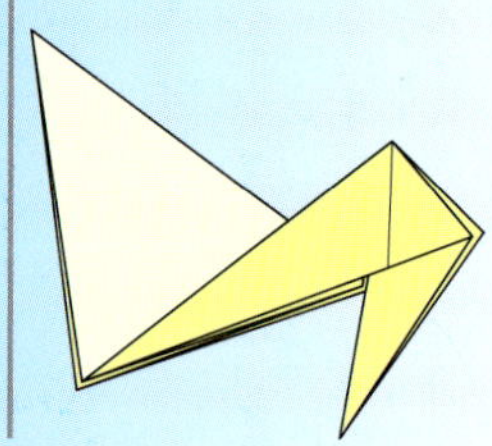

13. Schräge Linie falten, liegen lassen. Rückseite wiederholen.
Fold diagonal line and leave. Repeat back.

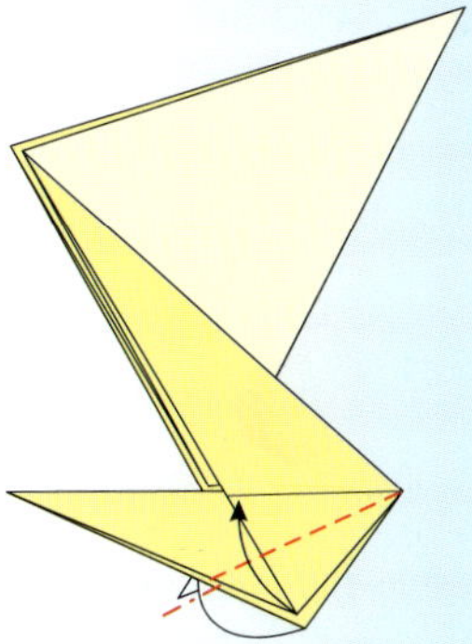

14. Waagerechte Linie falten, liegen lassen. Rückseite wiederholen.
Fold horizontal line and leave. Repeat back.

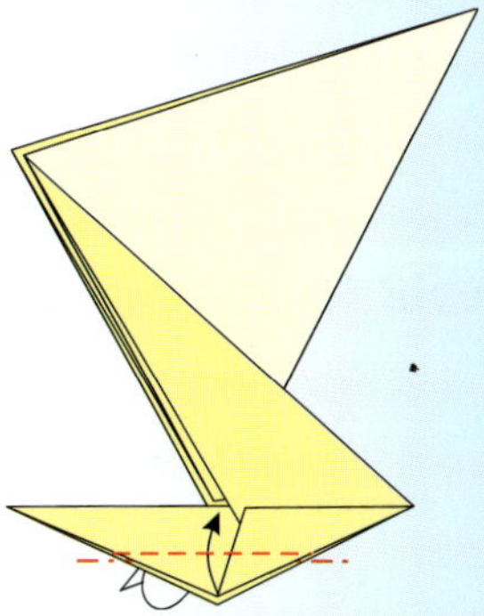

15. Nur mit der oberen Papierlage waagerechte Linie falten, liegen lassen.
Fold horizontal line only with top layer of paper and leave.

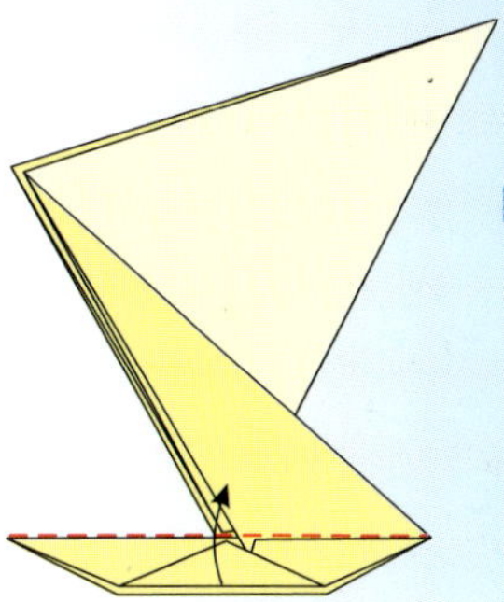

16. Die oberen Papierlagen nach außen ziehen, siehe Pfeile und nächste Zeichnung. Papier an der vorderen Spitze von oben etwas eindrücken.
Pull the top layers of paper outwards, see arrows and next chart. Push paper on front point from above downwards.

17. Am unteren Teil so drehen, bis das Papier waagerecht auf dem Tisch liegt.
Turn at the lower part in such a way until the paper lies horizontally on the table.

18. Die oberen Papierlagen nach außen öffnen, liegen lassen.
Open the top layers of paper outwards and leave.

19. Schräge Linie falten, liegen lassen. Rückseite wiederholen.
Fold diagonal line and leave. Repeat back.

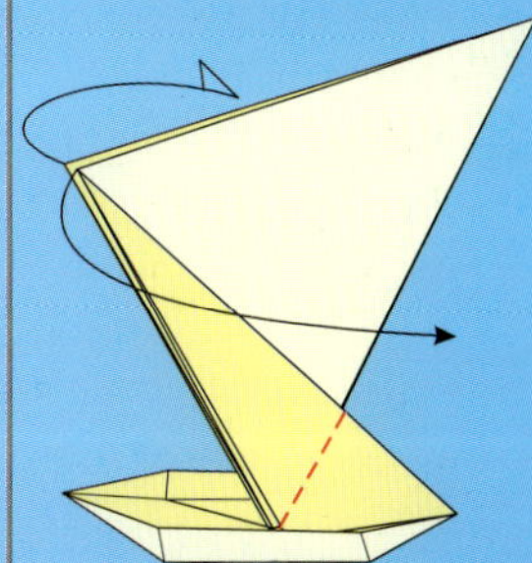

20. Fertiges Modell seitlich gesehen.
Finished model seen from the side.

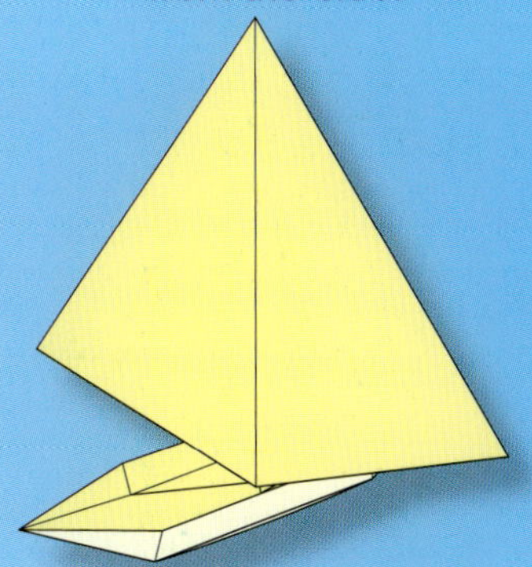

Segelboot mit Kajüte

MATERIAL
1 Bogen 20x20 cm AQUAPAPIER
1 sheet 20x20 cm AQUAPAPIER

1. Waagerecht falten, wieder öffnen. Senkrecht falten, liegen lassen.
Fold horizontally, open again. Fold vertically and leave.

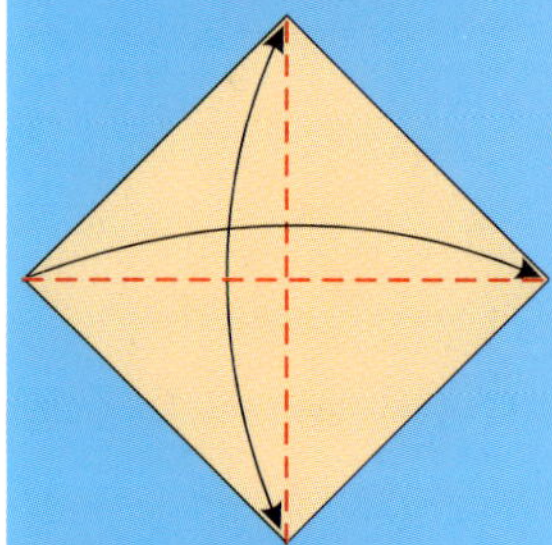

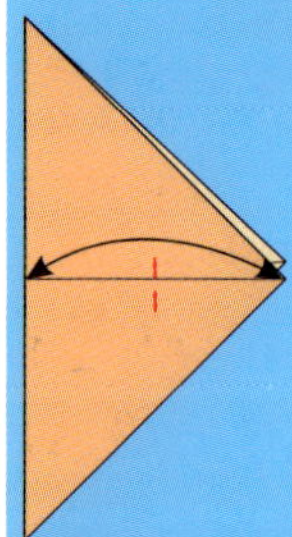

2. Markierung auf 1/2 anbringen.
Attach marking on 1/2 attach.

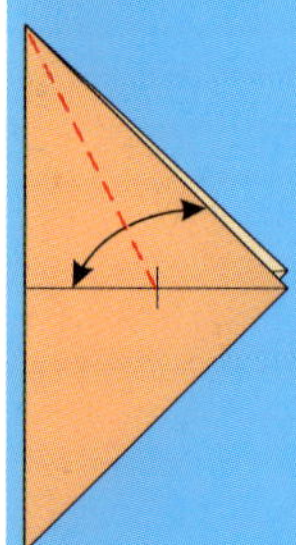

3. Schräge Linie falten, wieder öffnen.
Fold diagonal line and open again.

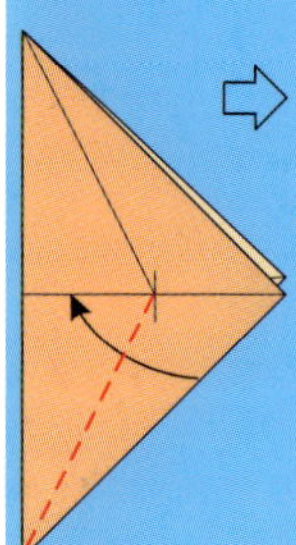

4. Schräge Linie falten, liegen lassen.
Fold diagonal line and leave.

5. Linien zu Bergfalten formen, dann die obere Papierlage, siehe Pfeil, formen. Danach die obere Spitze zur Rückseite falten, siehe auch nächste Zeichnung.
Form lines to mountain-fold, then form top layer of paper, see arrow. Fold then upper point to back, see also next chart.

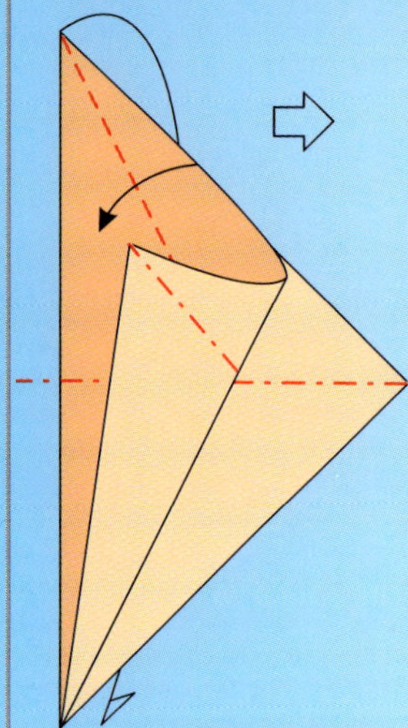

6. Schräge Linie falten, wieder öffnen. Rückseite wiederholen.
Fold diagonal line and open again. Repeat back.

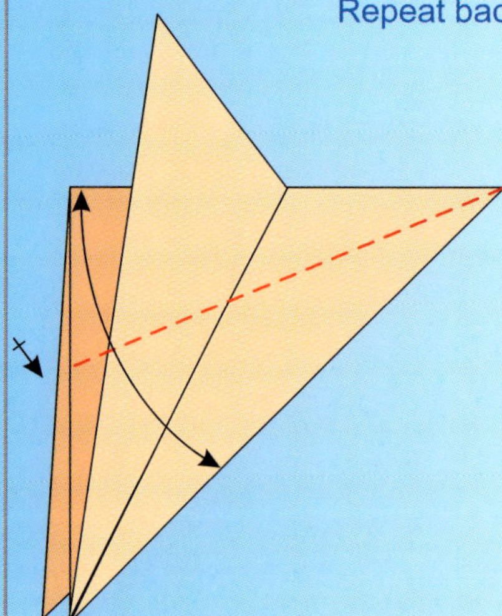

7. Schräge Linie falten, liegen lassen. Rückseite wiederholen.
Fold diagonal line and leave. Repeat back.

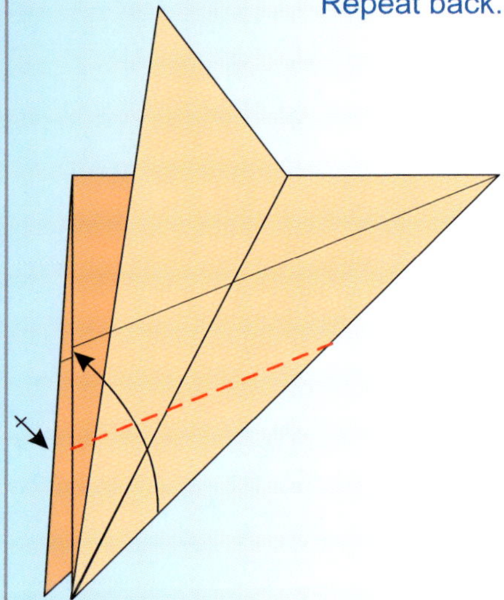

8. Schräge Linie von Nr.6 wieder nach oben legen, liegen lassen. Rückseite wiederholen. Modell etwas drehen.
Put diagonal line of no. 6 upwards and leave. Repeat back. Turn model somewhat.

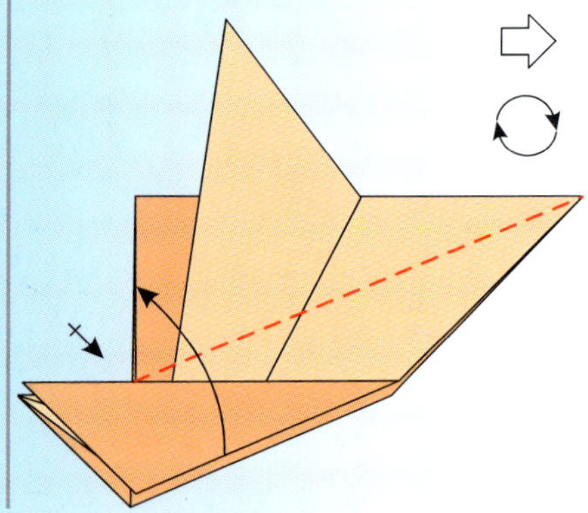

Sailing boat with cabin

9. Senkrechte Linie falten, liegen lassen.
Fold vertical line and leave.

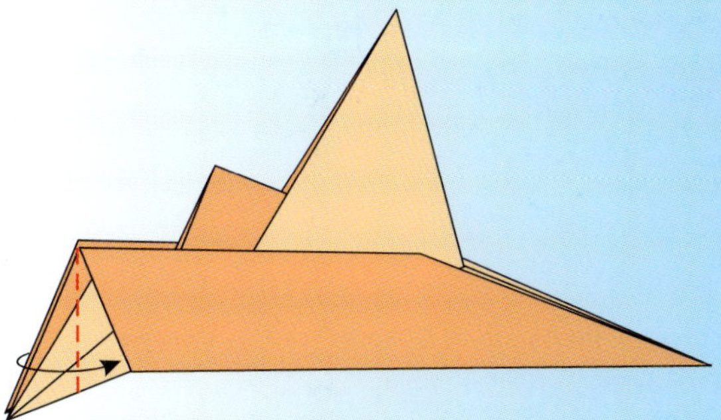

10. Schräge Linie zur Rückseite falten, liegen lassen.
Fold diagonal line to back and leave.

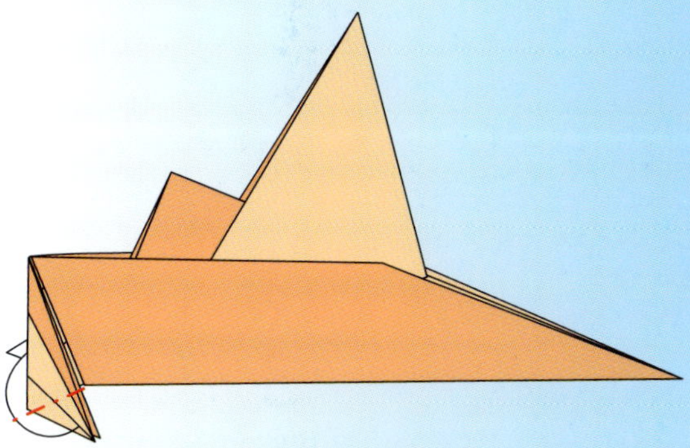

11. Schräge Linie falten, siehe Pfeil, dann zwischen die vorderen Papierlagen schieben.
Fold diagonal line, see arrow, push it then between the front layers of paper.

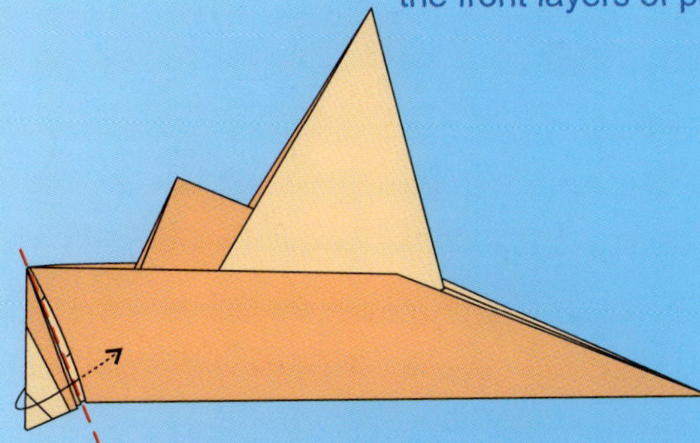

12. Papierlagen nach außen öffnen, siehe Pfeile. Vordere Spitze nach oben formen, dabei in der Mitte etwas eindrücken.
Open layers of paper outwards, see arrows. Form upper point upwards whilst pushing the middle.

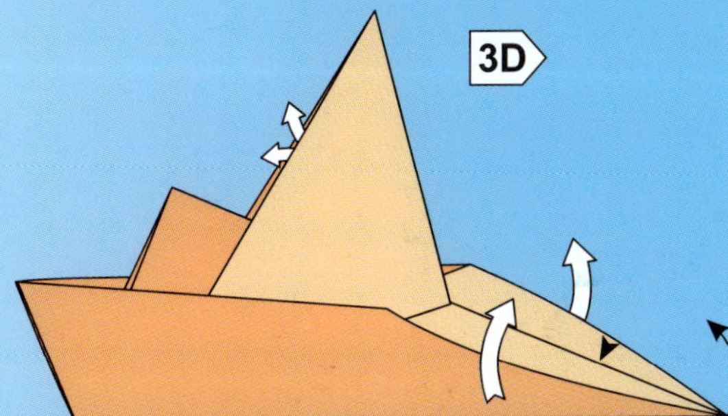

13. Fertiges Modell seitlich gesehen.
Finished model seen from the side.

Dieses Boot kann auch von einem Blatt aus der Natur hergestellt werden.
This boat can be made also of a nature leaf.

MATERIAL

1 Bogen 20x20 cm AQUAPAPIER
1 sheet 20x20 cm AQUAPAPIER

1. Papier an der waagerechten Linie durchschneiden.
Cut paper on the horizontal line.

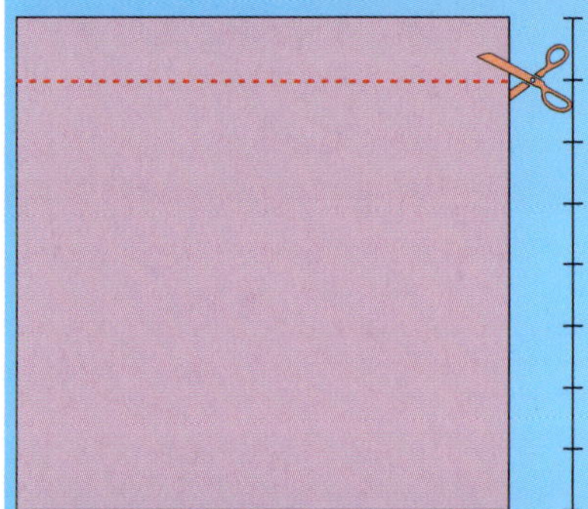

2. Waagerechte Linien falten, wieder öffnen.
Fold horizontal lines and leave.

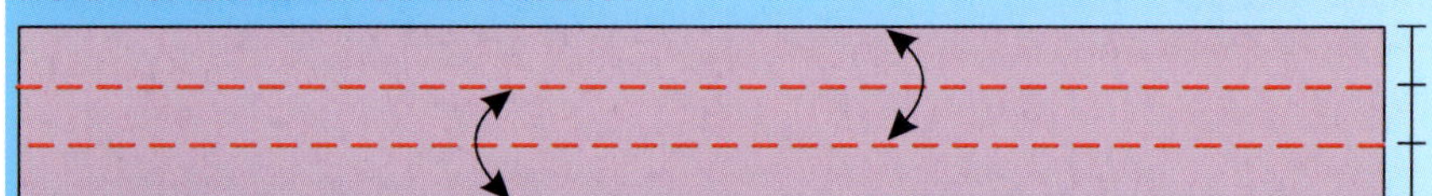

3. Senkrechte Linie falten, wieder öffnen.
Fold vertical lines and leave.

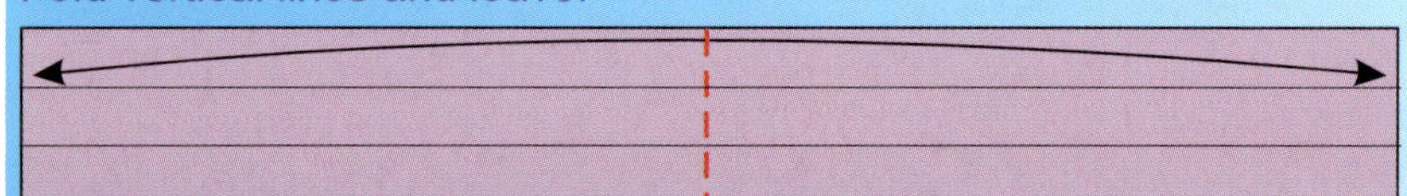

4. Senkrechte Linien falten, liegen lassen.
Fold vertical lines and leave.

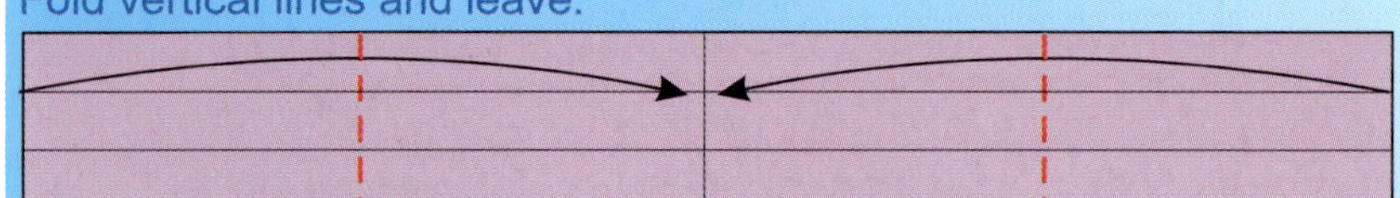

5. Papier an den waagerechten Linien einschneiden, siehe rote Punkte.
Cut paper on the horizontal lines, see red points.

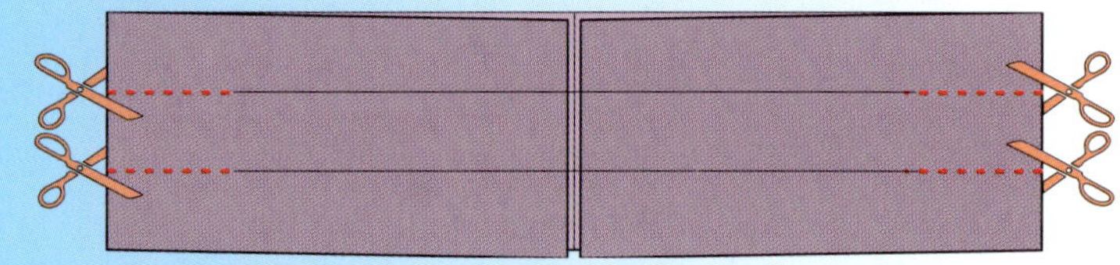

6. An den Seiten sind nun drei gleiche Papierstreifen zu sehen. Der rechte wird nun in den linken Streifen geschoben. Der mittlere Streifen liegt dann oben auf.
At the sides three equal paper strips are to be seen now. The right is pushed in the left strip now. The middle strip lies then on top.

3D

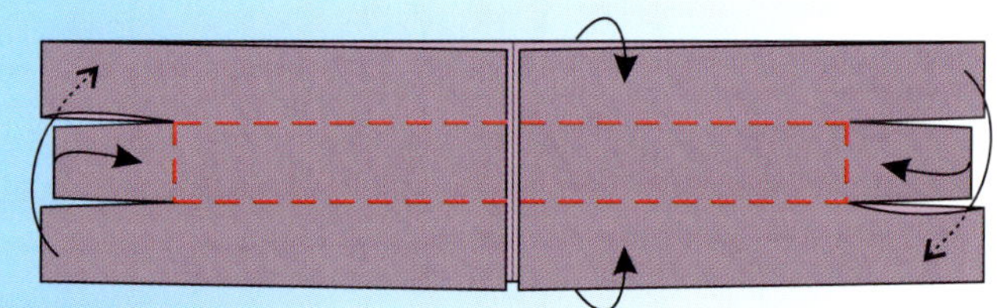

7. Fertiges Modell seitlich gesehen.
Finished model seen from the side.

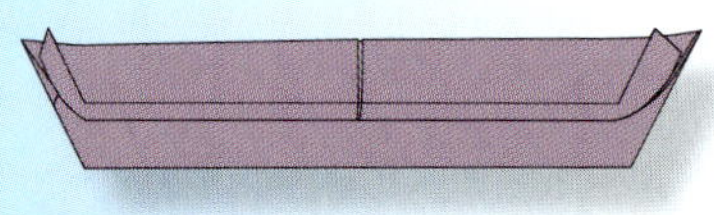

Cleopatra Schiff

Boat of Cleopatra

MATERIAL
1 Bogen 20x20 cm AQUAPAPIER
1 sheet 20x20 cm AQUAPAPIER

1. Markierung auf 1/2 anbringen.
Attach marking on 1/2.

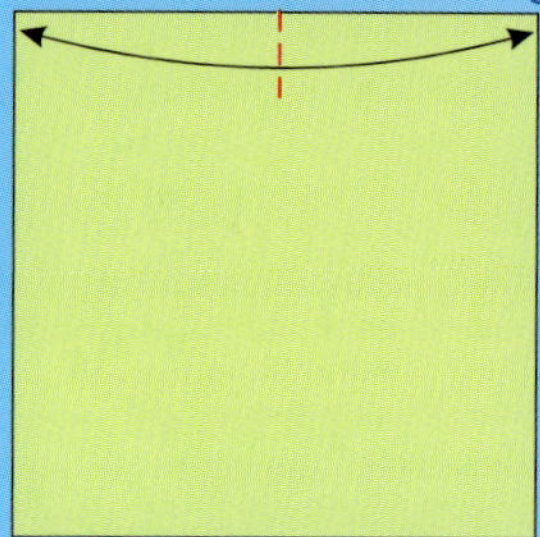

2. Schräge Linie falten, wieder öffnen.
Fold diagonal line and open again.

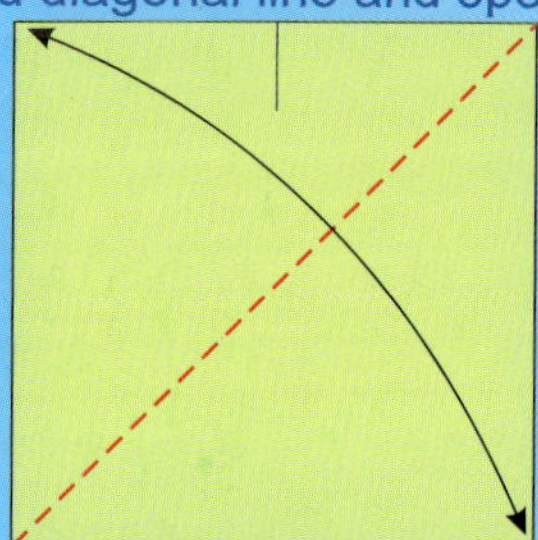

3. Schräge Linie falten, wieder öffnen.
Fold diagonal line and open again.

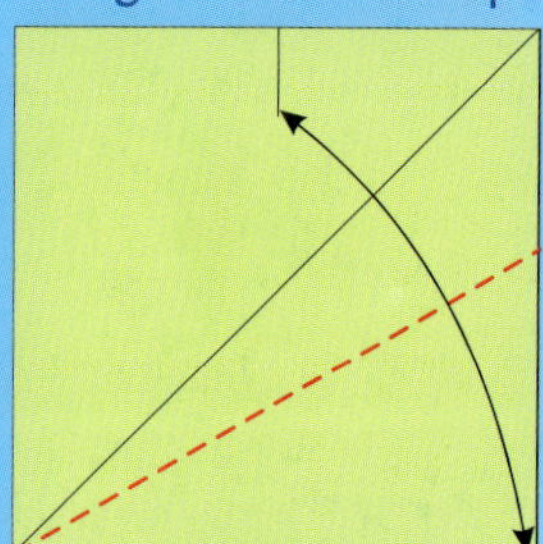

4. Schräge Linie falten, liegen lassen.
Fold diagonal line and leave.

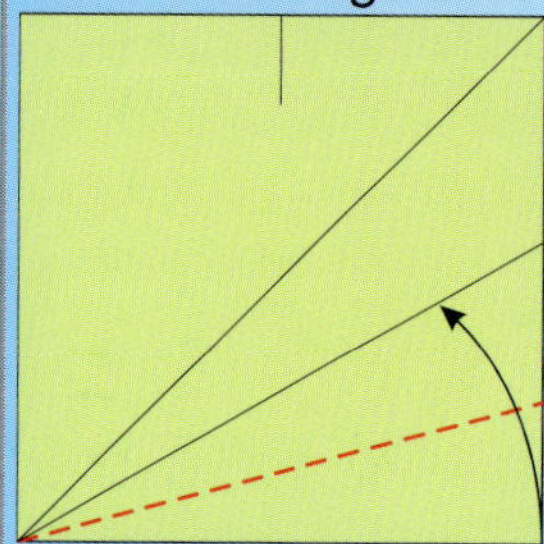

5. Schräge Linie falten, liegen lassen.
Fold diagonal line and leave.

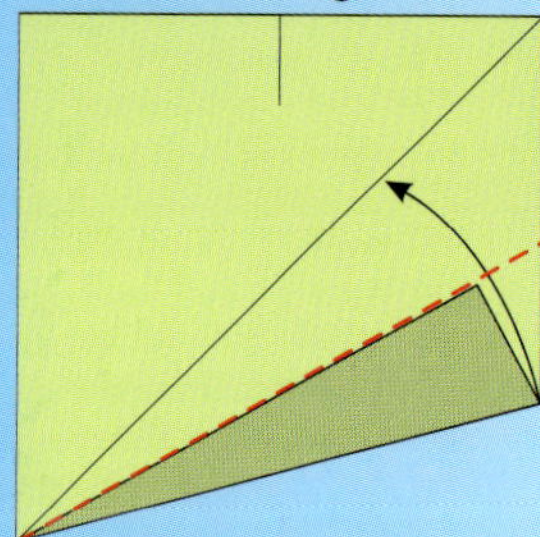

6. Schräge Linie falten, wieder öffnen.
Fold diagonal line and open again.

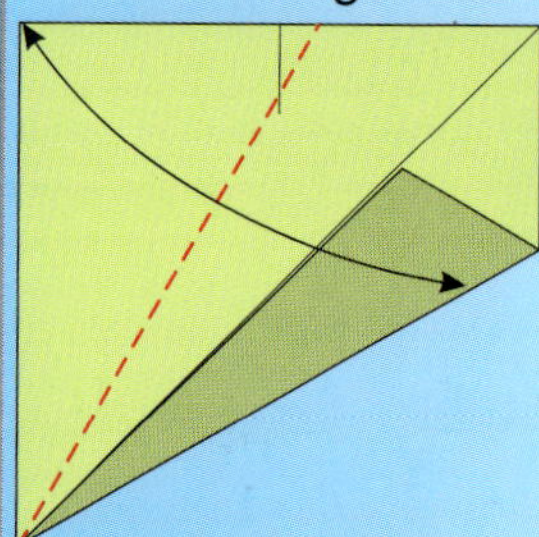

7. Schräge Linie falten, liegen lassen.
Fold diagonal line and leave.

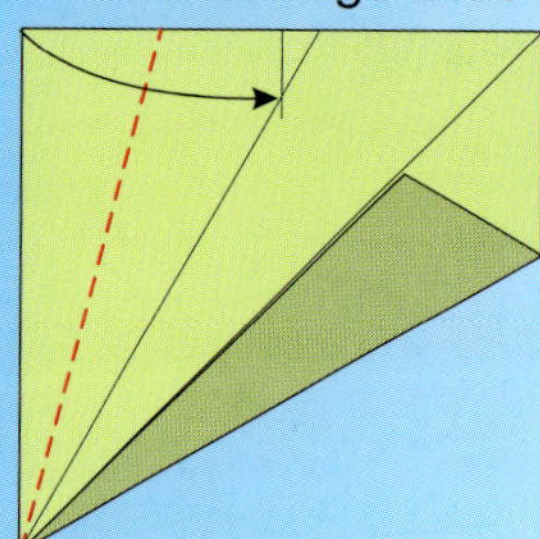

8. Schräge Linie falten, liegen lassen.
Fold diagonal line and leave.

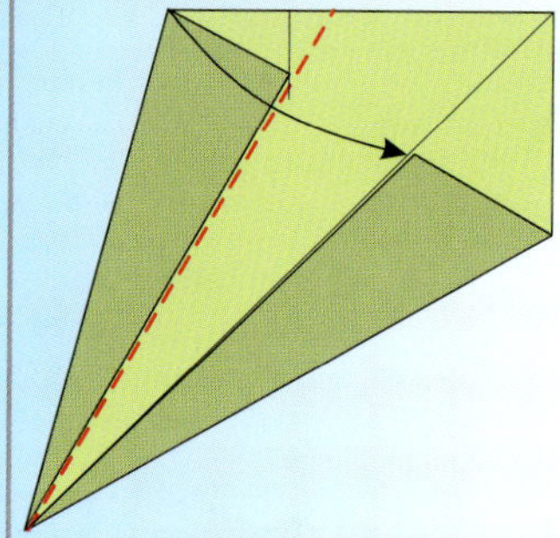

9. Schräge Linien falten, wieder öffnen.
Fold diagonal lines and open again.

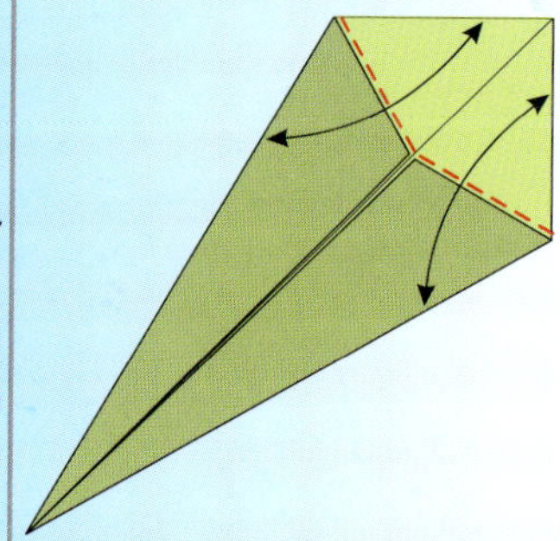

10. Obere Papierlage einmal wieder öffnen, siehe Pfeil.
Open only top layer of paper, see arrow.

11. Obere Spitze an den gefalteten Linien nach unten legen.
Put upper point at the folded lines downwards.

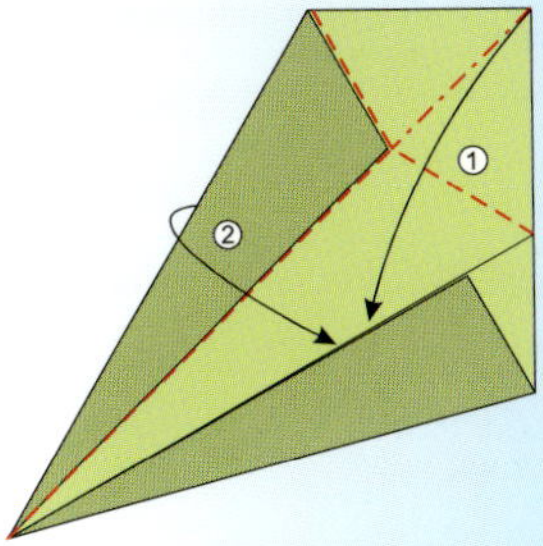

12. Siehe Pfeil, die rechte Papierlage in die neu gebildete Papiertasche schieben.
Push right layer of paper in new formed paper bag, see arrow.

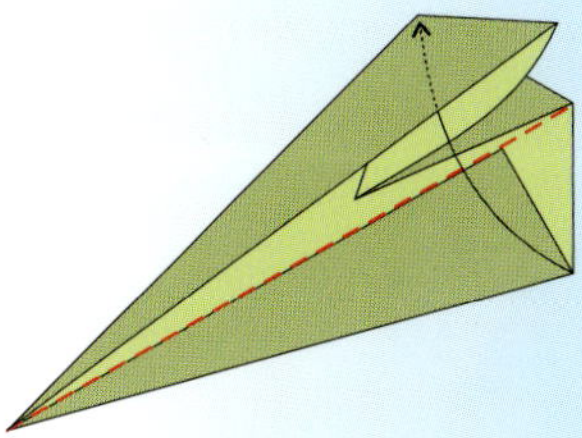

13. Senkrechte Linie falten, liegen lassen.
Fold vertical line and leave.

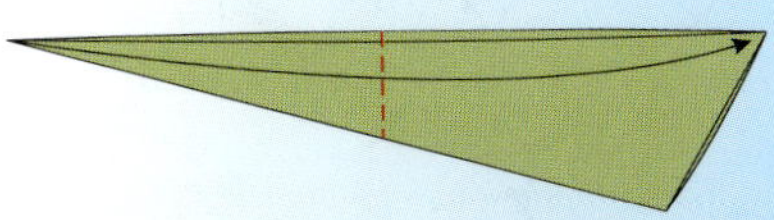

14. Senkrechte Linie falten, liegen lassen.
Fold vertical line and leave.

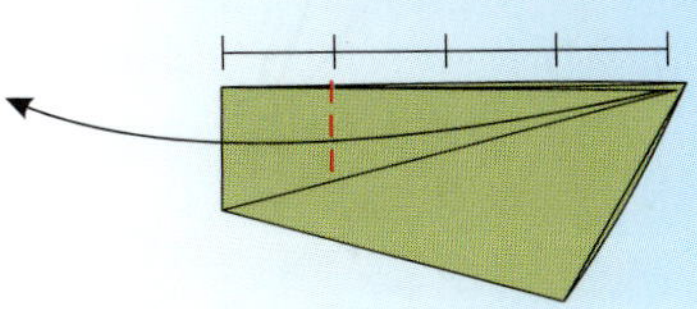

15. Schräge Linie falten, wieder öffnen bis Schritt Nr.13.
Fold diagonal line and open until step 13.

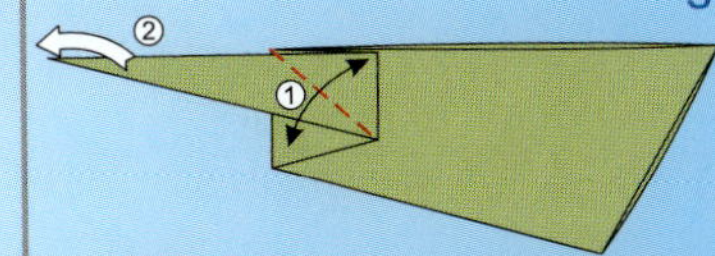

16. An den vorhandenen Linien Bergfalten formen und im Zickzack nach innen legen.
Form mountain-folds and put them in a zigzag line inwards.

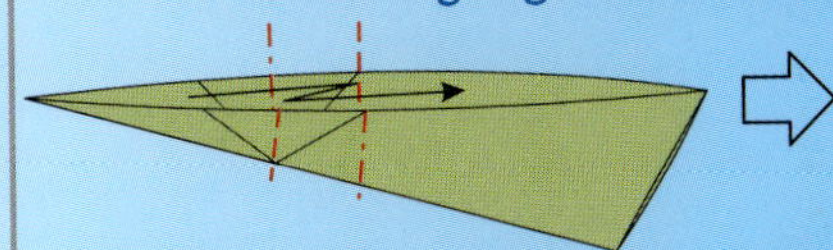

17. Die vorhandenen schrägen Linien, siehe Pfeile, nach innen legen. Zur Stabilisierung sehr wichtig.
Put the existing diagonal lines inwards, see arrows. Very important for stabilization.

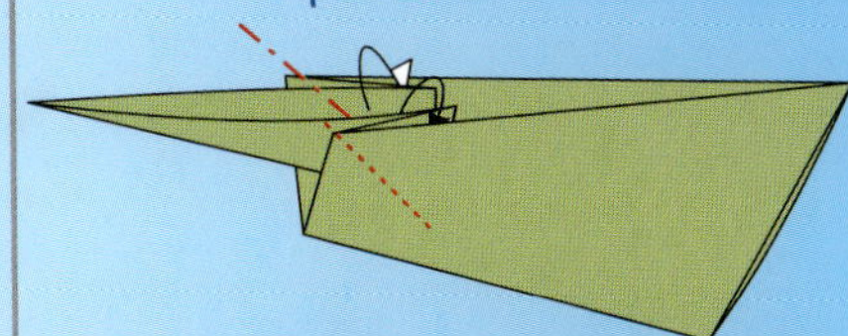

18. Waagerechte Linie falten, wieder öffnen. Hintere Spitze nach oben drücken.
Fold horizontal line and open again. Push rear point upwards.

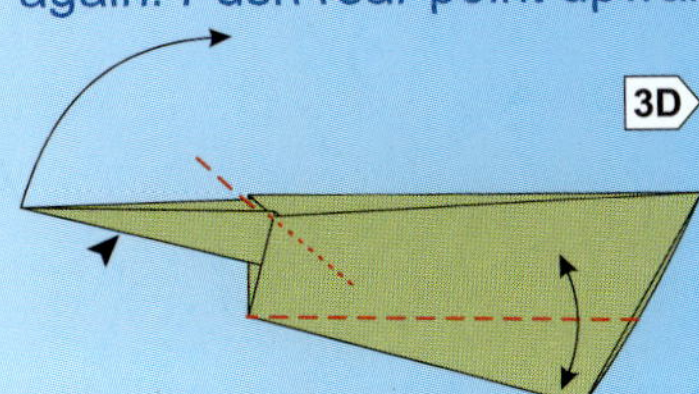

19. Linien zur Bergfalten formen, siehe Pfeile, damit das Boot schwimmen kann.
Fold lines to mountain-folds, see arrows, so that the boat can swim.

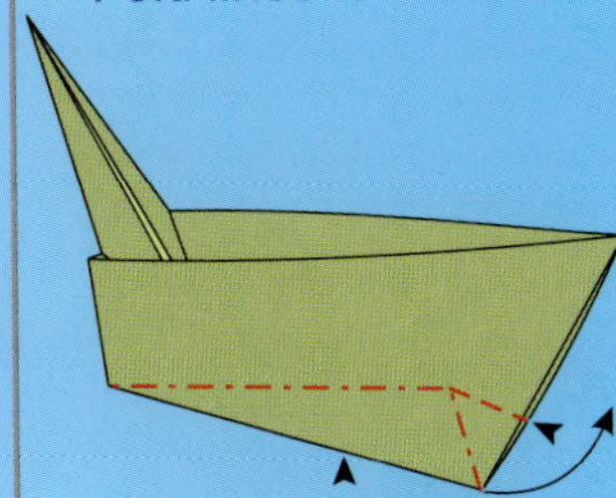

20. Papierlagen nach außen öffnen, siehe Pfeile.
Open layers of paper outwards, see arrows.

21. Papierlagen über ein Falzbein rollen.
Roll layers of paper over a bonefolder.

22. Fertiges Modell.
Finished model.

Dieses Boot ist mit Zahnstochern, als Ruder sehr schön.

This boat is very beautiful with tooth picks as rudders.

MATERIAL

1 Bogen 20x20 cm AQUAPAPIER

1 sheet 20x20 cm AQUAPAPIER

1. Zweimal die Mitte falten, wieder öffnen.
Fold twice the middle and open again.

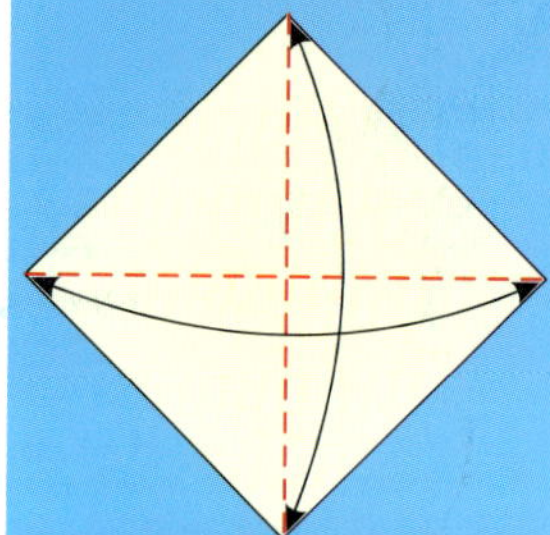

2. Schräge Linien falten, wieder öffnen.
Fold diagonal lines and open again.

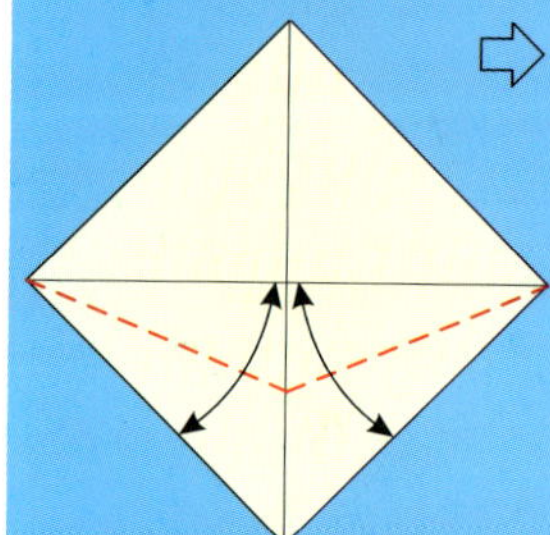

3. Linien, siehe Pfeile, nach oben legen, liegen lassen.
Put lines upwards, see arrows, and leave.

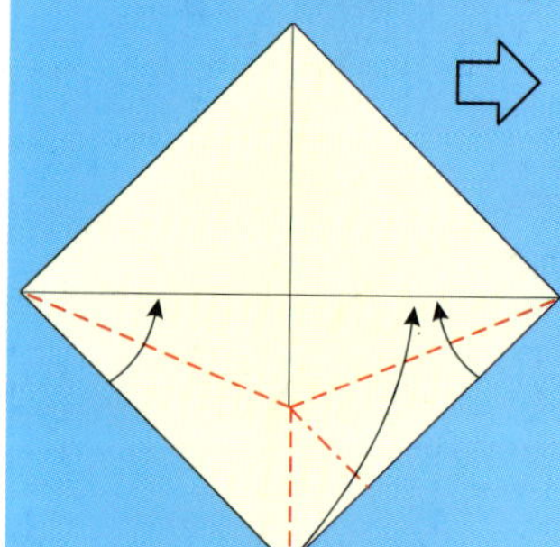

4. Schräge Linie falten, wieder öffnen. Dann im Gegenbruch nach links legen.
Fold diagonal line and open again. Then put left in reverse fold.

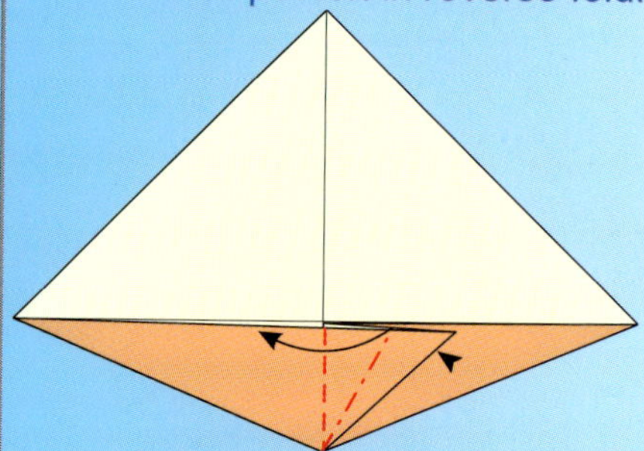

5. Waagerechte Linie nach innen falten, liegen lassen. An der oberen Spitze die Schritte Nr. 2-5 wiederholen.
Fold horizontal line inwards and leave. Repeat steps no 2-5 on upper point.

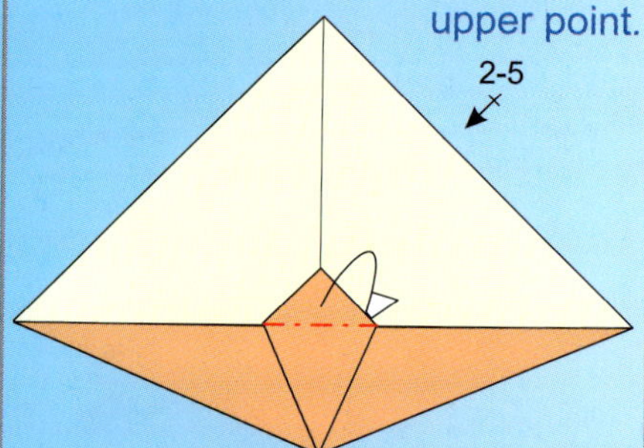

6. Waagerechte Linie falten, liegen lassen.
Fold horizontal line and leave.

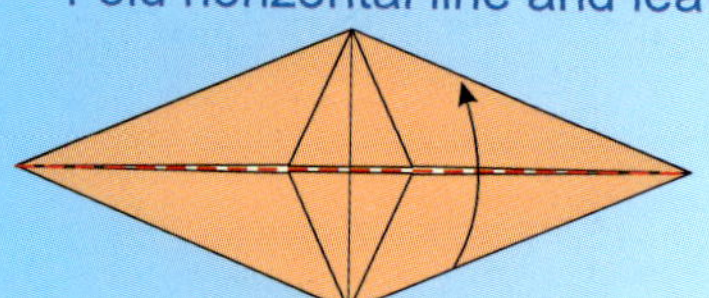

7. Schräge Linien falten und im Gegenbruch nach innen und oben legen.
Fold diagonal lines and put them inside upwards, in reverse fold.

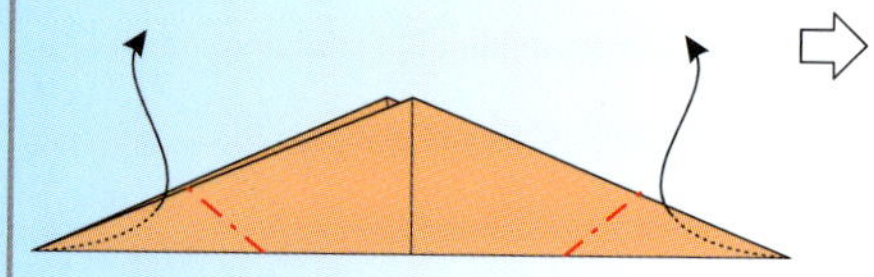

8. An der linken Spitze schräge Linie falten und im Gegenbruch nach außen legen. An der rechten Seite senkrechte Linie falten und im Gegenbruch nach außen legen.
Fold diagonal line on the left point and put it outwards in reverse fold. Fold vertical line on the right point and put it outwards in revese fold.

9. Waagerechte Linie falten, wieder öffnen.
Fold horizontal line and open again.

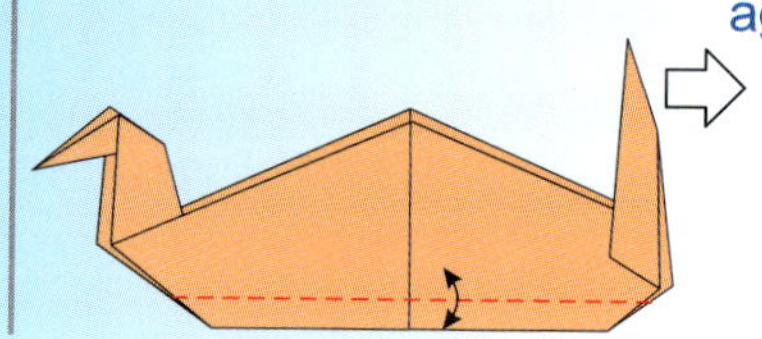

10. An der linken Spitze schräge Linien falten und im Gegenbruch nach innen, dann nach oben legen. An der rechten Seite schräge Linie falten und im Gegenbruch nach außen legen.

Fold diagonal lines on the left point and put them inwards and then upwards in reverse fold. Fold diagonal line and put it outwards in reverse fold.

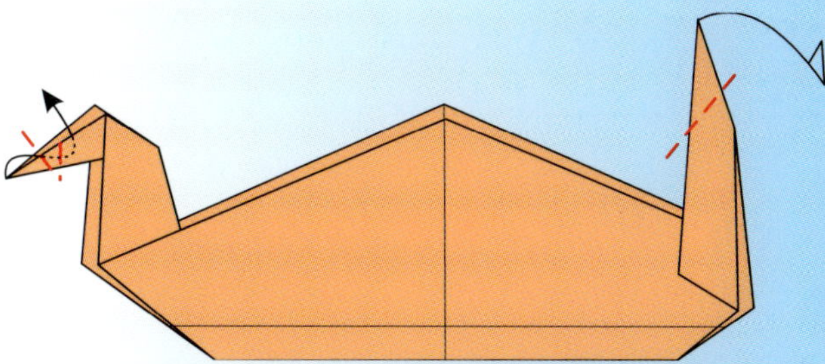

11. Am Drachenkopf Linien mit den Fingern formen. An der rechten Seite schräge Linie falten und im Gegenbruch nach unten legen.

Form lines on the dragon head with your fingers. Fold diagonal line on the right side and put it downwards in reverse fold.

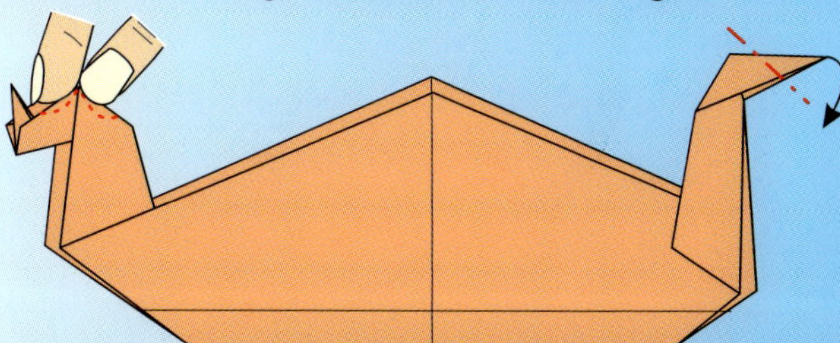

12. An der linken Seite senkrechte Linie nach außen falten. Rückseite wiederholen. Waagerechte Linie falten, liegen lassen. Rückseite wiederholen.

Fold vertical line on the left side outwards. Repeat back. Fold horizontal line and leave. Repeat back.

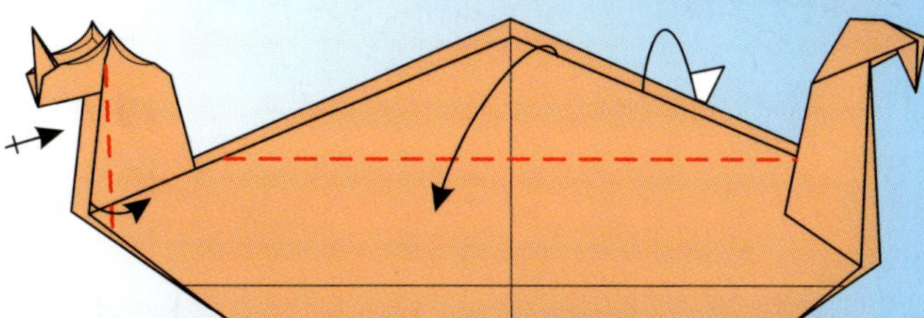

13. Waagerechte Linie zur Bergfalte formen und im Gegenbruch nach innen legen.

Form horizontal line to mountain-fold and put it inwards in reverse fold.

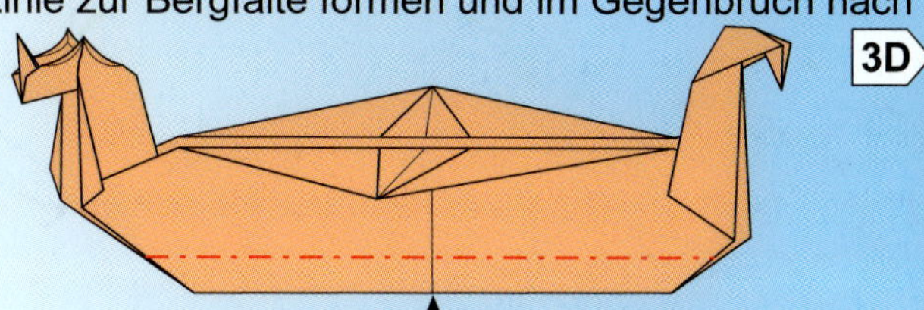

14. Fertiges Modell seitlich gesehen.

Finished model seen from the side.

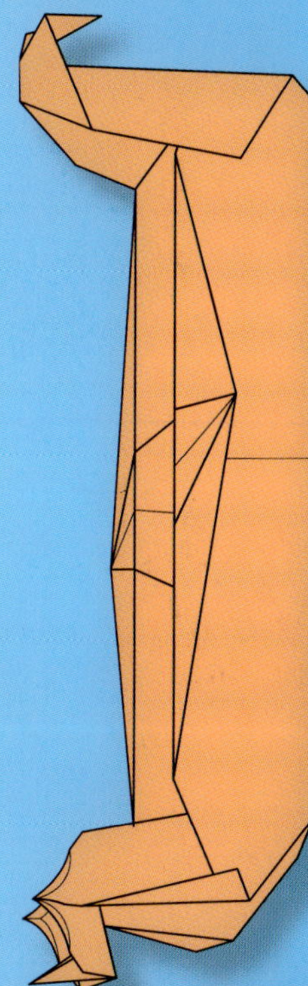

Chinesisches Schiff — Chinese ship

Boot mit glatten Segeln
Boat with smooth sails

MATERIAL

1 Bogen 20x20 cm AQUAPAPIER
1 sheet 20x20 cm AQUAPAPIER

1. Zweimal diagonal die Mitte falten, wieder öffnen. Rückseite nach oben legen.
Fold twice the middle diagonally and open again. Put back upwards.

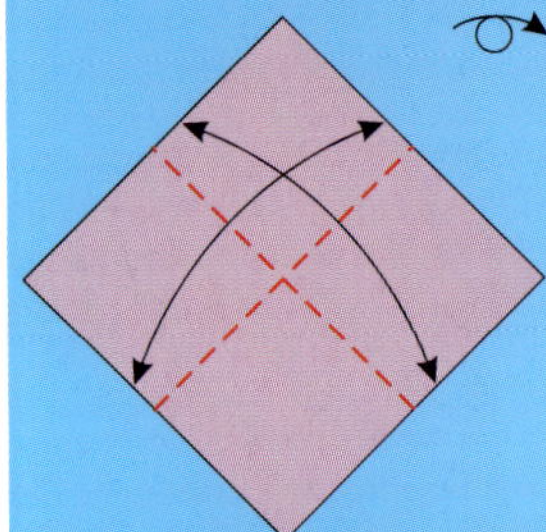

2. Zweimal waagerecht die Mitte falten, wieder öffnen. Rückseite nach oben legen.
Fold twice the middle horizontally and open again. Put back upwards.

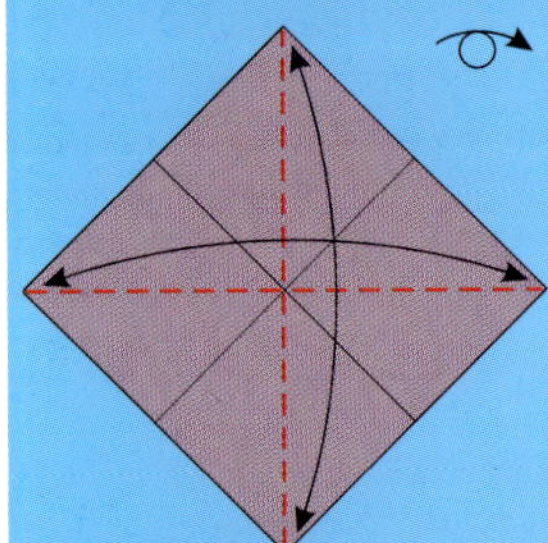

3. Drei Ecken zur Mitte falten, liegen lassen.
Fold all three corners to the middle and leave.

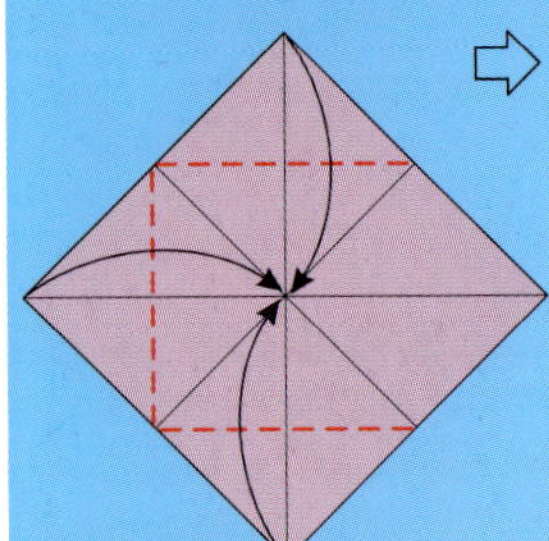

4. Senkrechte Linie falten, liegen lassen.
Fold vertical line and leave.

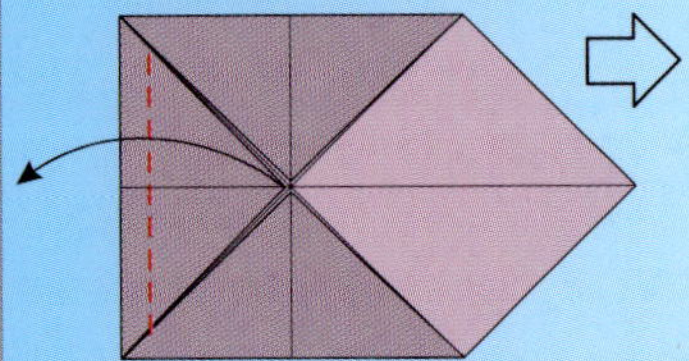

5. An den schrägen Linien in der Mitte zusammenlegen, dabei die Spitzen rechts und links nach oben drücken.
Form a center on diagonal lines by pushing the points to the right and the left upwards.

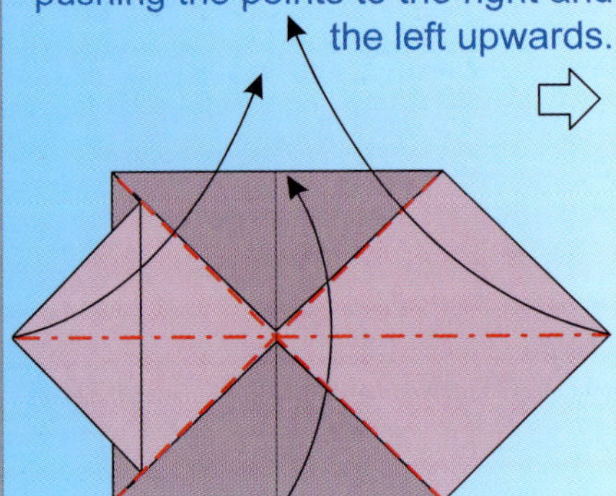

6. Waagerechte Linie falten, wieder öffnen.
Fold horizontal line and open again.

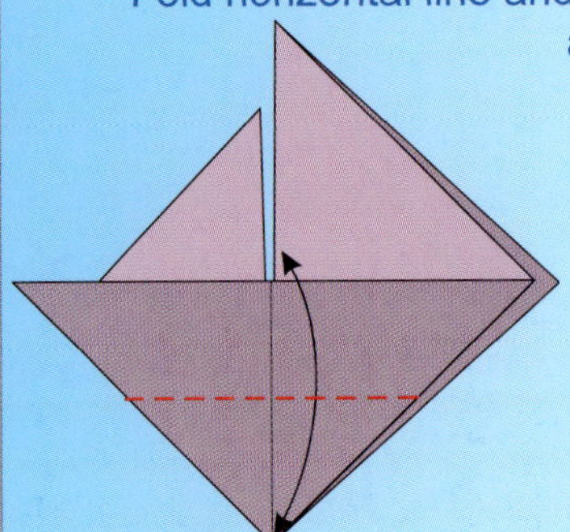

7. Waagerechte Linie zur Bergfalte formen und im Gegenbruch nach innen legen.
Form horizontal line to mountain-fold and put it inwards in reverse fold.

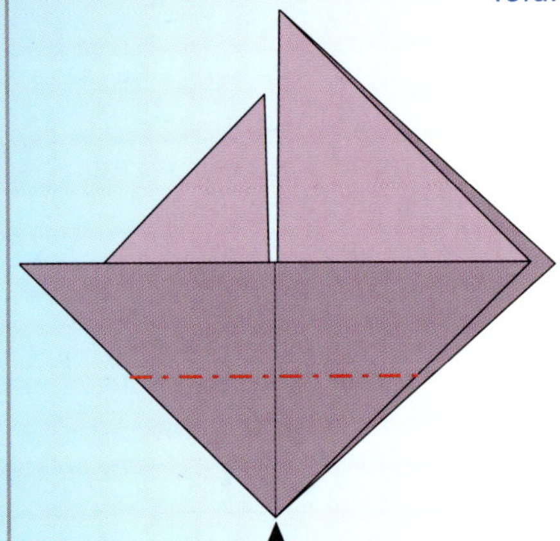

8. Fertiges Modell seitlich gesehen.
Finished model seen from the side.

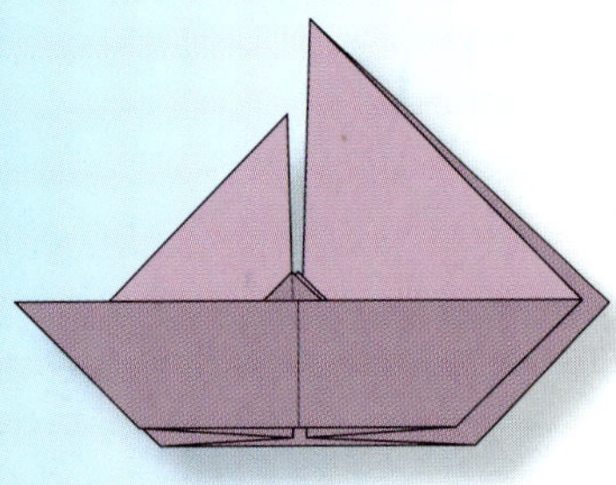

Chinesisches Schiff - Variation

Boot mit chinesischen Segeln
Boat with chinese sails

MATERIAL

1 Bogen 20x20 cm AQUAPAPIER
1 sheet 20x20 cm AQUAPAPIER

Start. Diagramme von Seite 44 bis Nr.8 falten.
Fold charts of page 44 until step no.8.

1. Papierlagen nach außen öffnen, siehe Pfeile und nächste Zeichnung.
Open layers of paper outwards, see arrows and next chart.

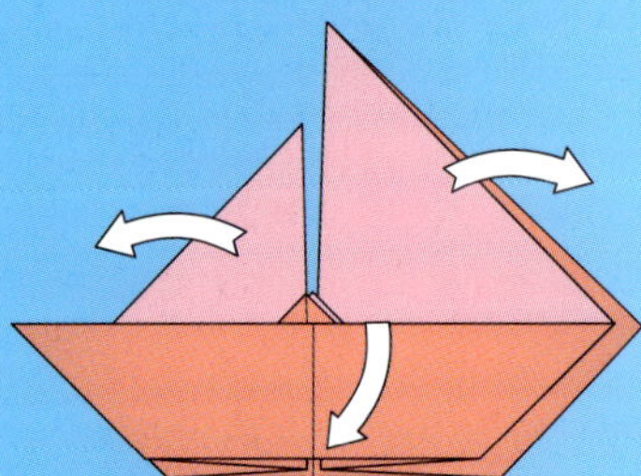

2. Waagerechte Linie zur Rückseite falten, liegen lassen.
Fold horizontal line to the back and leave.

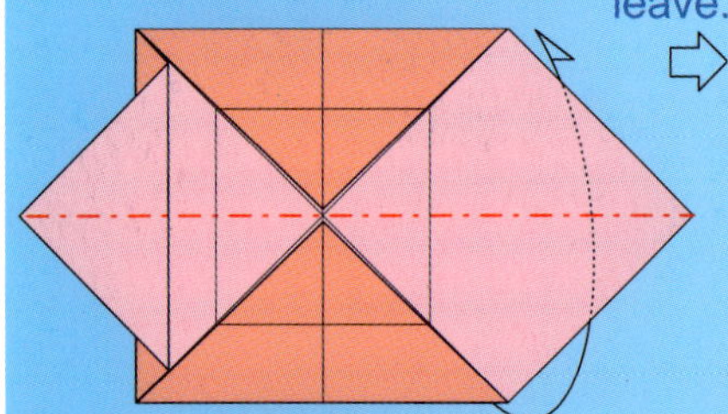

3. Schräge Linien falten, wieder öffnen.
Fold diagonal lines and open again.

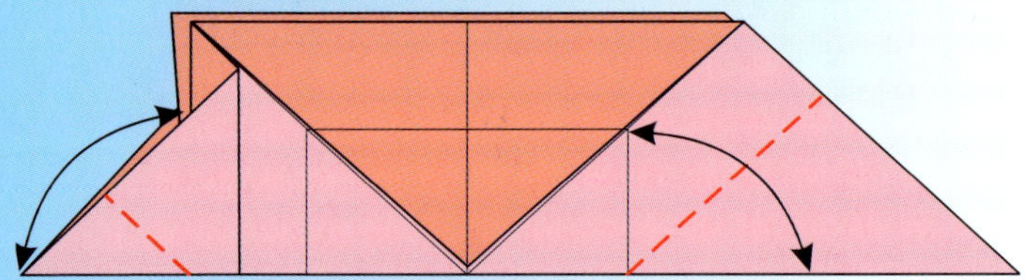

4. Schräge Linien falten, wieder öffnen.
Fold diagonal lines and open again.

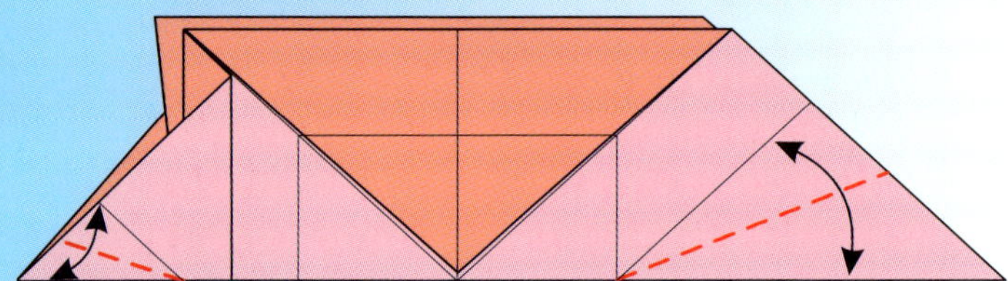

5. Schräge und senkrechte Linie falten, wieder öffnen.
Fold diagonal and vertical lines and open again.

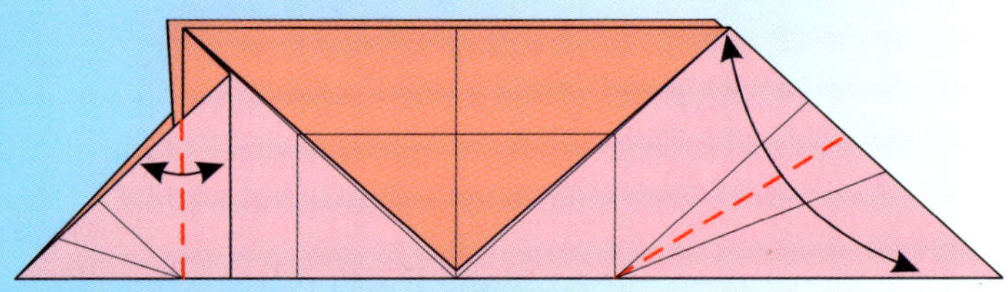

6. Schräge Linien falten, wieder öffnen.
Fold diagonal lines and open again.

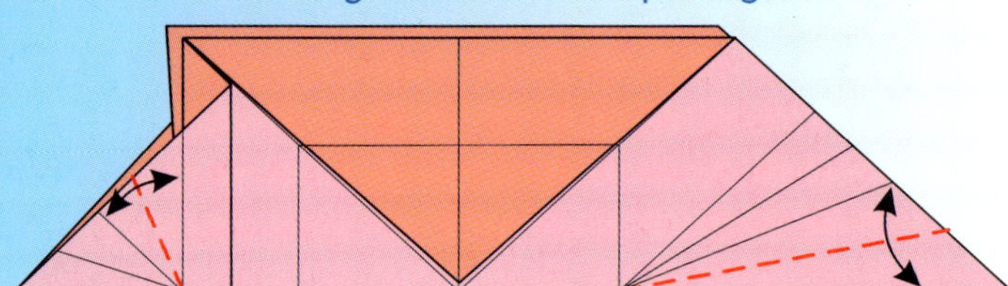

7. Jetzt wird zwischen den gefalteten Linien an der rechten Seite jeweils noch eine Zickzackfaltung durchgeführt.
Between the folded lines at the right side in each case a zigzag folding is accomplished now.

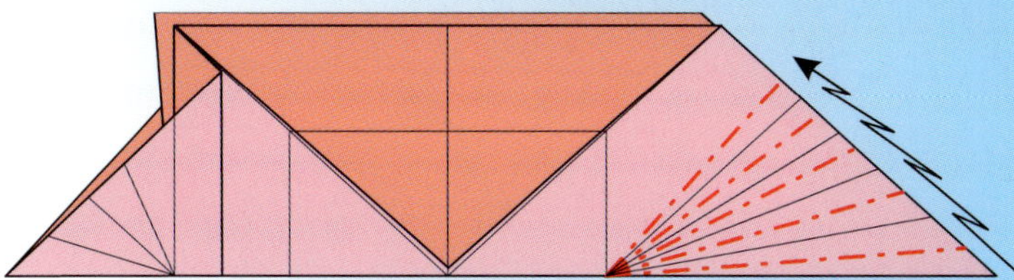

8. Jetzt wird zwischen den gefalteten Linien an der linken Seite jeweils noch eine Zickzackfaltung durchgeführt.
Between the folded lines at the left side in each case a zigzag folding is accomplished now.

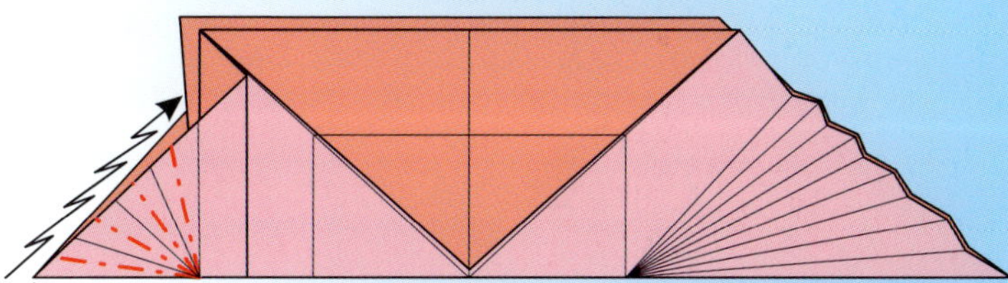

9. Papierlagen nach außen öffnen, siehe Pfeil und nächste Zeichnung.
Open layers of paper outwards, see arrow and next chart.

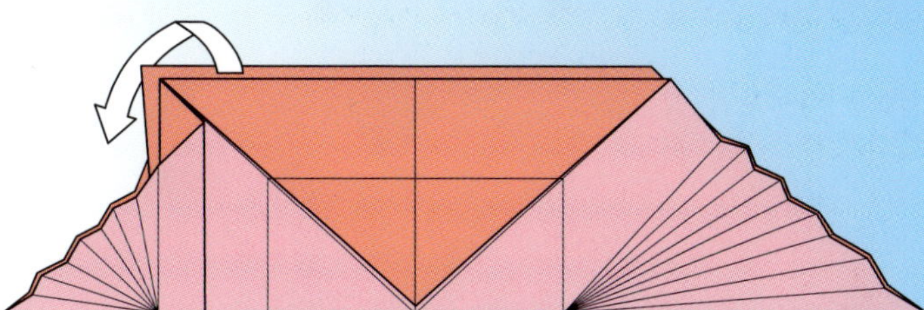

10. An den schrägen Linien in der Mitte zusammenlegen, dabei die Spitzen rechts und links nach oben drücken.
Form a center on diagonal lines by pushing the points to the right and the left upwards.

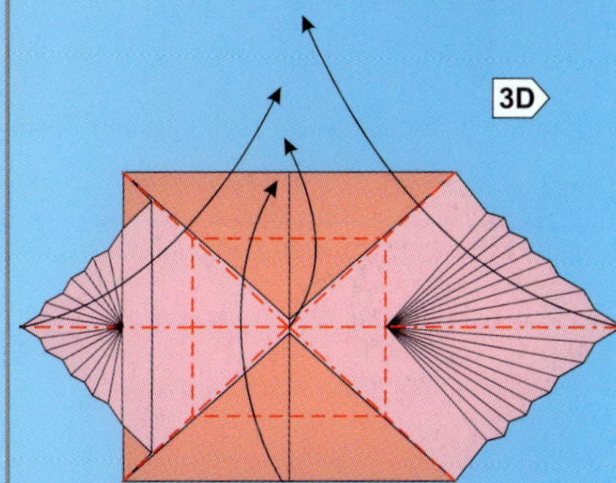

8. Fertiges Modell seitlich gesehen.
Finished model seen from the side.

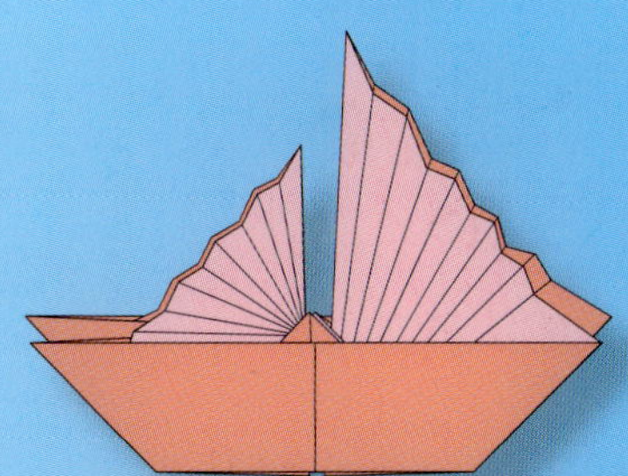

Frachtschiff

Cargo ship

MATERIAL
1 Bogen 20x20 cm AQUAPAPIER
1 sheet 20x20 cm AQUAPAPIER

1. Zweimal diagonal die Mitte falten, wieder öffnen.
Fold twice the middle diagonally and open again.

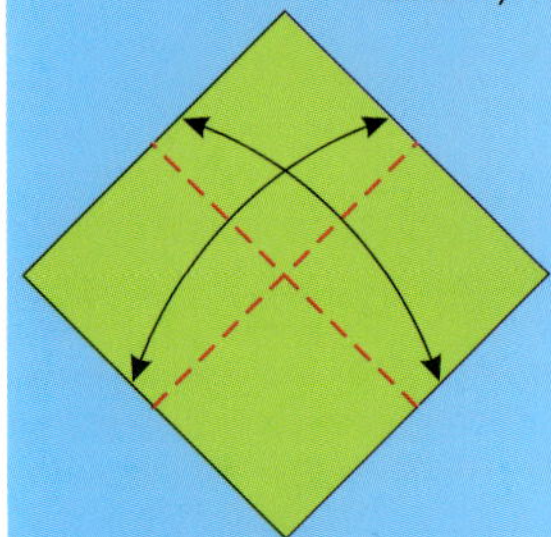

2. Einmal waagerecht die Mitte falten, wieder öffnen. Rückseite nach oben legen.
Fold once the middle horizontally and open again. Put back upwards.

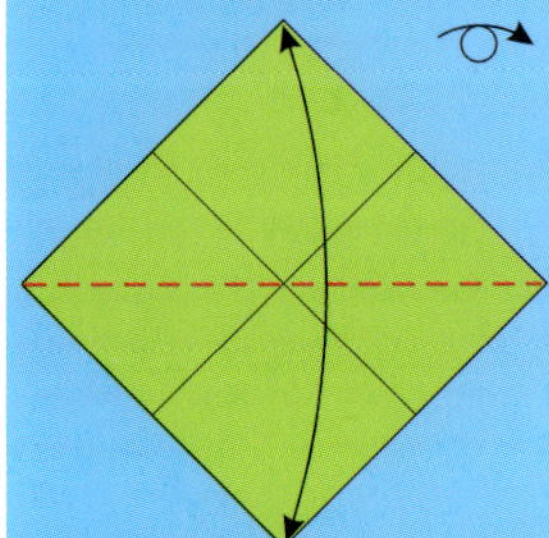

3. Zweimal waagerechte Linien falten, liegen lassen.
Fold twice the horizontal lines and leave.

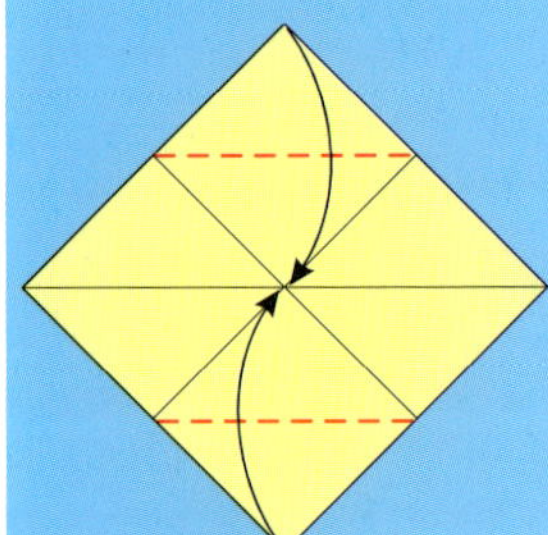

4. Waagerechte Linien falten, wieder öffnen.
Fold horizontal lines and open again.

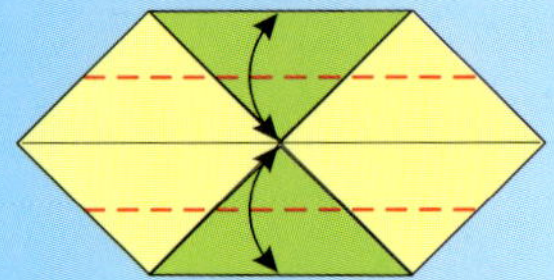

5. Spitzen nach innen falten, liegen lassen.
Fold points inwards and leave.

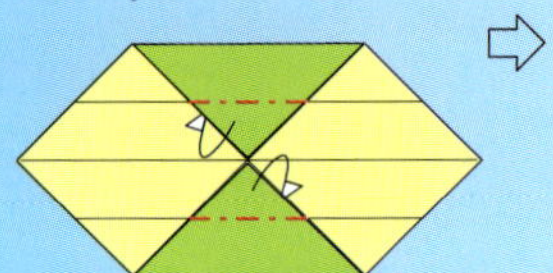

6. Senkrechte Linie falten, wieder öffnen.
Fold vertical line and open again.

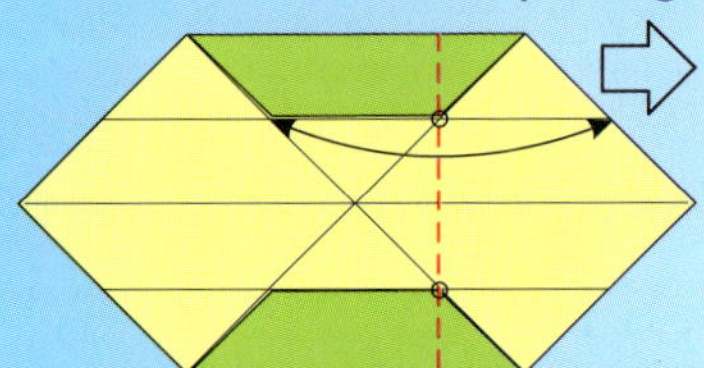

7. Linien zu Berg- oder Talfalten formen, dann siehe Pfeile, zusammenlegen.
Form lines to mountain and valley-folds and put them together, see arrows.

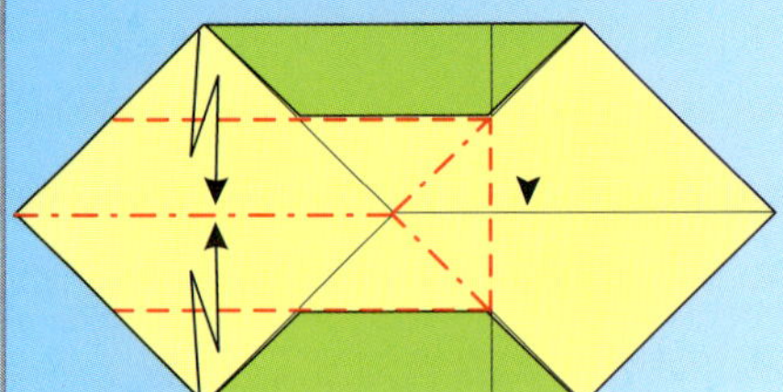

8. An der rechten Spitze Linien zu Berg- oder Talfalten formen, siehe Pfeil, Spitze nach oben legen.
Form lines to mountain and valley-folds on the right point, see arrow. Put point downwards.

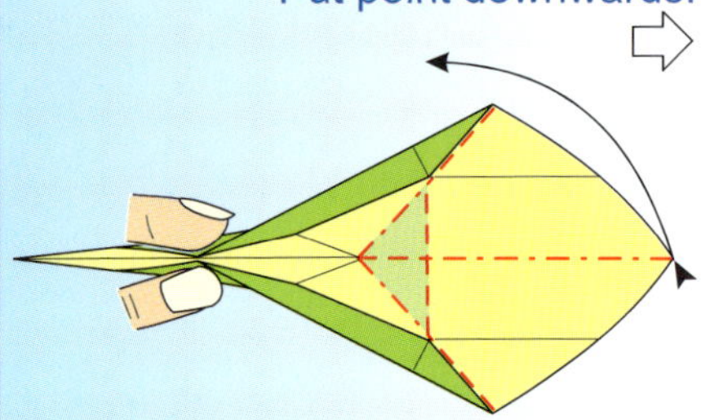

9. Waagerechte und schräge Linie falten, wieder öffnen.
Fold horizontal and diagonal line and open again.

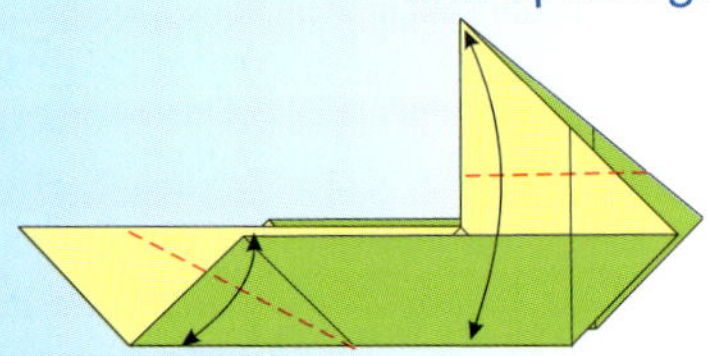

10. Rechte Seite schräge Linie falten, wieder öffnen. Linke Seite Papierlagen nach außen drehen, siehe Pfeile und im Gegenbruch nach oben legen.
Fold diagonal line on the right side and open again. Turn layers of paper on the left side outwards, see arrows, and put them upwards in reverse fold.

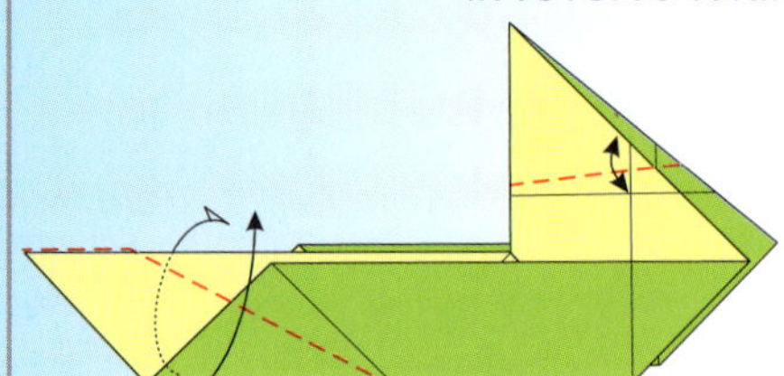

11. Rechte Seite Bergfalte formen und im Gegenbruch, siehe Pfeile, nach unten legen. Obere Spitze im Gegenbruch nach vorne legen.
Form right side to mountain-fold and in reverse fold, see arrows, and put it downwards. Put upper point forwards in reverse fold.

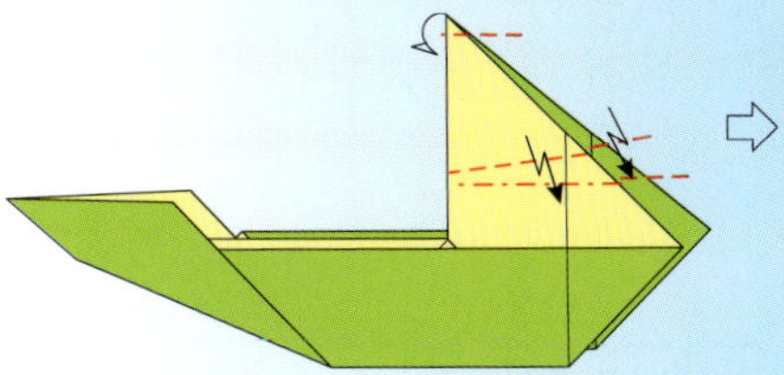

12. Schräge und senkrechte Linie falten, wieder öffnen.
Fold diagonal and vertical line and open again.

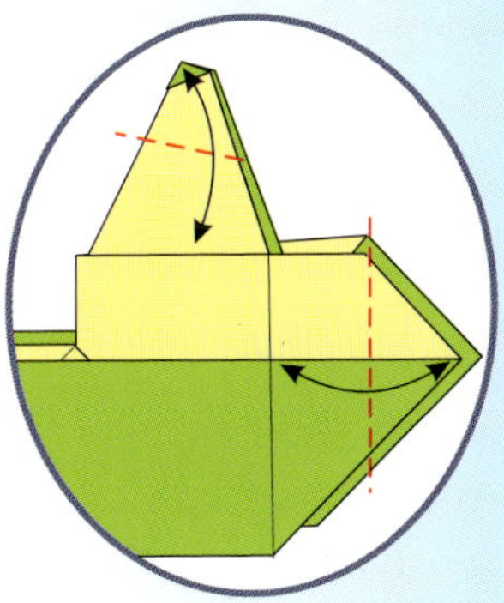

13. Schräge und senkrechte Linie falten, wieder öffnen.
Fold diagonal and vertical line and open again.

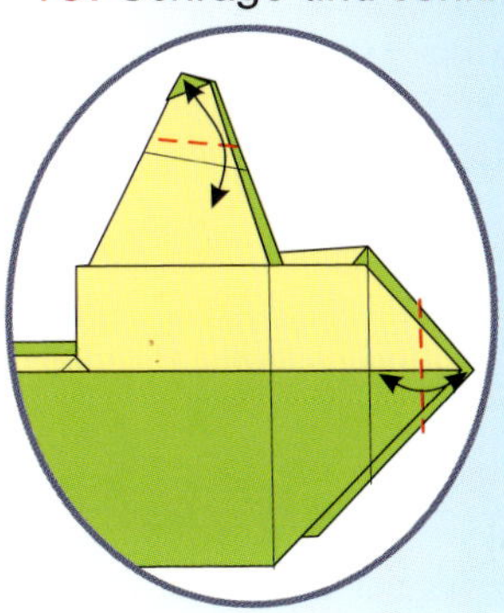

14. An der oberen Spitze Linien im Gegenbruch nach innen legen. Rechte Seite schräge Linie falten, wieder öffnen.
Put lines on the upper point inwards in reverse fold. Fold diagonal line on the right side and open again.

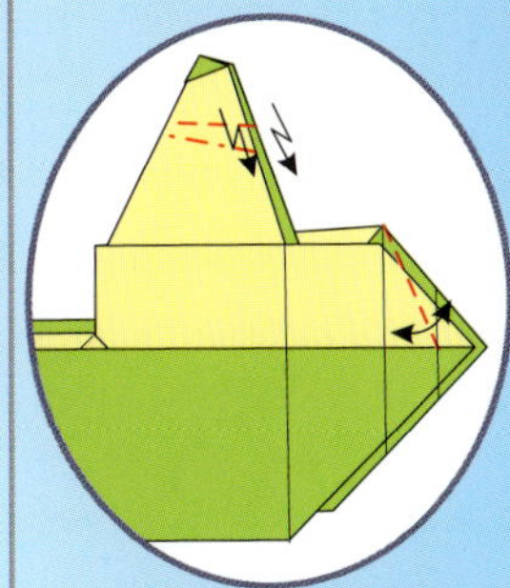

15. Rechte Spitze von der oberen Papierlage im Gegenbruch nach innen legen.
Put right point of top layer of paper inwards in reverse fold.

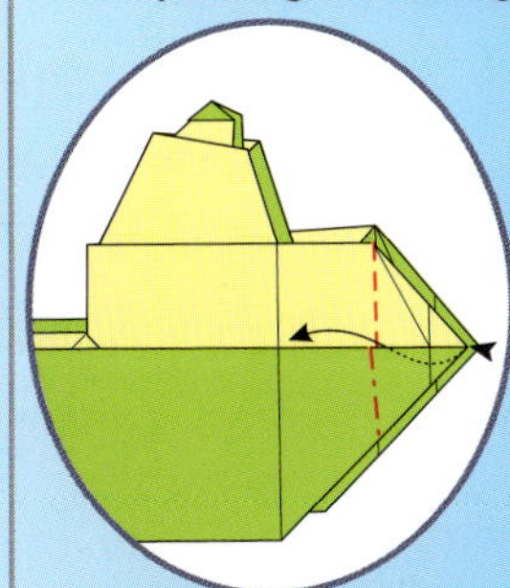

16. Rechte Spitze von der unteren Papierlage im Gegenbruch nach innen legen. Von beiden Papierlagen liegen jetzt die Spitzen aufeinander.
Put right point of lower layer of paper inwards in reverse fold. For both layers of paper the points lie on top of one another now.

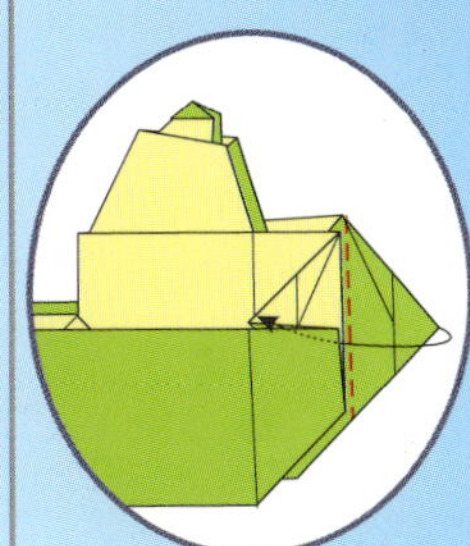

17. Beide Spitzen nun nach innen falten.
Fold both points inwards.

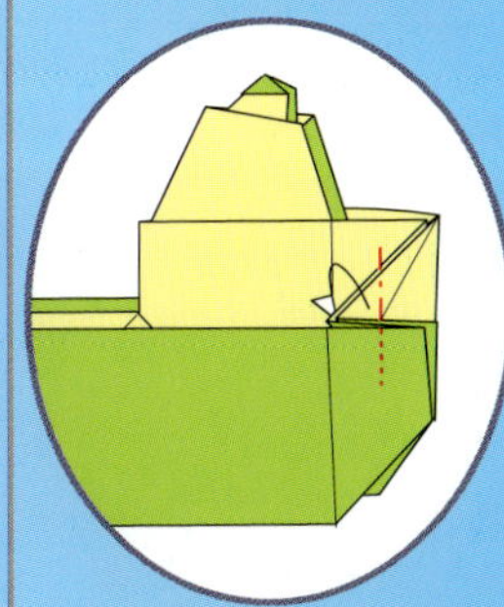

18. Nochmals schräge Linie nach innen falten.
Fold diagonal line once again inwards.

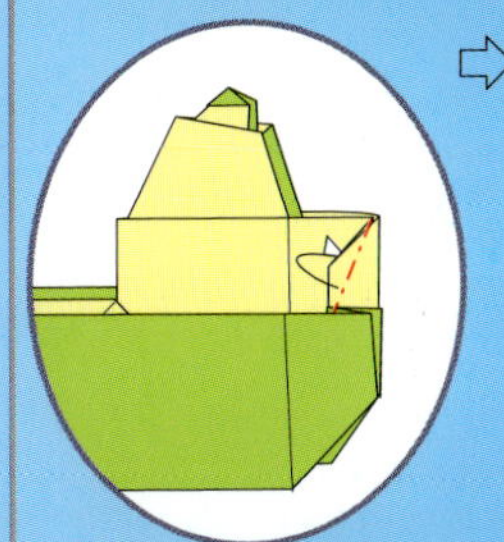

19. Bergfalten formen, damit das Schiff breiter wird.
Form mountain-folds in order the ship becomes broader.

20. Fertiges Modell seitlich gesehen.
Finished model seen from the side.

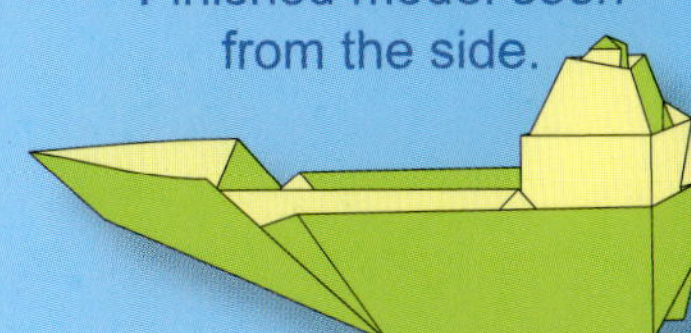

Flugzeugträger — Aircraft carrier

MATERIAL
1 Bogen 20x20 cm AQUAPAPIER
1 sheet 20x20 cm AQUAPAPIER

1. Waagerechte Linie falten, wieder öffnen.
Fold horizontal line and open again.

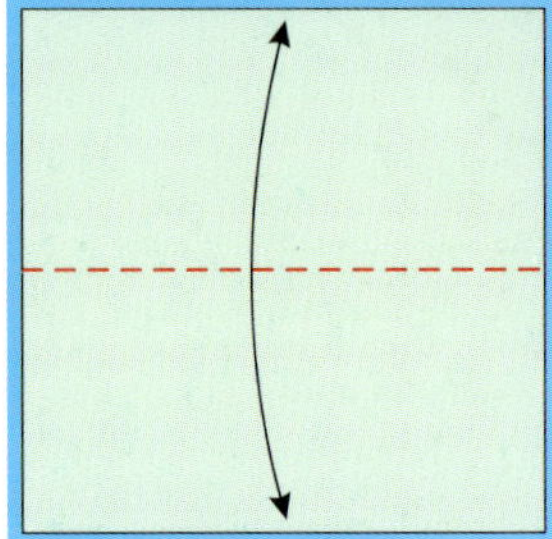

2. Waagerechte Linien falten, wieder öffnen.
Fold horizontal line and open again.

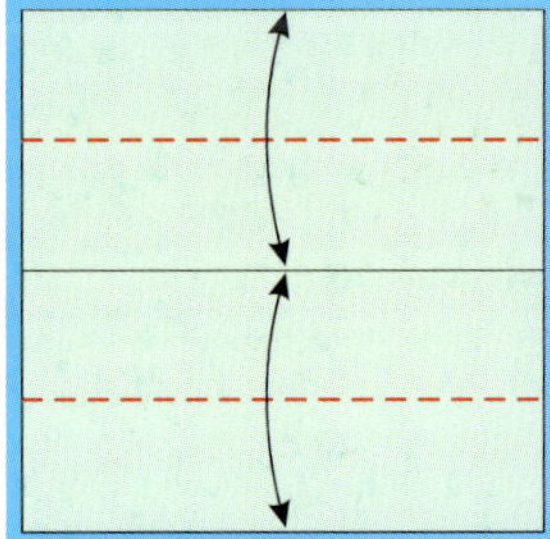

3. Waagerechte Linie falten, liegen lassen.
Fold horizontal line and leave.

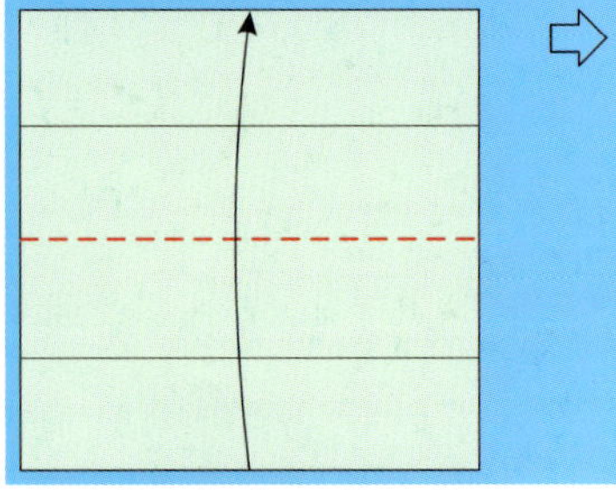

4. Markierung auf 1/2 anbringen.
Attach marking on 1/2.

5. Waagerechte Linie falten, wieder öffnen.
Fold horizontal line and open again.

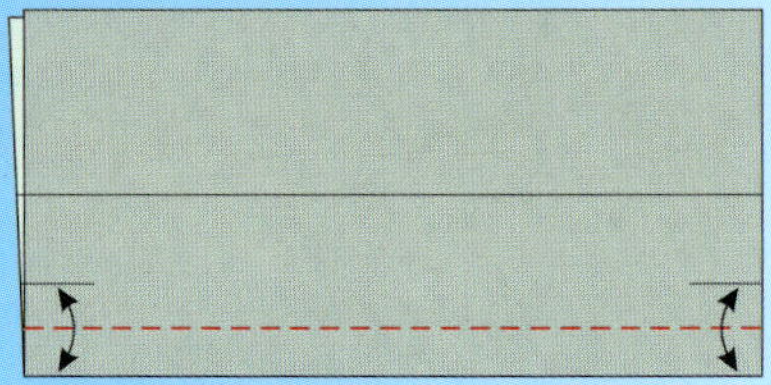

6. Waagerechte Linie falten, wieder öffnen. Rückseite wiederholen.
Fold horizontal line and open again. Repeat back.

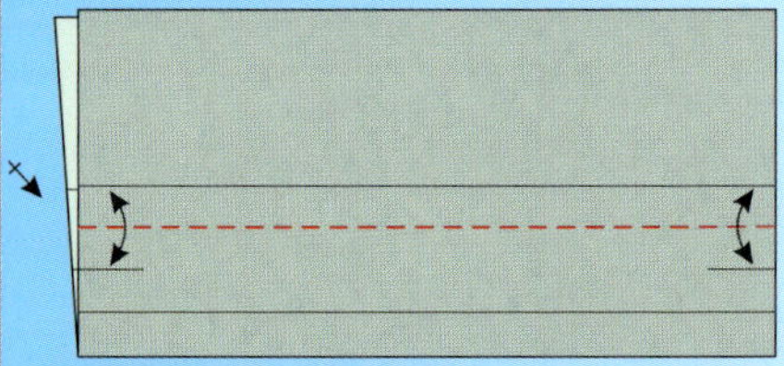

7. Schräge Linien falten, wieder öffnen.
Fold diagonal lines and open again.

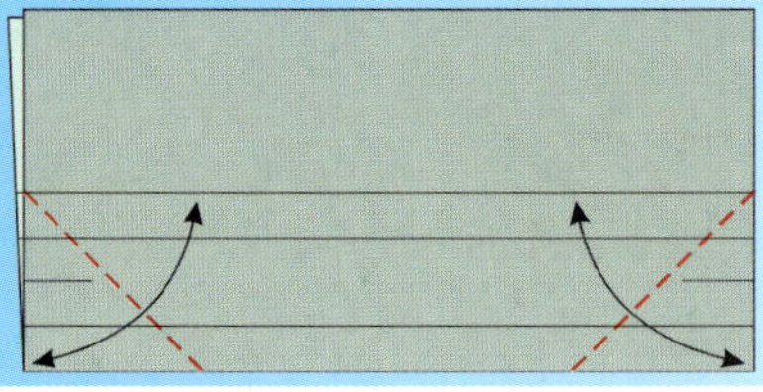

8. Schräge Linien falten, wieder öffnen. Danach komplett öffnen.
Fold diagonal lines and open again. Open completely afterwards.

9. An den gekennzeichneten Linien Talfalten anbringen. Rückseite nach oben legen.
Put valley-folds on characterized lines. Put back upwards.

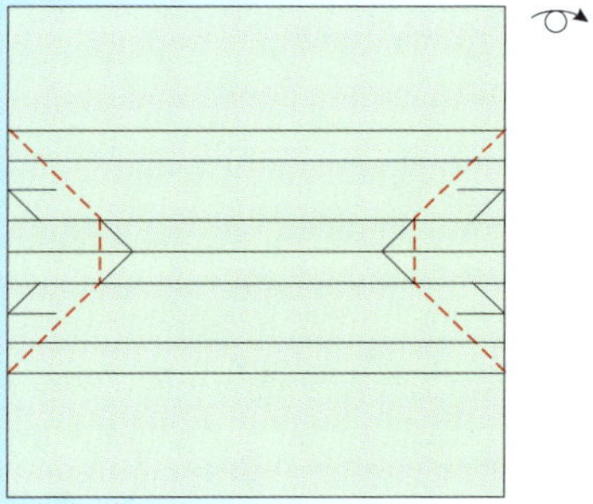

10. Senkrechte Linien falten, wieder öffnen. Drehen und Rückseite nach oben legen.
Fold vertical lines and open again. Turn and put back upwards.

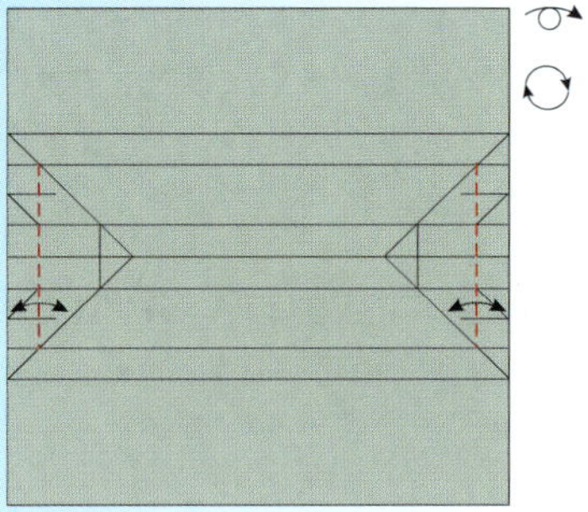

11. An der oberen Papierkante, die gekennzeichneten Linien zu Tal- und Bergfalten formen, dann siehe Pfeile zusammen legen. An der unteren Papierkante wiederholen.

Along the upper paper edge, form valley and mountain-folds on characterized lines, then lay together see arrows. Repeat on the lower paper edge.

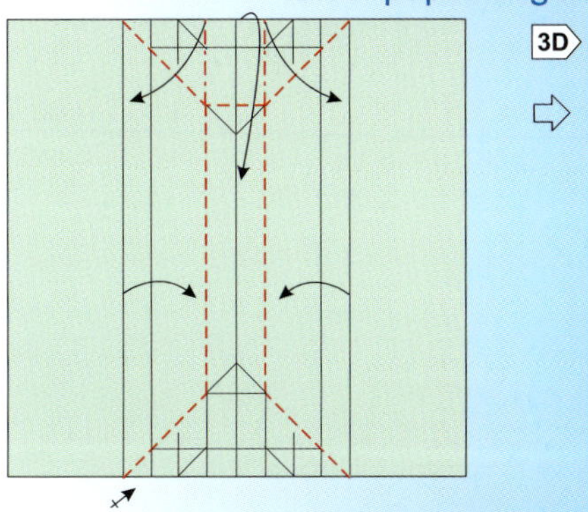

12. An den gekennzeichneten Linien Tal- und Bergfalten anbringen, siehe Pfeile.

Fold valley and mountain-folds on characterized lines, see arrows.

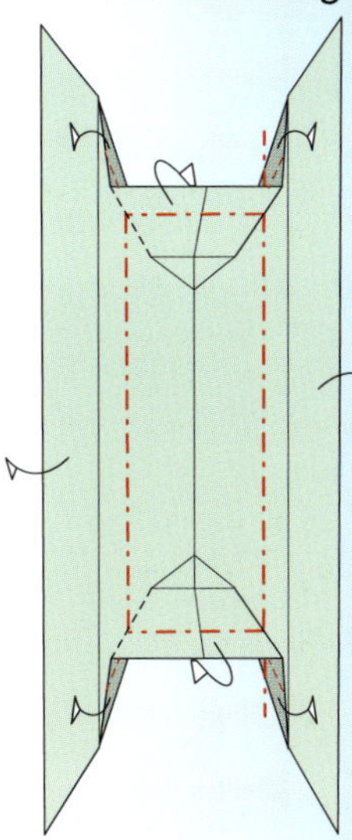

13. Senkrechte Linien falten, liegen lassen. Rückseite nach oben legen.

Fold vertical lines and leave. Put back upwards.

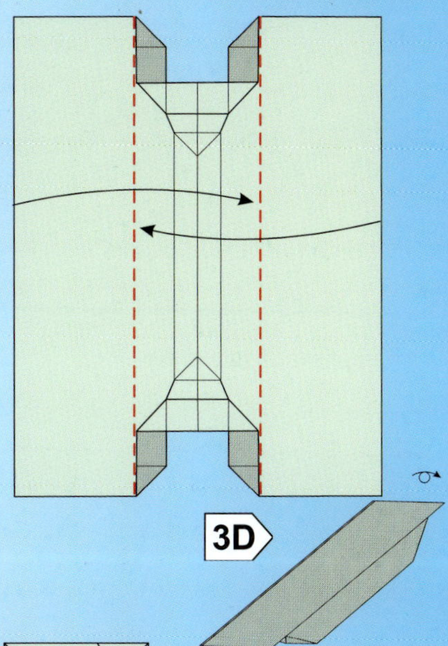

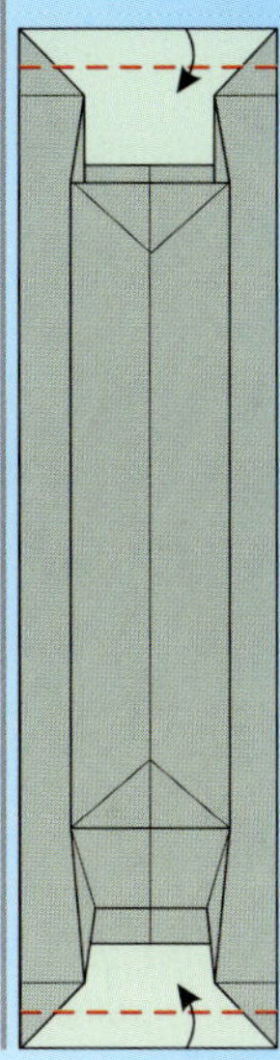

14. Waagerechte Linien falten, liegen lassen.

Fold horizontal lines and leave.

15. Schräge Linien falten, liegen lassen.

Fold diagonal lines and leave.

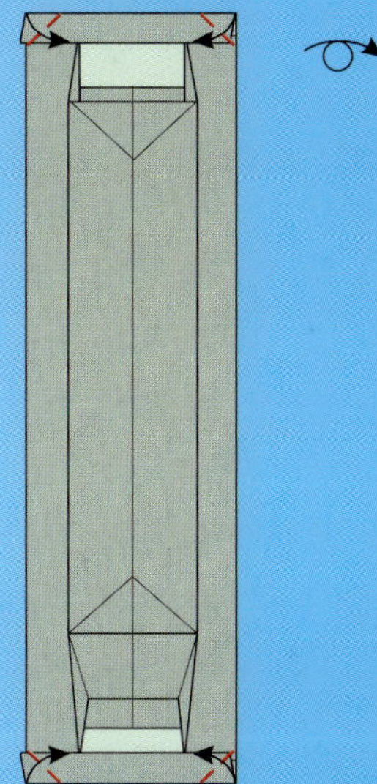

16. Fertiges Modell seitlich gesehen.

Finished model seen from the side.

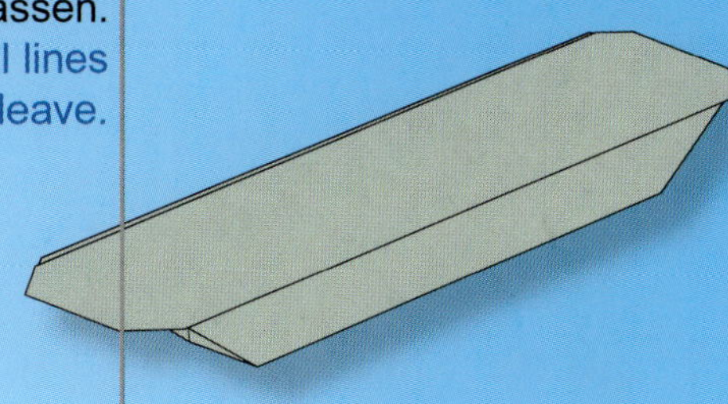

Flugzeugträger - Kommandoturm

MATERIAL
1 Bogen 20x20 cm AQUAPAPIER
1 sheet 20x20 cm AQUAPAPIER

1. Papier an der senkrechten Linie durchschneiden.
Cut paper on the vertical line.

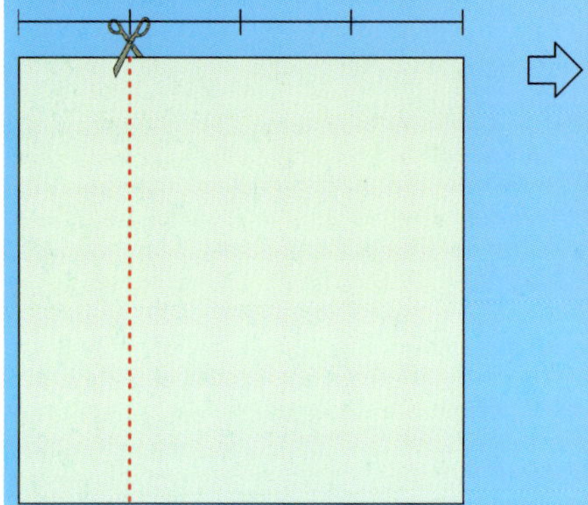

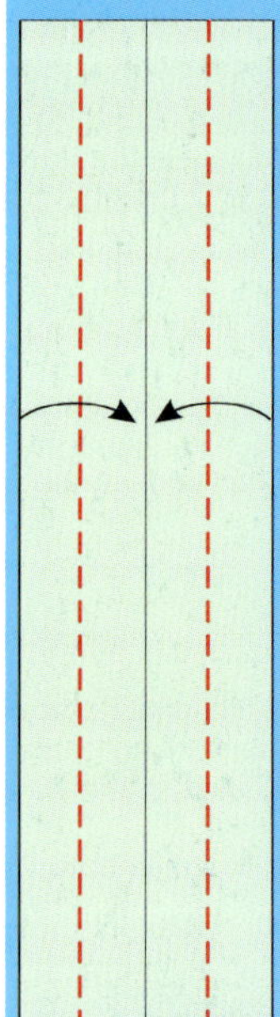

2. Senkrechte Linie falten, liegen lassen.
Fold vertical line and leave.

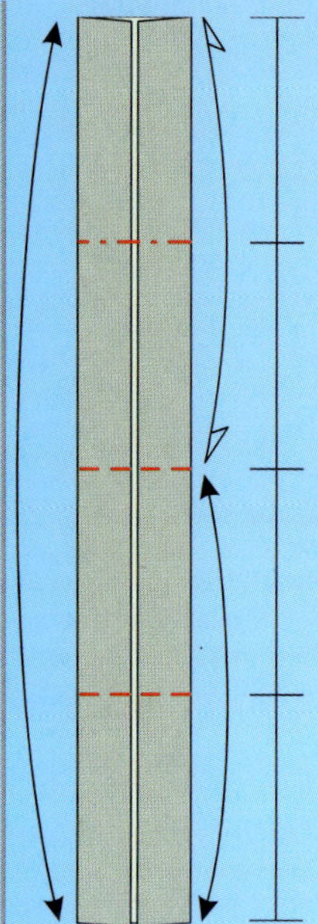

3. Waagerechte Linien falten, wieder öffnen. Obere Linie zur Rückseite falten, wieder öffnen.
Fold horizontal lines and open again. Fold upper line to back and open again.

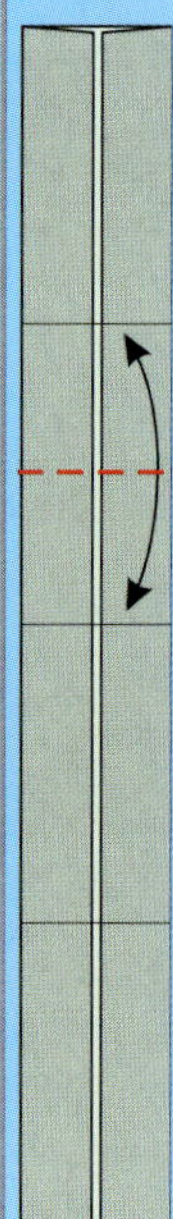

4. Waagerechte Linie falten, wieder öffnen.
Fold horizontal lines and open again.

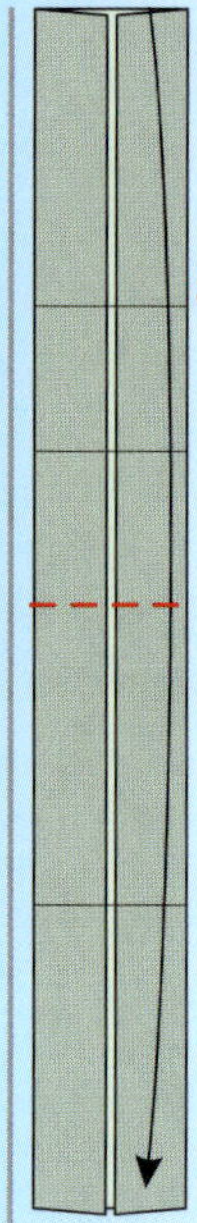

5. Waagerechte Linie falten, liegen lassen.
Fold horizontal line and leave.

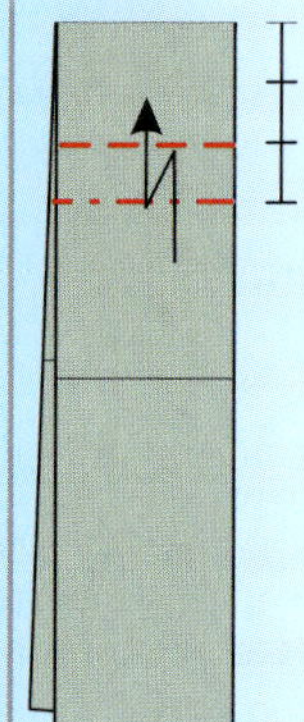

6. Waagerechte Linien im Zickzack nach oben legen, liegen lassen.
Put horizontal lines in a zigzag line upwards and leave.

7. Waagerechte Linie auf der Rückseite falten, liegen lassen.
Fold horizontal line on the back and leave.

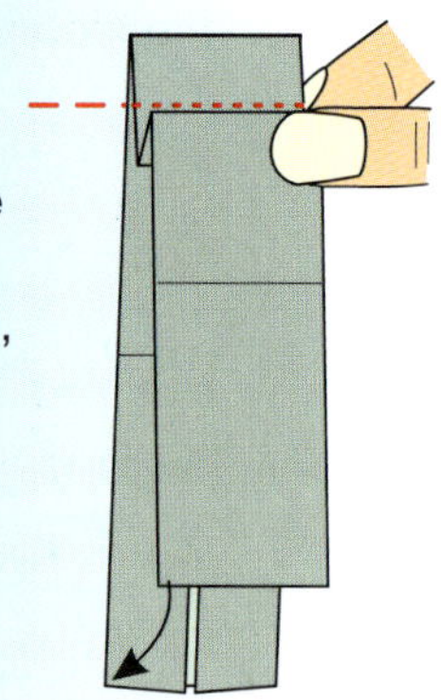

Aircraft carrier - tower of command

8. Kante nach oben schieben, siehe kleiner Pfeil. Waagerechte Linie mit beiden Teilen falten, liegen lassen.
Push corner upwards, see small arrow. Fold horizontal line with both parts and leave.

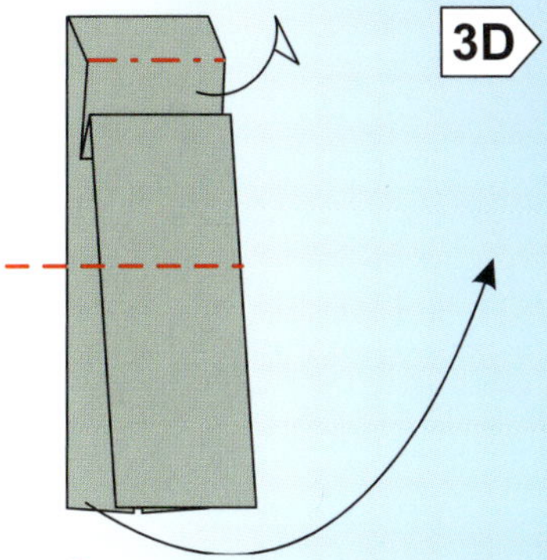

9. Fertige Kommandobrücke seitlich gesehen.
Finished ship bridge seen from the side.

10. Kommandobrücke seitlich in den Flugzeugträger schieben, fertig.
Push ship bridge in aircraft carrier, ready.

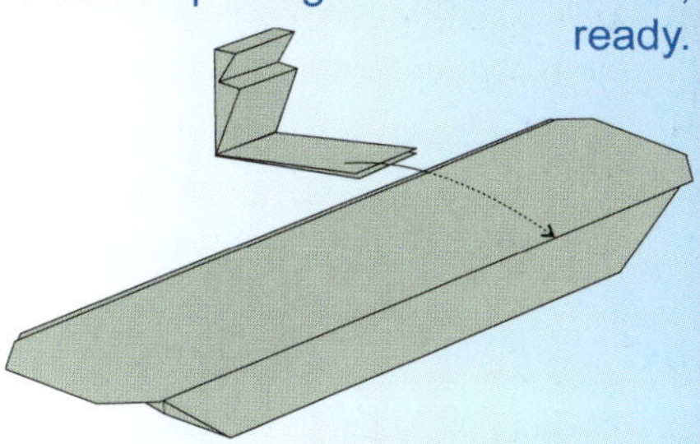

11. Fertiges komplett Modell, seitlich gesehen.
Finished model seen from the side.

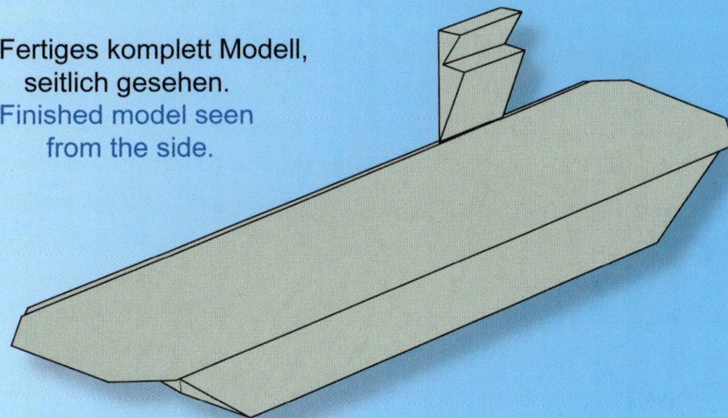

Flugzeug

Aircraft

MATERIAL
1 Bogen 3,5 x 3,5 cm
1 sheet 3,5 x 3,5 cm

1. Waagerechte Linie falten, wieder öffnen.
Fold horizontal line and open again.

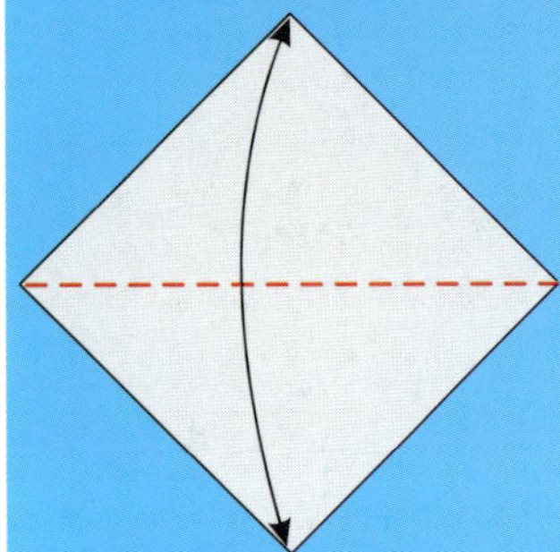

2. Schräge Linien falten, siehe Pfeile, liegen lassen.
Fold diagonal lines, see arrows, and leave.

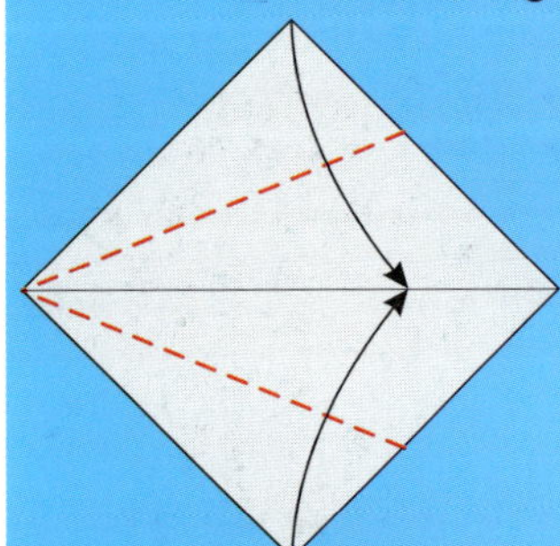

3. Waagerechte Linie falten, liegen lassen.
Fold horizontal line and leave.

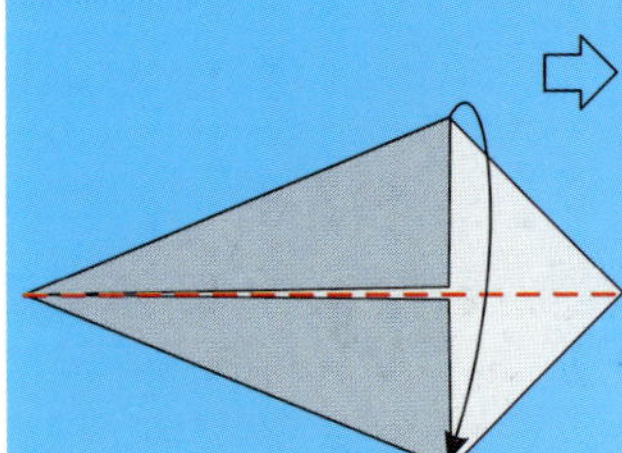

4. Schräge Linien falten, siehe Pfeile, wieder öffnen.
Fold diagonal lines, see arrows, and open again.

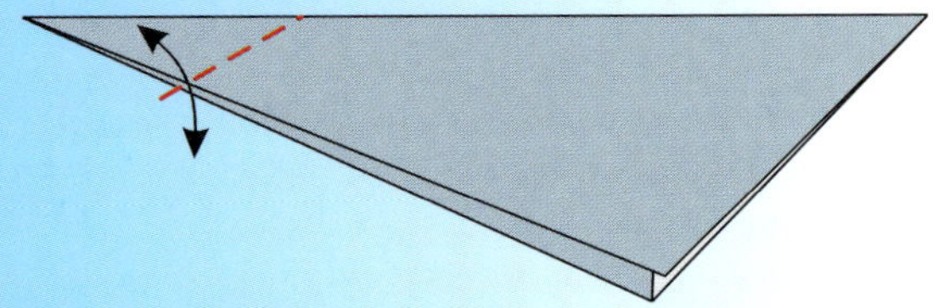

5. Schräge Linie im Gegenbruch nach innen legen, liegen lassen.
Put diagonal line inwards in reverse fold and leave.

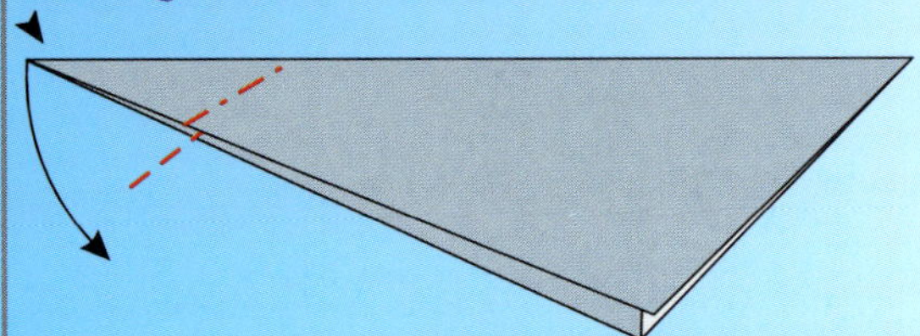

6. Linie nach oben falten, siehe Pfeil, liegen lassen. Rückseite wiederholen.
Fold line upwards, see arrow, and leave. Repeat back.

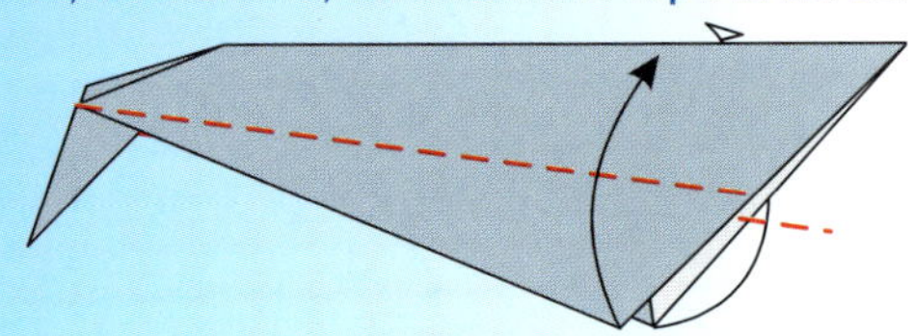

7. Nach unten drücken, siehe Pfeil, liegen lassen. Rückseite wiederholen.
Push downwards, see arrow, and leave. Repeat back.

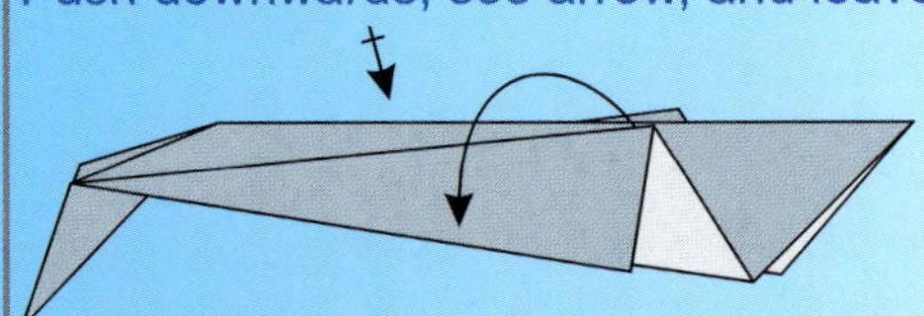

8. Fertiges Modell seitlich gesehen.
Finished model seen from the side.

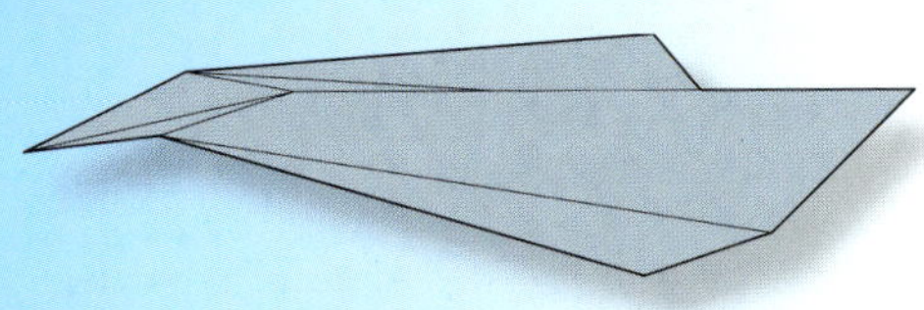

Düsenjäger Jet fighter

MATERIAL
1 Bogen 3,5 x 3,5 cm
1 sheet 3,5 x 3,5 cm

1. Waagerechte Linie falten, wieder öffnen.
Fold horizontal line and open again.

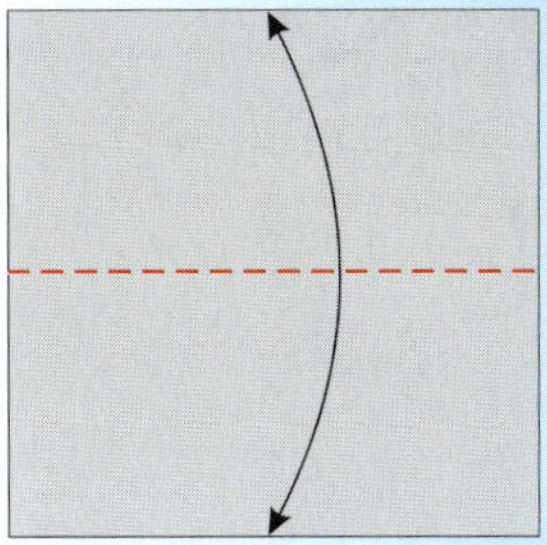

2. Schräge Linien falten, liegen lassen.
Fold diagonal lines and leave.

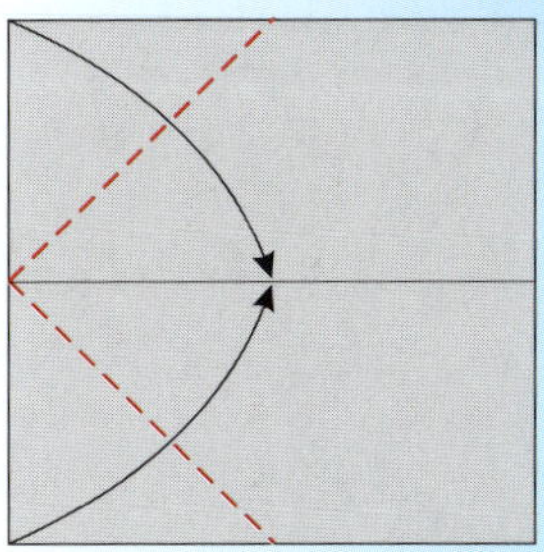

3. Schräge Linien falten, liegen lassen.
Fold diagonal lines and leave.

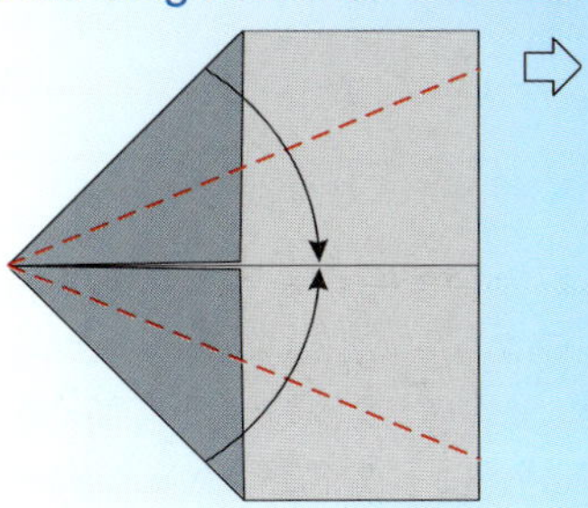

4. Waagerechte Linie zur Rückseite falten, liegen lassen.
Fold horizontal line to back and leave.

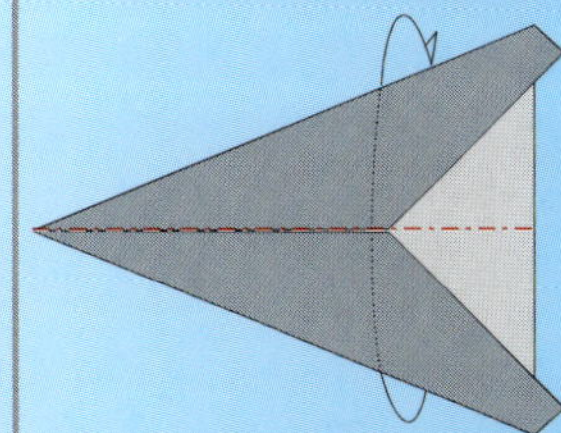

5. Waagerechte Linie falten, wieder öffnen. Rückseite wiederholen.
Fold horizontal line and open again. Repeat back.

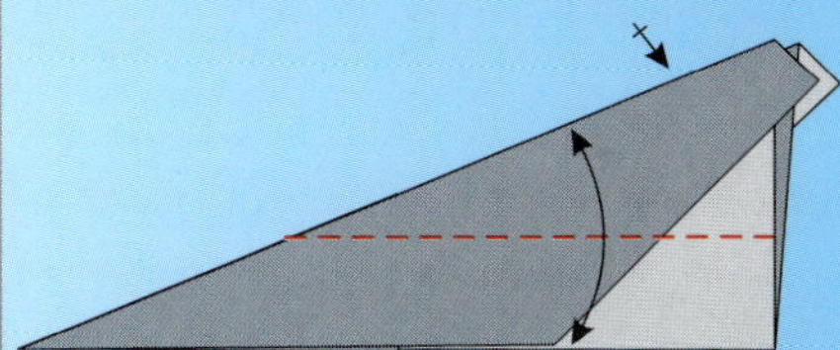

6. Schräge Linien falten, wieder öffnen.
Fold diagonal lines and open again.

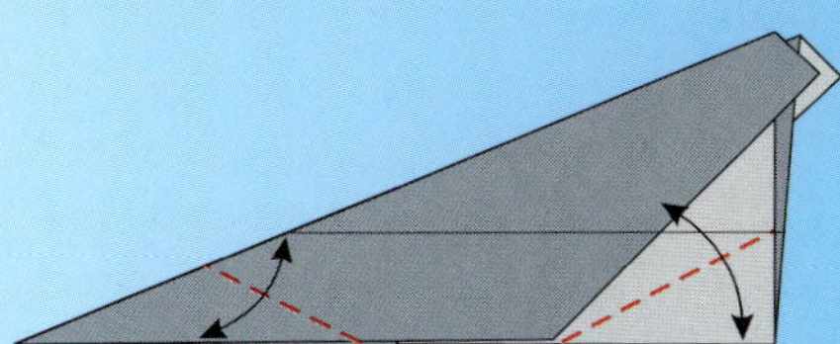

7. Linke Seite Linie im Gegenbruch nach oben leben, rechte Seite nach innen legen.
Put left side upwards in reverse fold. Put right side inwards.

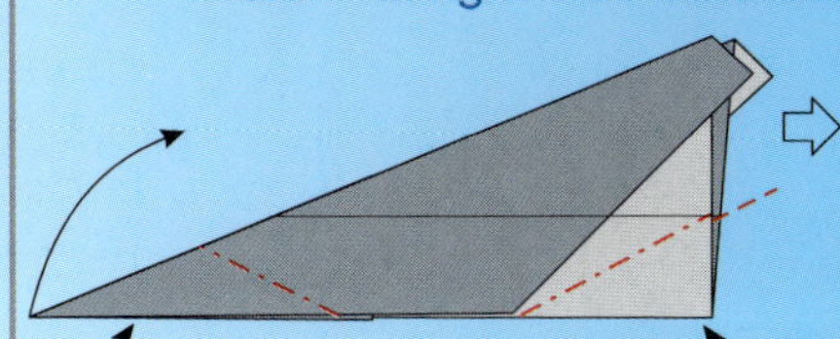

8. Schräge Linie falten, wieder öffnen.
Fold diagonal line and open again.

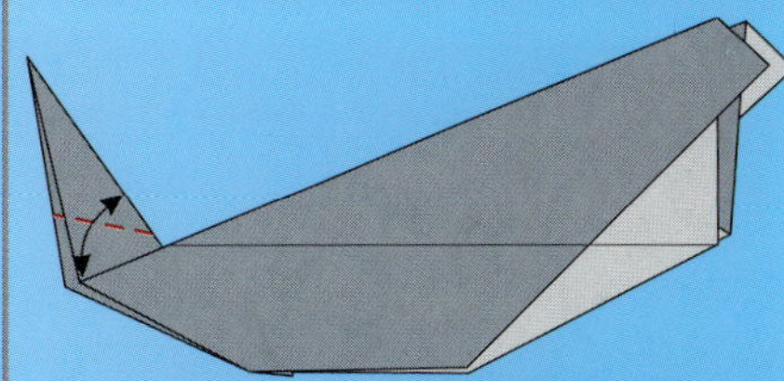

9. Schräge Linie im Gegenbruch nach links legen, liegen lassen.
Put diagonal line to the left in reverse fold and leave.

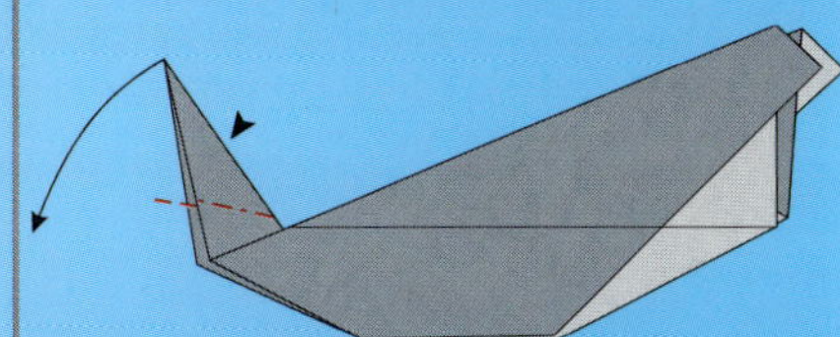

10. Waagerechte Linie nach unten falten, liegen lassen. Rückseite wiederholen.
Fold horizontal line downwards and leave. Repeat back.

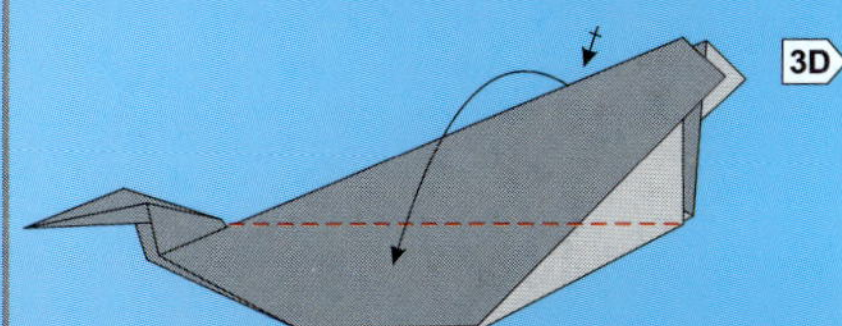

11. Fertiges Modell seitlich gesehen.
Finished model seen from the side.

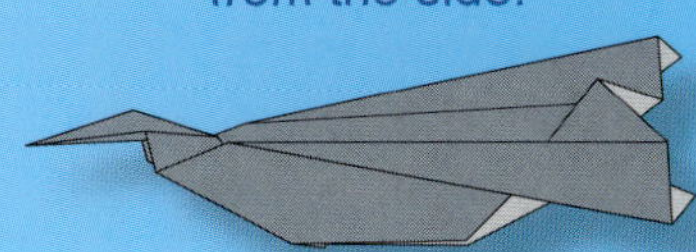

MATERIAL
1 Bogen 20x20 cm AQUAPAPIER.
1 sheet 20x20 cm AQUAPAPIER

1. Senkrecht falten, wieder öffnen. Waagerecht falten, liegen lassen.
Fold vertically, open again. Fold horizontally and leave.

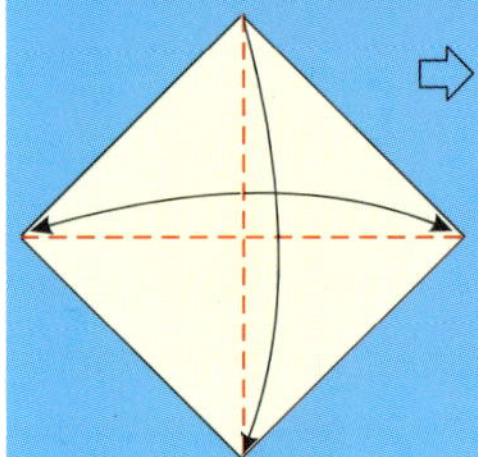

2. Markierung auf 1/2 anbringen. Waagerechte Linie falten, liegen lassen.
Attach marking on 1/2. Fold horizontal line and leave.

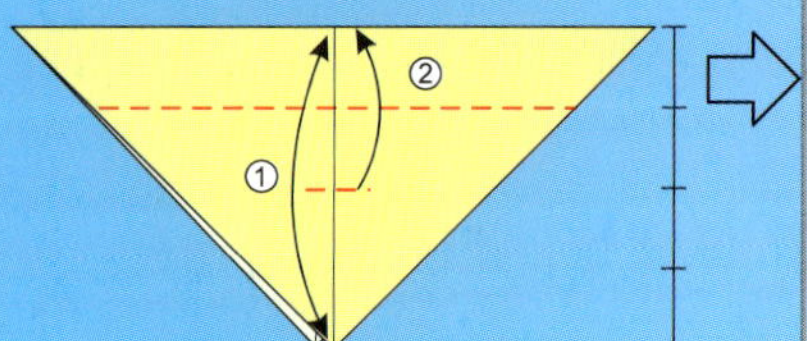

3. Nur mit der oberen Papierlage schräge Linien falten, wieder öffnen.
Fold diagonal lines only with top layers of paper and open again.

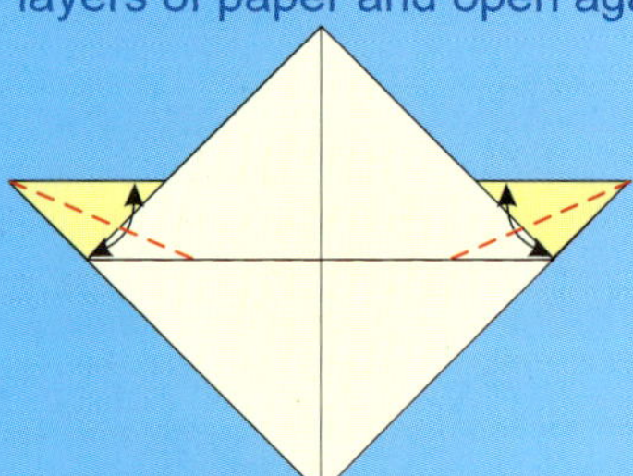

4. Senkrechte Linie falten, liegen lassen.
Fold vertical line and leave.

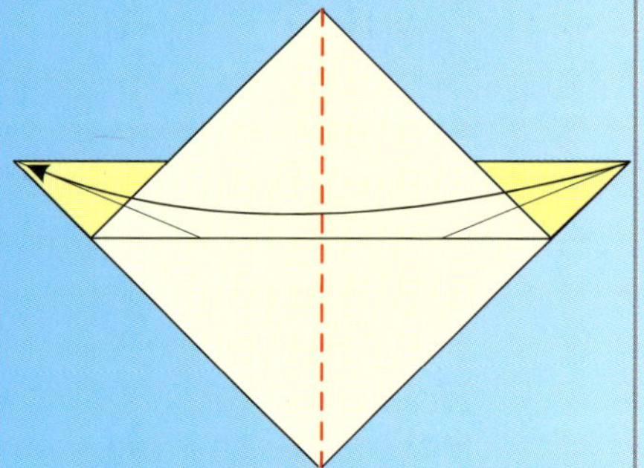

5. Die obere Spitze etwas nach links ziehen. Siehe auch nächste Zeichnung.
Pull the upper point somewhat to the left. See also next chart.

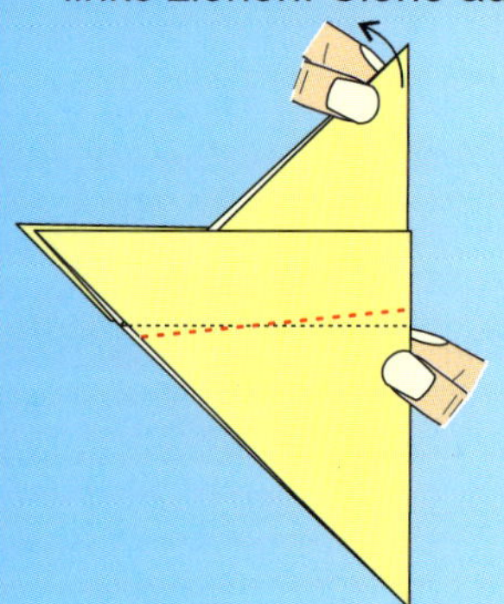

6. Modell nach rechts öffnen, liegen lassen.
Open model to the left and leave.

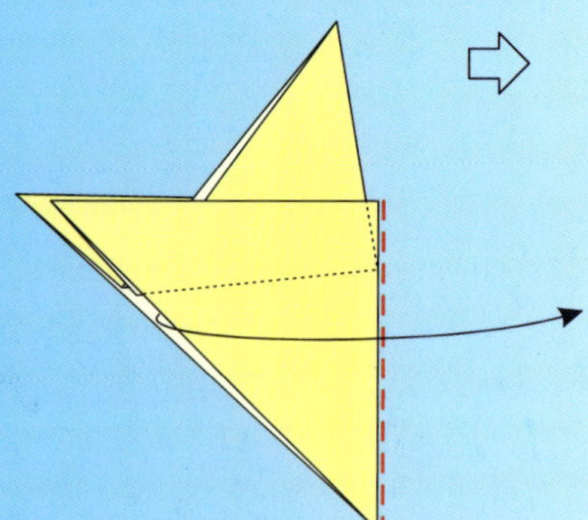

7. Schräge Linie, kleiner Pfeil, nach oben legen, liegen lassen. Dann die senkrechte Linie falten, siehe Pfeil, liegen lassen. Siehe auch nächste Zeichnung.
Put diagonal line upwards, see small arrow, and leave. Fold the vertical line, see arrow, and leave. See also next chart.

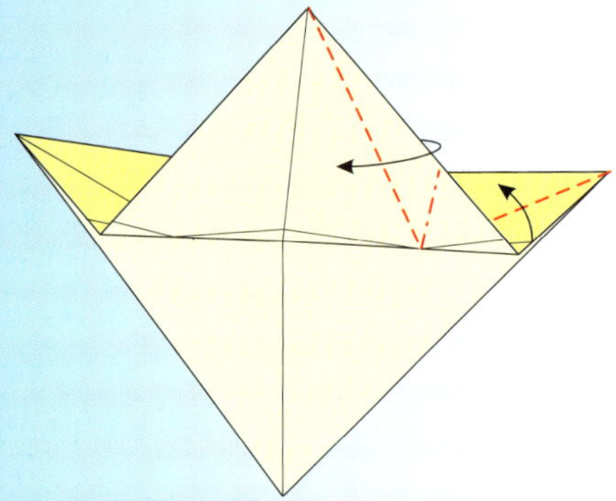

8. Schräge Linie falten, liegen lassen, siehe auch nächste Zeichnung.
Fold diagonal line and leave. See also next chart.

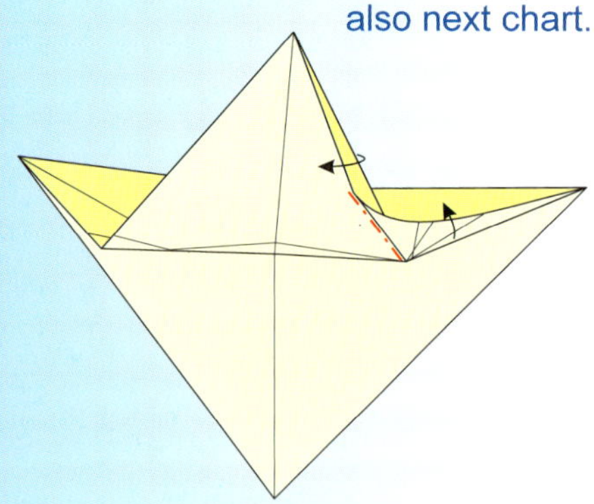

9. Schritte von Nr. 7-9 an der linken Seite wiederholen, liegen lassen.

Repeat steps from no. 7-9 on left side and leave.

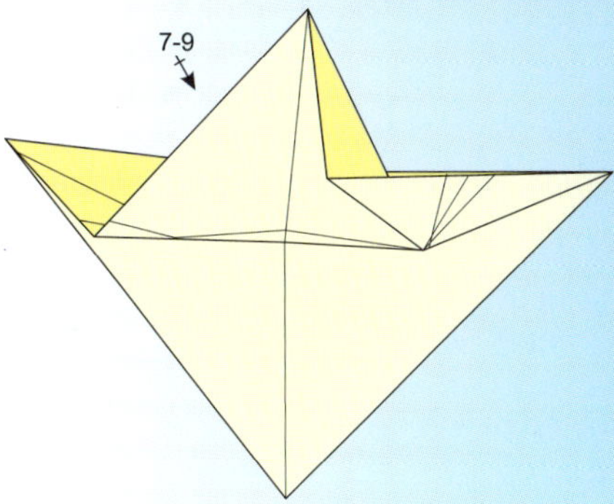

10. Modell wieder zusammenlegen, siehe Pfeil, liegen lassen.

Fold up model again, see arrow, and leave.

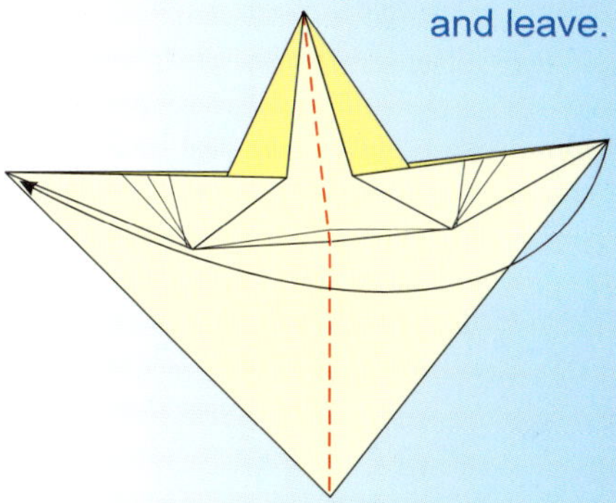

11. An der oberen Spitze waagerechte Linie falten, wieder öffnen.
Schräge Linie falten, wieder öffnen.

Fold horizontal line on upper point and open again. Fold diagonal line and open again.

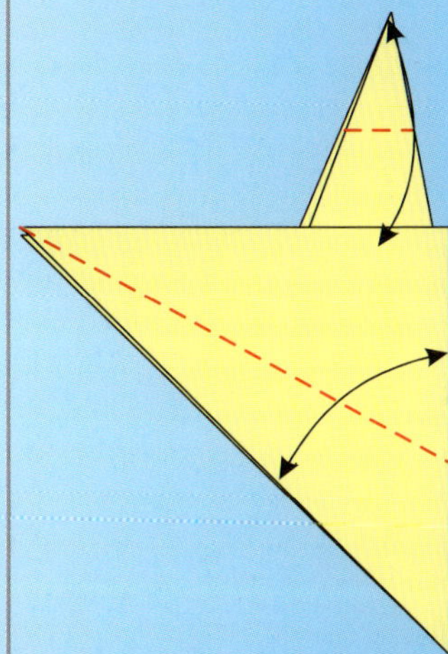

12. An der oberen Spitze waagerechte Linie falten, wieder öffnen. Schräge Linie nach außen drehen, dann im Gegenbruch nach oben legen. Modell etwas drehen.

Fold horizontal line on upper point and open again. Turn diagonal line outwards and put then upwards in reverse fold. Turn model somewhat.

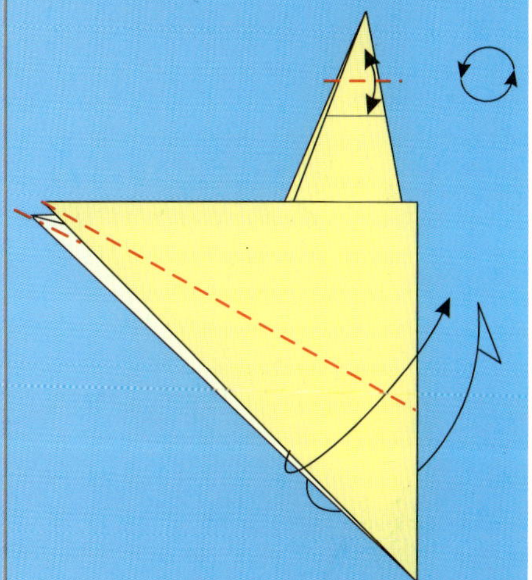

Lotsenboot

13. An der oberen Spitze Linien im Zickzack nach innen legen. Links schräge Linie nach rechts falten, liegen lassen.
Put lines on upper point inwards in zigzag line. Fold left diagonal line to the right and leave.

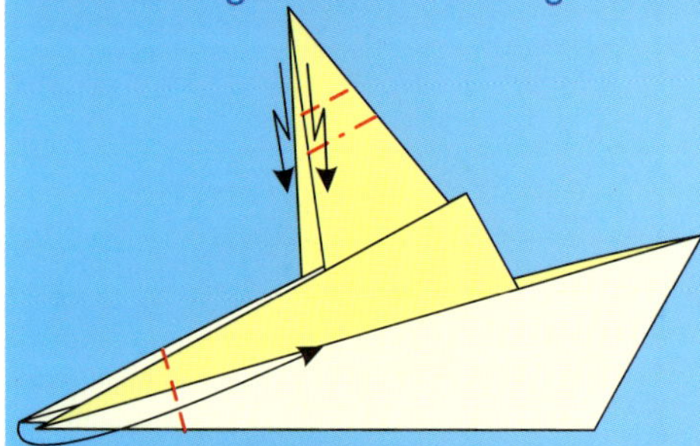

14. Mit der Spitze links schräge Linie nach oben falten, liegen lassen.
With the left point fold diagonal line upwards and leave.

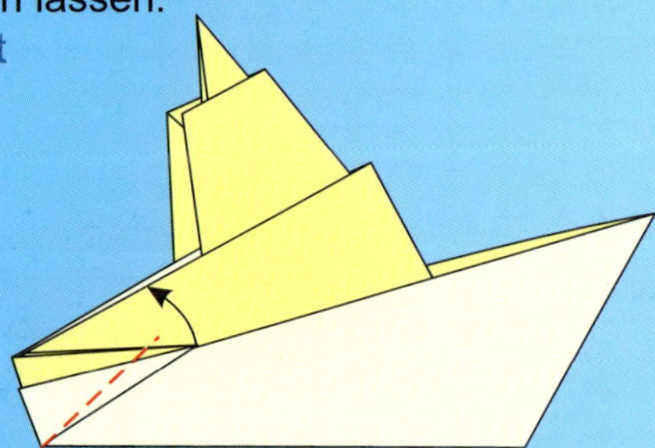

15. Links schräge Linie nach innen falten, dann bis Schritt Nr.13 wieder öffnen. Rückseite nach oben legen.
Fold left diagonal line inwards, then open until step no.13. Put back upwards.

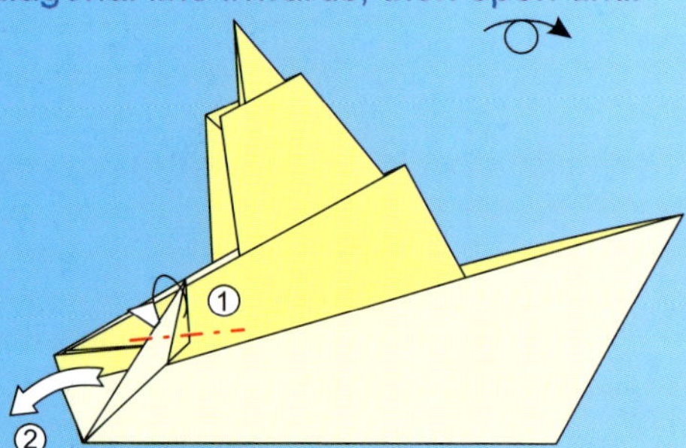

16. An der rechten Seite die Spitze der unteren Papierlage an der Linie von Nr.13 nach innen legen, liegen lassen.
Put on the right side the point of the lower layer of paper on the line of step no. 13 inwards and leave.

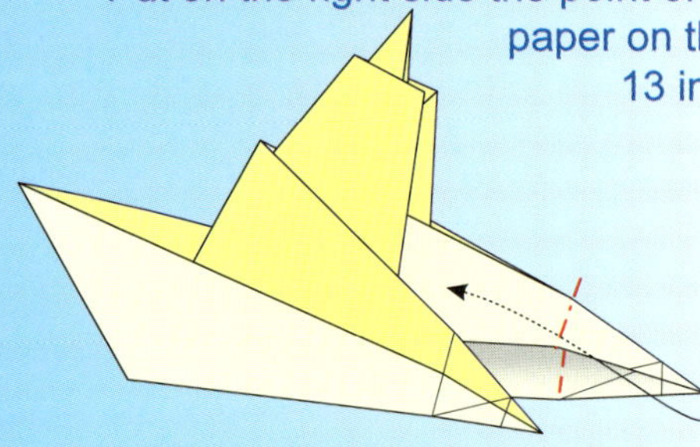

17. Nun die obere Spitze, siehe Pfeil, bei der unteren Papierlage nach innen legen, liegen lassen. Rückseite nach oben legen.
Put the upper point, see arrow, of the lower layer of paper inwards and leave. Put back upwards.

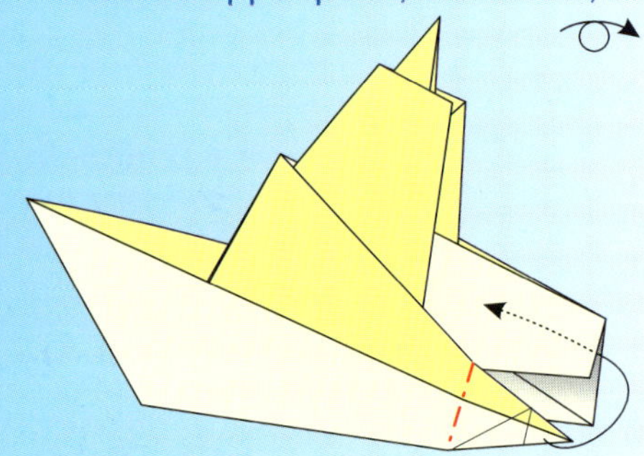

18. Schräge Linie von Nr.14 mit den inneren Spitzen nach oben legen, liegen lassen.
Put diagonal line of step no.14 with inside points upwards and leave.

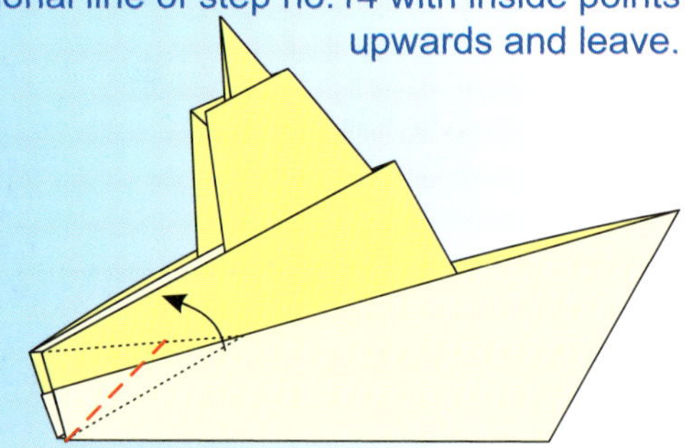

19. Schräge Linie von Nr.15 mit den inneren Spitzen nach hinten legen, liegen lassen.
Put diagonal line of step no.15 with inside points to the back and leave.

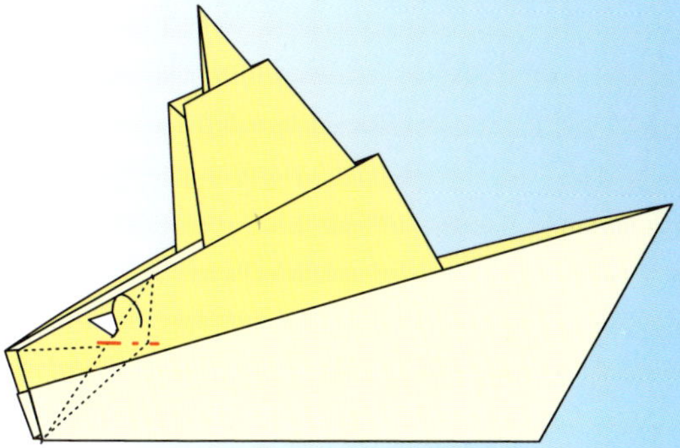

20. Bergfalten formen, damit das Schiff breiter wird, fertig.
Form mountain-folds in order the boat becomes broader, ready.

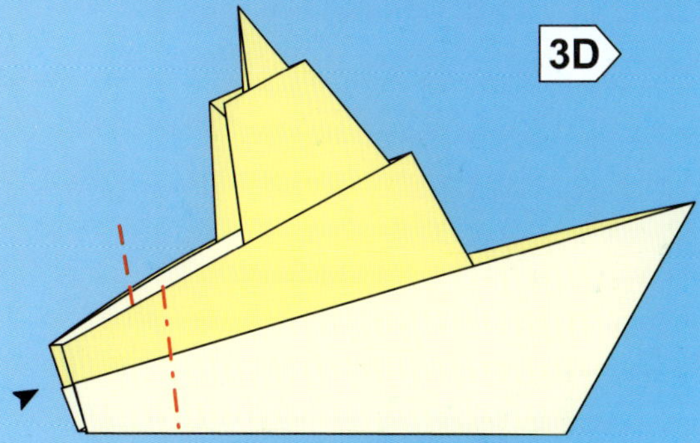

21. Fertiges Modell seitlich gesehen.
Finished model seen from the side.

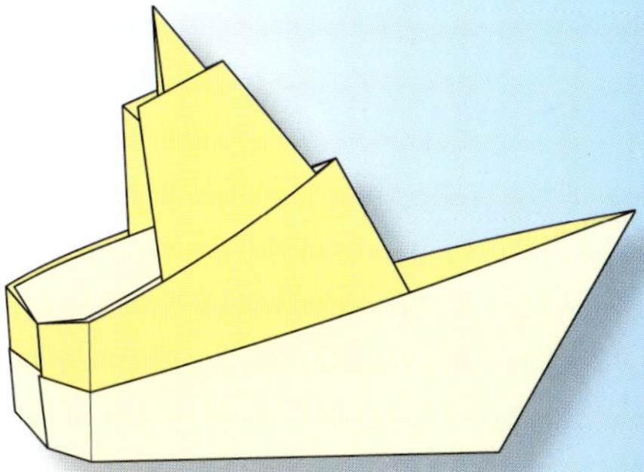

Rettungsboot

Lifeboat

MATERIAL
1 Bogen 20x20 cm AQUAPAPIER
1 sheet 20x20 cm AQUAPAPIER

1. Waagerechte Linien falten, liegen lassen.
Fold horizontal lines and leave.

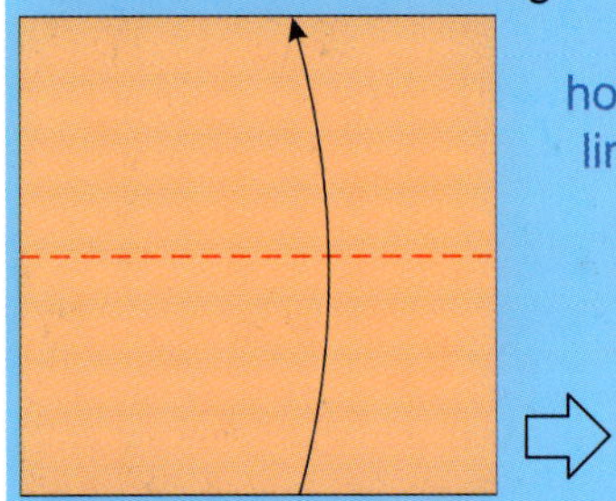

2. Nur mit der oberen Papierlage waagerechte Linie falten, wieder öffnen. Rückseite wiederholen.
Fold horizontal line only with upper layer and open again. Repeat back.

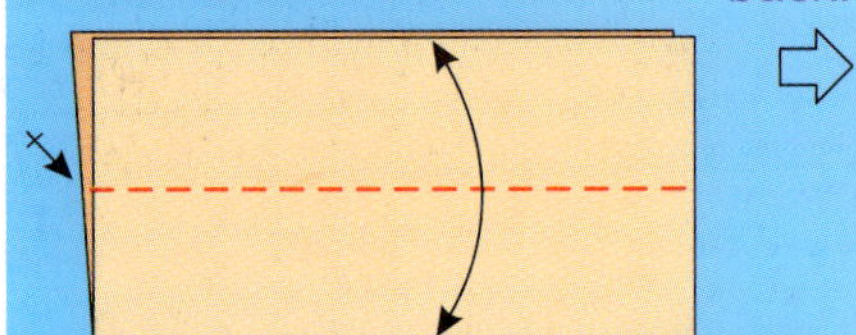

3. Nur mit der oberen Papierlage drei Ecken falten, siehe Pfeile, liegen lassen.
Fold three corners only with top layer of paper, see arrows, and leave.

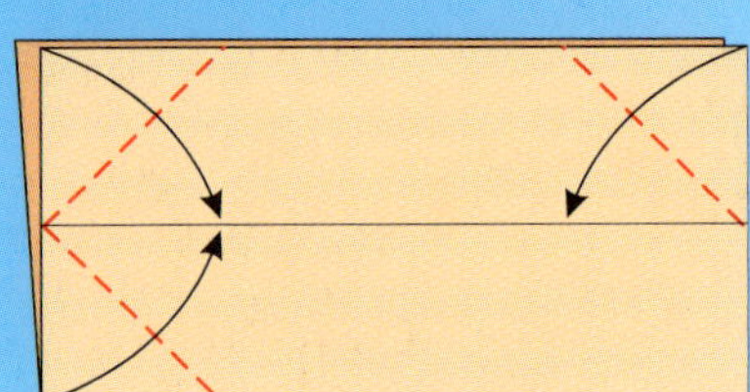

4. Nur mit der oberen Papierlage waagerechte Linie falten, liegen lassen.
Fold horizontal line only with top layer of paper and leave.

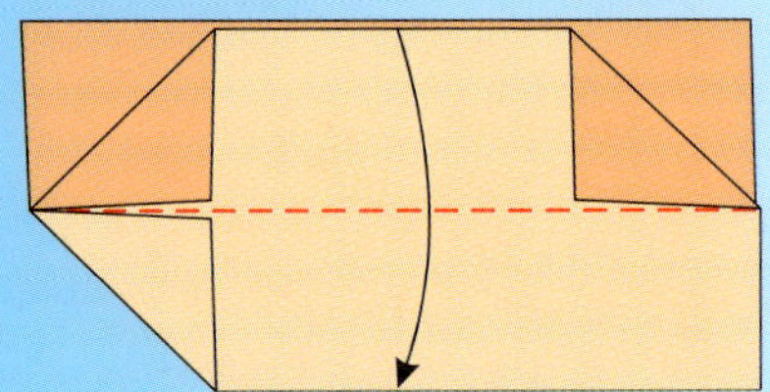

5 . Rückseite nach oben legen.
Put back upwards.

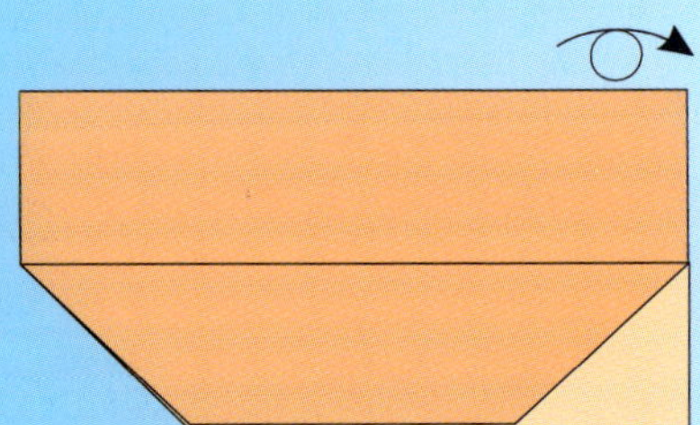

6. Drei Ecken falten, siehe Pfeile, liegen lassen.
Fold three corners, see arrows, and leave.

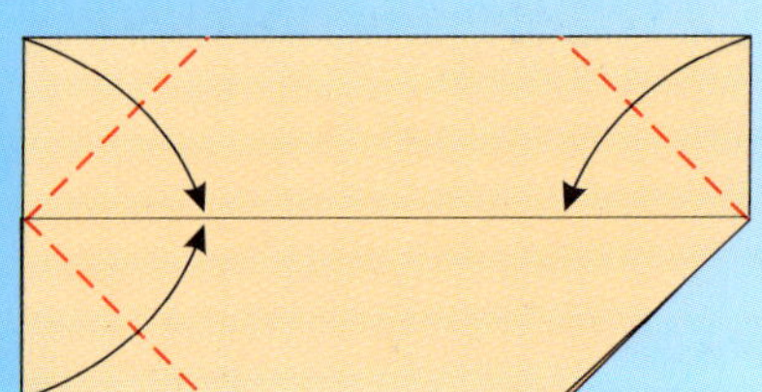

7. Waagerechte Linie falten, liegen lassen.
Fold horizontal line and leave.

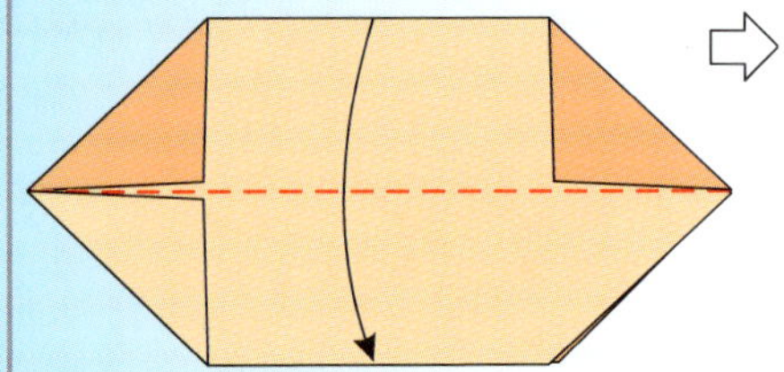

8. Waagerechte Linie falten, wieder öffnen.
Fold horizontal line and open again.

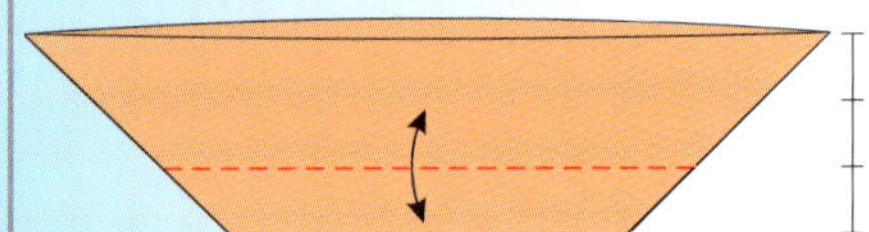

9. Schräge Linien falten, siehe Pfeile, liegen lassen.
Fold diagonal lines, see arrows, and leave.

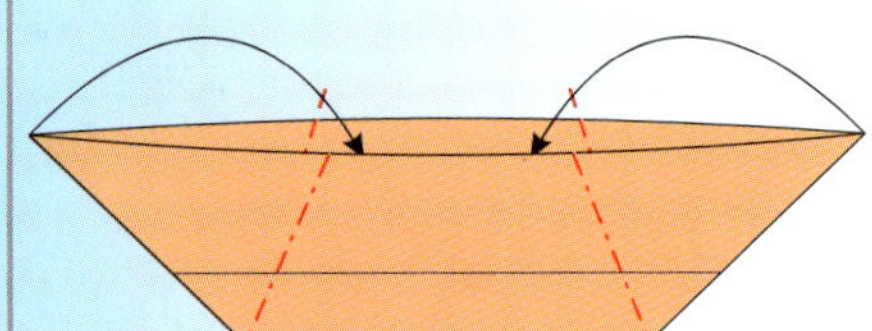

10. Senkrechte Linien falten, siehe Pfeile, liegen lassen.
Fold vertical lines, see arrows, and leave.

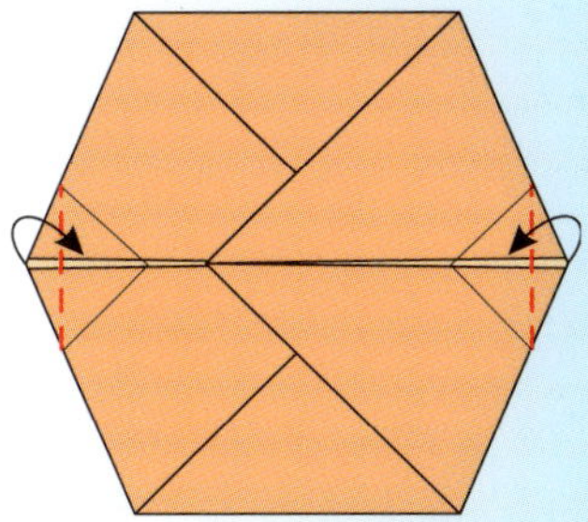

11. Rechte Spitze nach außen falten, liegen lassen.
Fold right point outwards and leave.

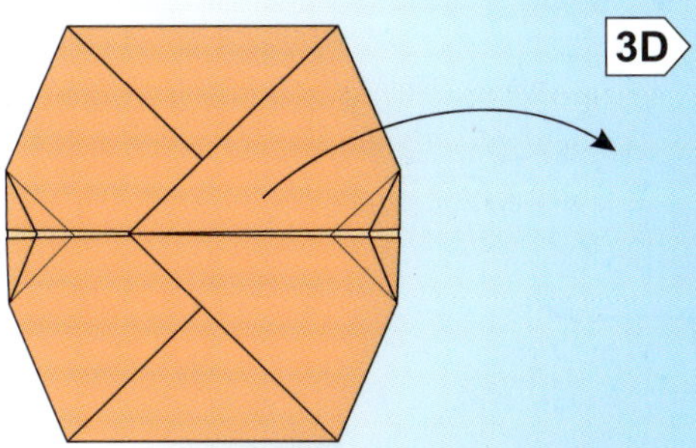

12. Linke Spitze nach außen falten, liegen lassen. Modell drehen, fertig.
Fold left point outwards and leave. Turn model, ready.

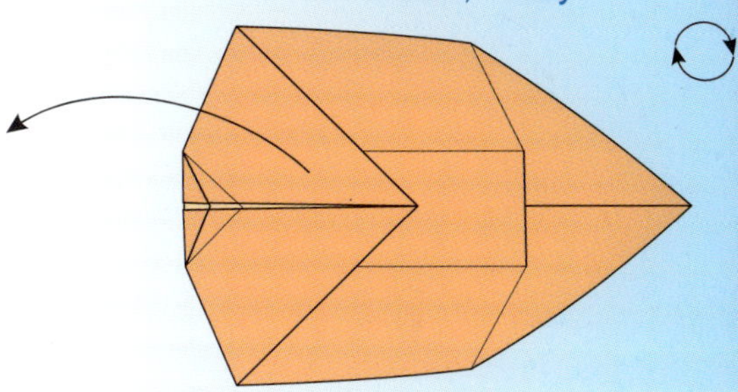

13. Fertiges Modell seitlich gesehen.
Finished model seen from the side.

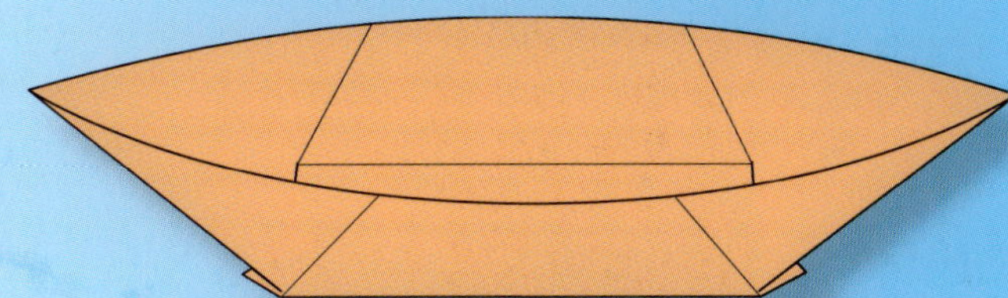

Autofähre

Car ferry

Lieblingsboot: lade Autos hinein
Favourite boat: load cars

MATERIAL

1 Bogen 20x20 cm AQUAPAPIER
1 sheet 20x20 cm AQUAPAPIER

1. Zweimal die Mitte falten, wieder öffnen.
Fold twice the middle and open again.

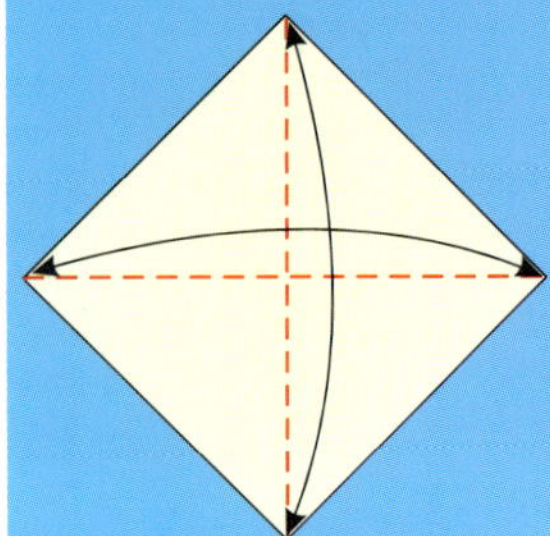

2. Markierungen auf 1/4 anbringen.
Attach marking on 1/4.

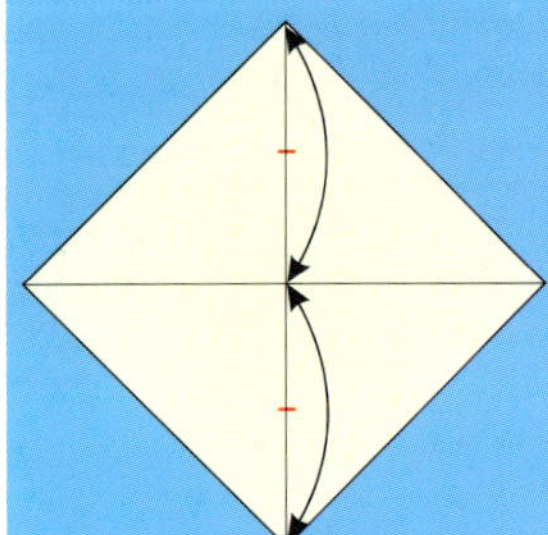

3. Waagerechte Linien falten, wieder öffnen. Rückseite nach oben legen.
Fold horizontal lines and open again. Put back upwards.

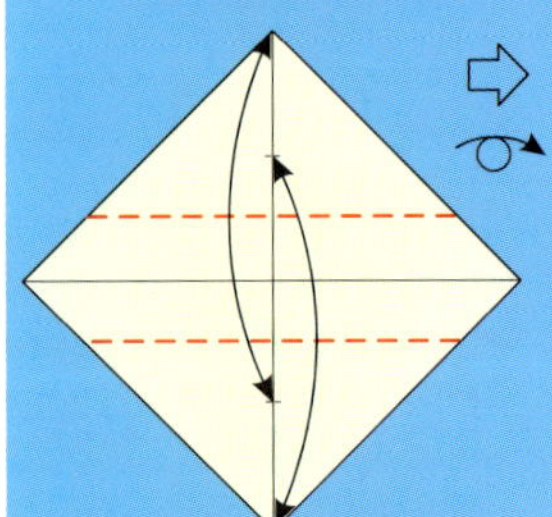

4. Schräge Linien falten, wieder öffnen. Rückseite nach oben legen.
Fold diagonal lines and open again. Put back upwards.

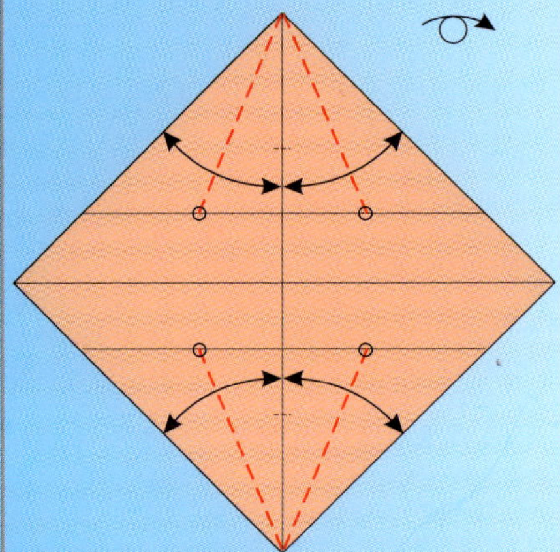

5. Senkrechte Linien falten, wieder öffnen.
Fold vertical lines and open again.

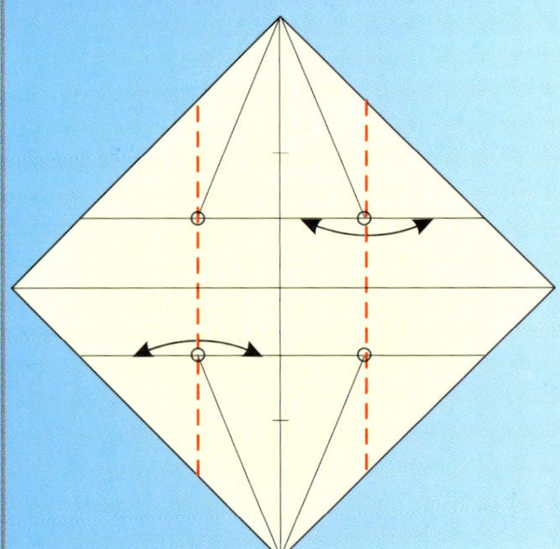

6. Senkrechte Linien falten, liegen lassen.
Fold vertical lines and leave.

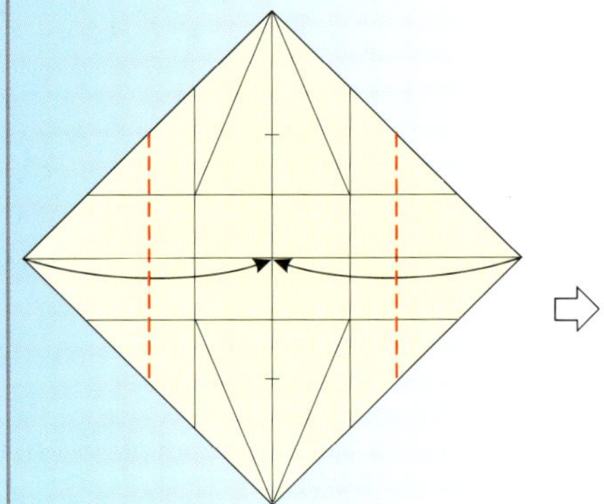

7. Nur mit der oberen Papierlage, Markierung auf 1/2 anbringen.
Using only the top layer of paper, attach marking on 1/2.

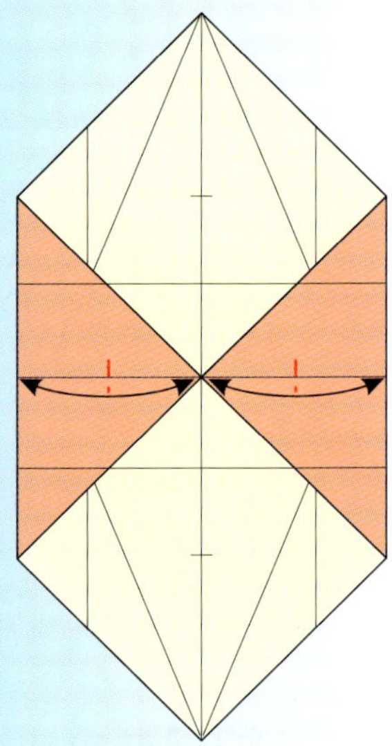

8. Nur mit der oberen Papierlage, senkrechte Linien falten, liegen lassen.

Using only the top layer of paper, fold vertical lines and leave.

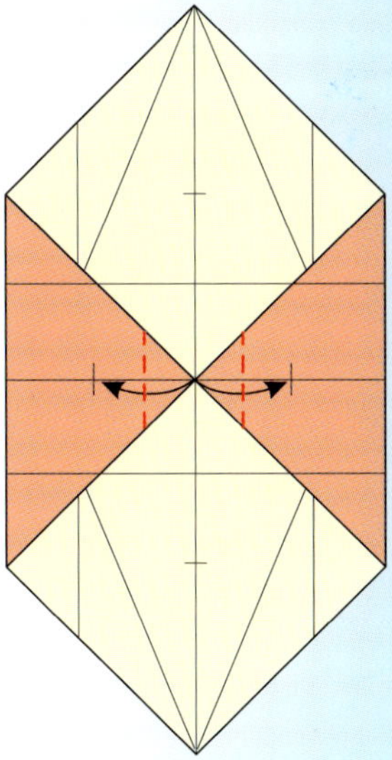

9. Nur mit der oberen Papierlage, senkrechte Linien falten, liegen lassen.

Using only the top layer of paper, fold vertical lines and leave.

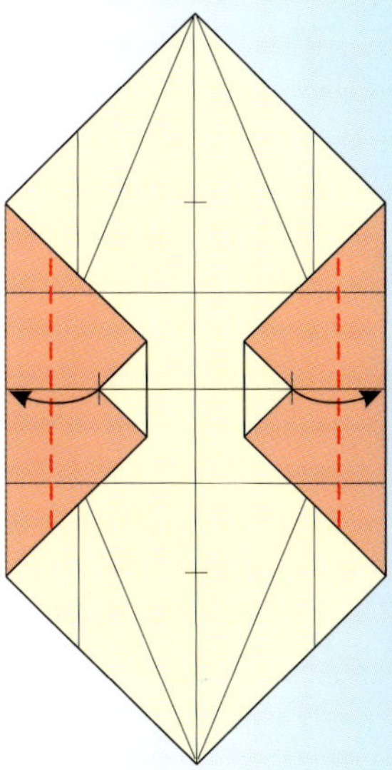

10. Schräge Linien falten, liegen lassen.

Fold diagonal lines and leave.

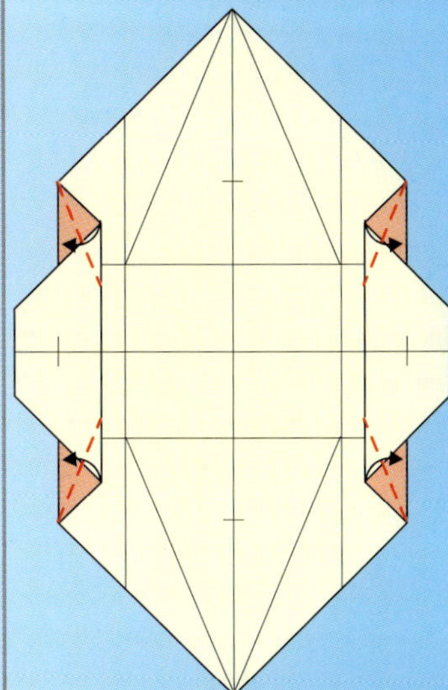

11. Schräge Linien zur Rückseite falten, liegen lassen.

Fold diagonal lines to the back and leave.

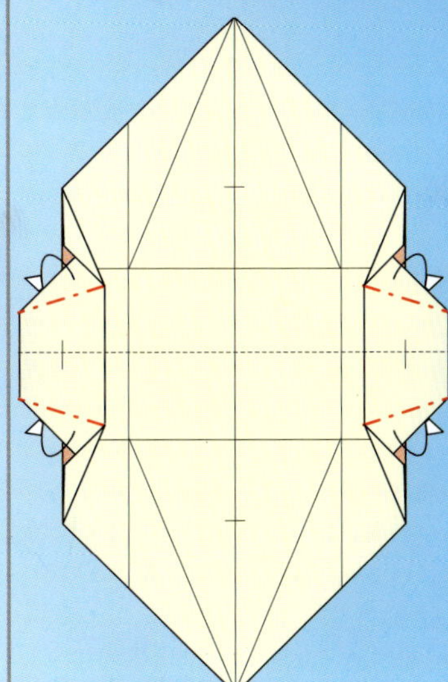

12. Schräge Linien falten, liegen lassen.

Fold diagonal lines and leave.

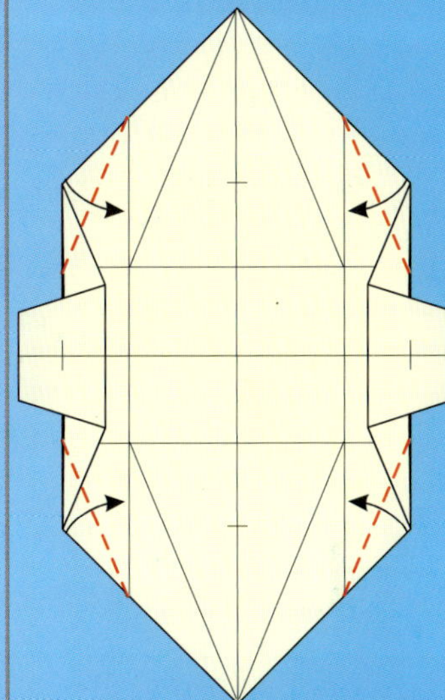

13. Waagerechte Linien falten, wieder öffnen.

Fold horizontal lines and open again.

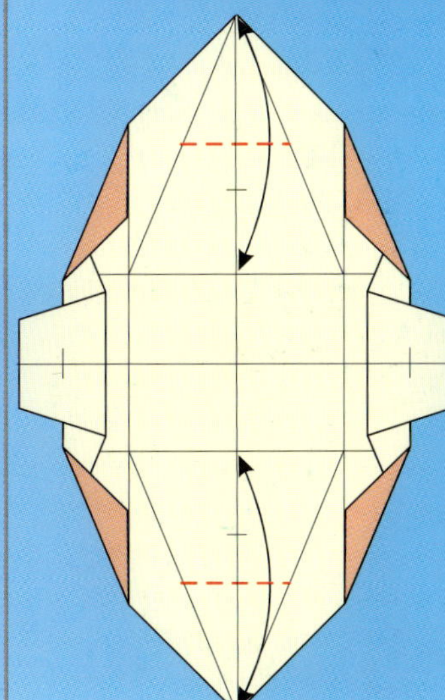

14. Waagerechte Linien zur Rückseite falten, wieder öffnen.
Fold horizontal lines to the back and open again.

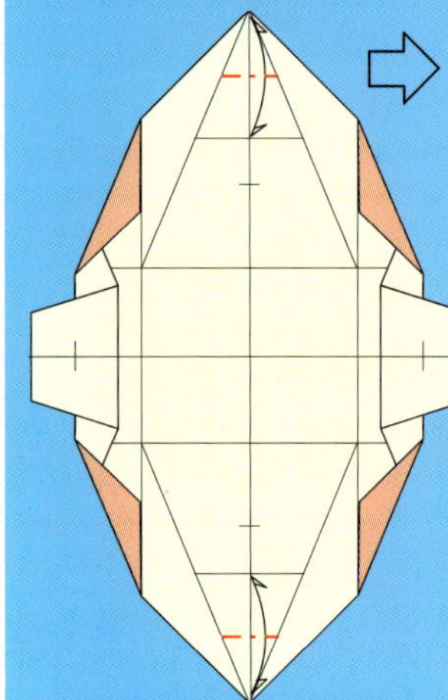

15. Obere Spitze, Linien zu Berg- oder Talfalten formen, dann siehe Pfeile, zusammenlegen. An der unteren Spitze wiederholen.
Form lines to mountain and valley-folds on the upper point and put them together. Repeat on the lower point.

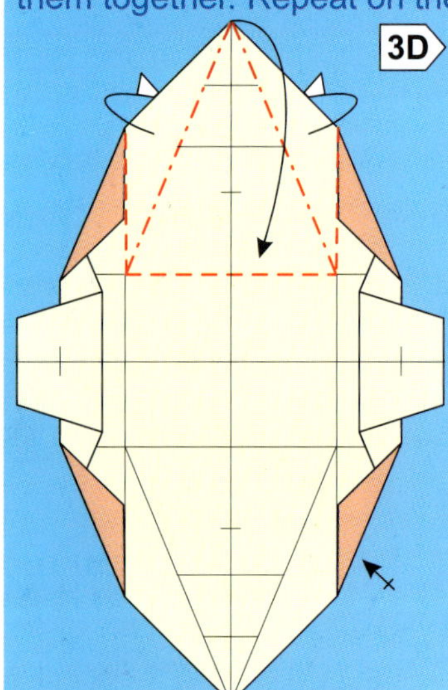

16. Waagerechte Linien falten, liegen lassen.
Fold horizontal lines and leave.

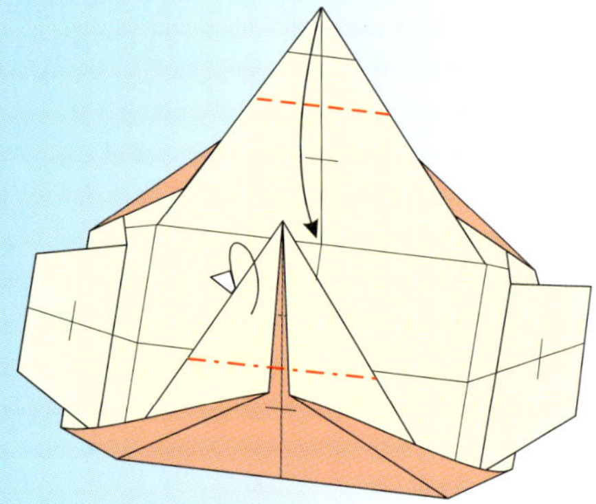

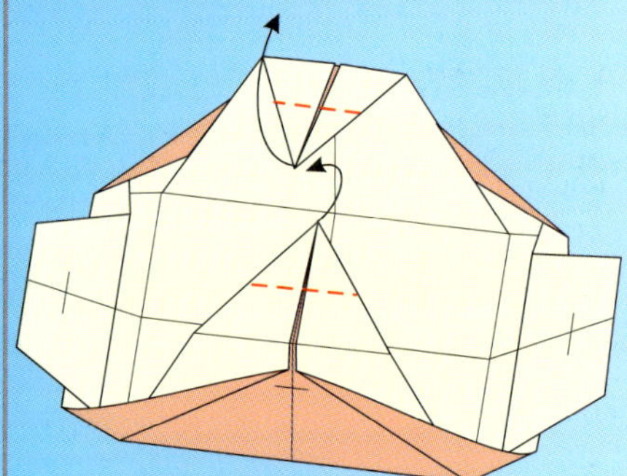

17. Waagerechte Linien nach oben falten, liegen lassen.
Fold horizontal lines upwards and leave.

18. Schräge Linien nach innen falten, liegen lassen. Obere Spitzen zusammenkleben.
Fold diagonal lines inwards and leave. Stick upper points.

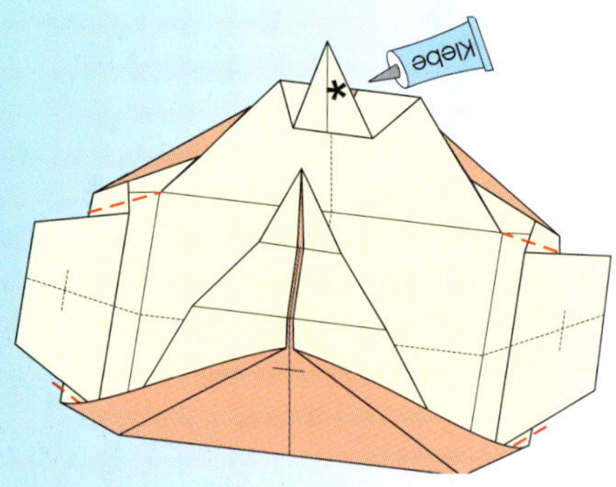

19. Siehe Pfeile, nach außen biegen, fertig.
Bend outwards, see arrows, ready.

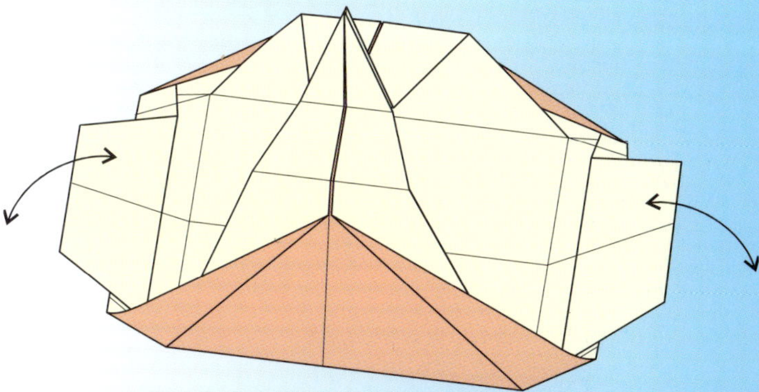

20. Fertiges Modell seitlich gesehen.
Finished model seen from the side.

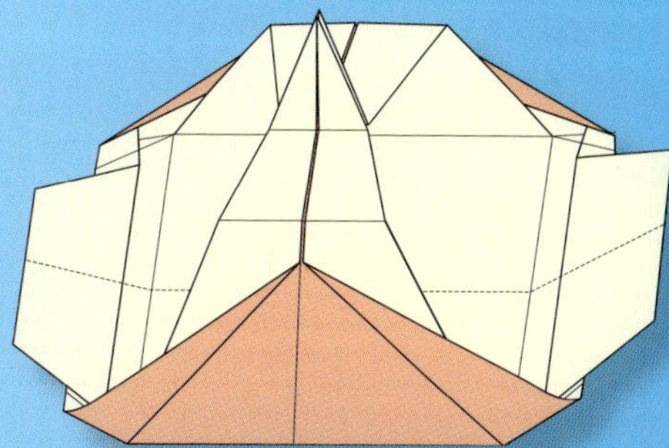

Flaches Kartenmodell
Flat map model

MATERIAL
1 Bogen 9 x 9 cm
1 sheet 9 x 9 cm

1. Senkrechte Linie falten, wieder öffnen.
Fold vertical line and open again.

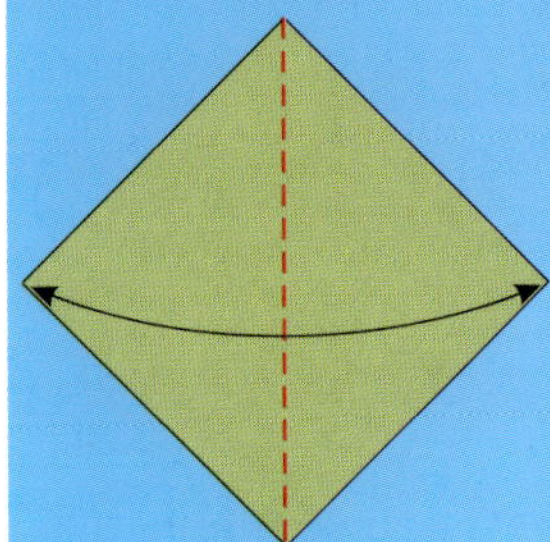

2. Schräge Linien falten, liegen lassen.
Fold diagonal lines and leave.

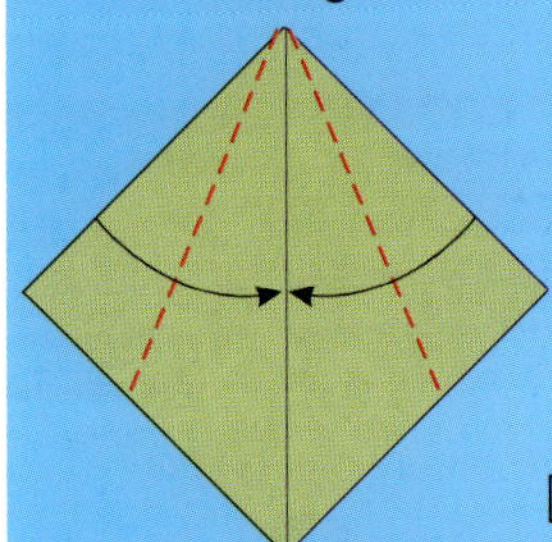

3. Waagerechte Linie zur Rückseite falten, liegen lassen.
Fold horizontal line to the back and leave.

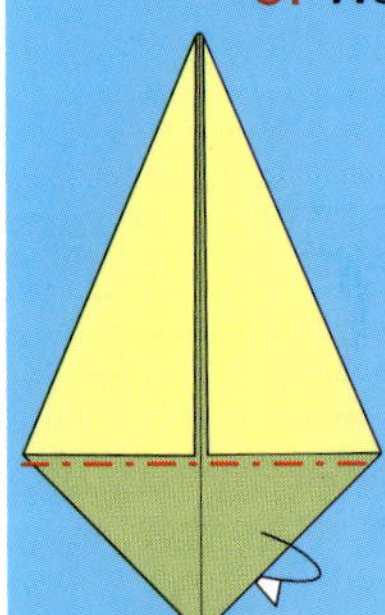

4. Waagerechte Linie falten, liegen lassen.
Fold horizontal line and leave.

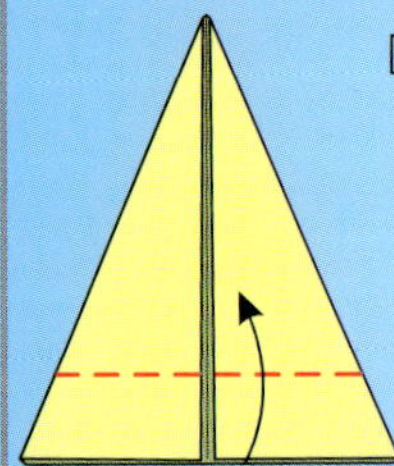

5. Schräge Linien falten und nach innen schieben, fertig.
Fold diagonal lines, push inwards, ready.

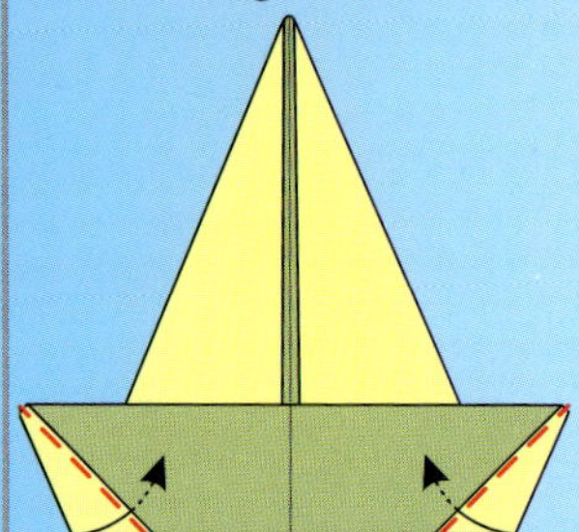

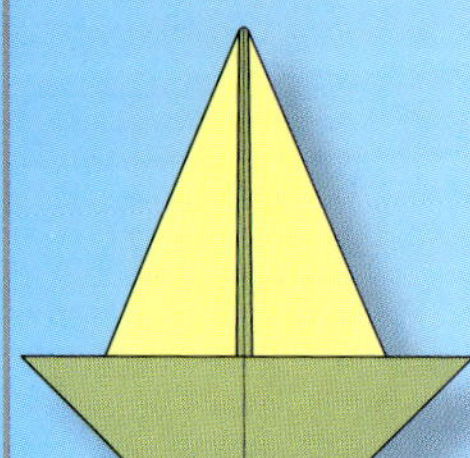

6. Fertiges Modell.
Finished model.

Flaches Kartenmodell
Flat map model

MATERIAL
1 Bogen 9 x 9 cm
1 sheet 9 x 9 cm

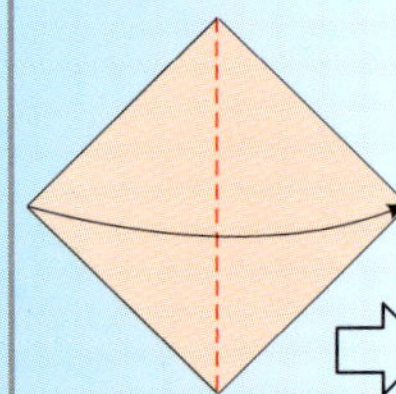

1. Senkrechte Linie falten, liegen lassen.
Fold vertical line and leave.

2. Nur obere Papierlage senkrechte Linie falten, liegen lassen.
Fold vertical line on top layer of paper only and leave.

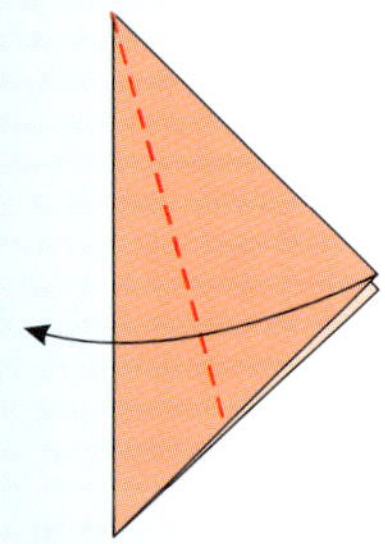

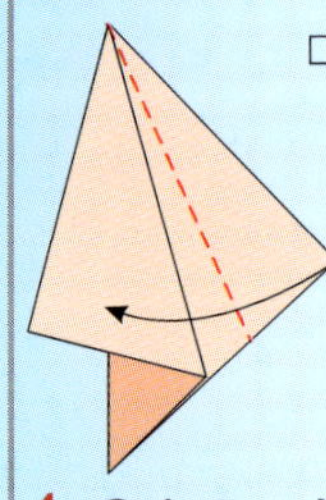

3. Senkrechte Linie falten, liegen lassen.
Fold vertical line and leave.

4. Schräge Linie falten, liegen lassen. Modell etwas drehen.
Fold diagonal line and leave. Turn model somewhat.

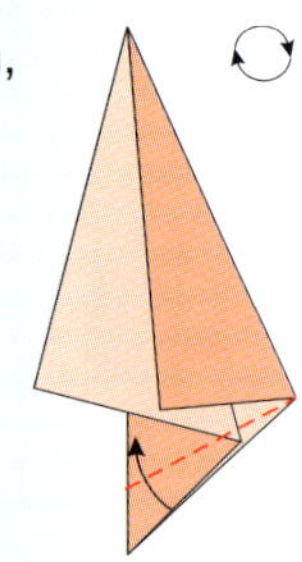

5. Fertiges Modell.
Finished model.

Briefeckenboot

Letter corner boat

Modell von Paula Versnick
Model by Paula Versnick

Briefeckenboot
Letter corner boat

MATERIAL
1 Bogen 9 x 9 cm
1 sheet 9 x 9 cm

1. Zweimal waagerecht die Mitte falten, wieder öffnen. Rückseite nach oben legen.
Fold twice the middle horizontally and open again. Put back upwards.

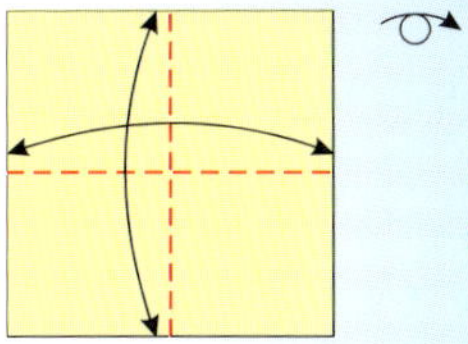

2. Zweimal diagonal die Mitte falten, wieder öffnen.
Fold twice the middle diagonally and open again.

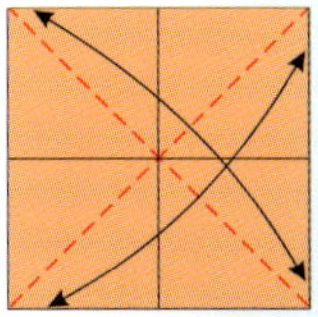

3. Waagerechte Linie falten, liegen lassen.
Fold horizontal line and leave.

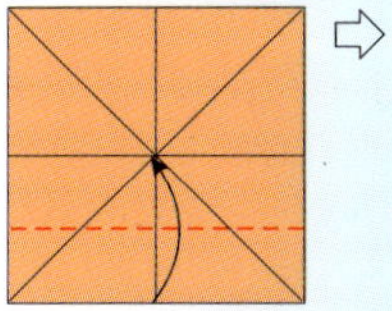

4. Schräge Linien falten und nach innen legen.
Fold diagonal lines and put them inwards.

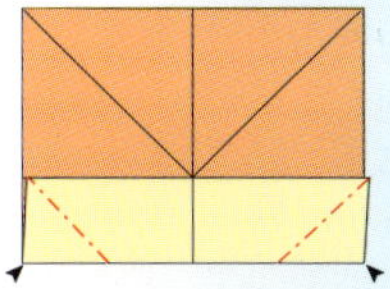

5. Linien zu Berg- oder Talfalten formen, dann siehe Pfeile, zusammenlegen.
Fold lines to mountain and valley-folds, see arrows, and put them together.

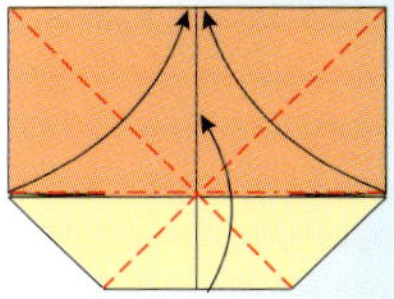

6. Nur obere Papierlage nach links falten, liegen lassen.
Fold top layer of paper to the left only and leave.

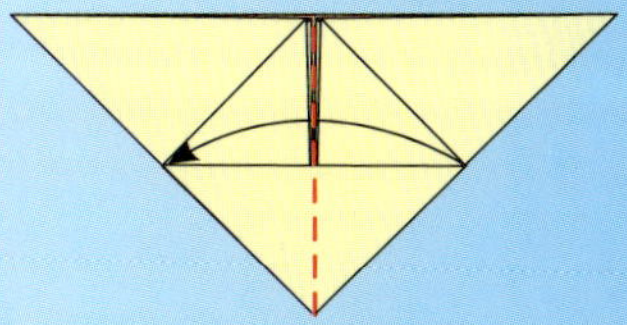

7. Nur obere Papierlage schräge Linie falten, wieder öffnen.
Fold top layer of paper to diagonal line only and open again.

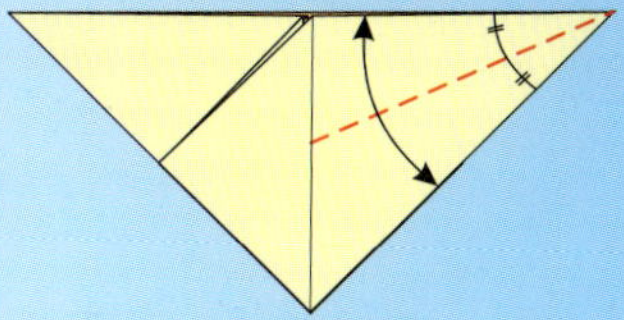

8. Nur obere Papierlage schräge Linie falten, wieder öffnen.
Fold top layer of paper to diagonal line only and open again.

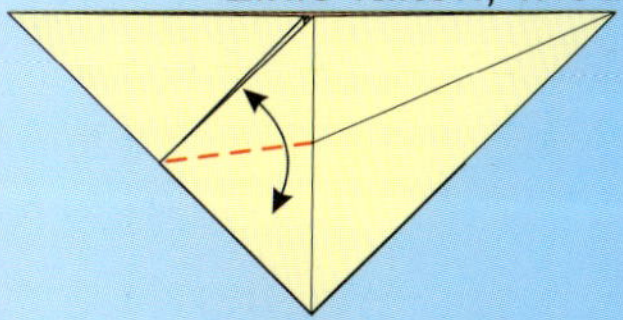

9. Linie Nr.1 nach unten, dann Linie Nr. 2 nach rechts legen.
Put line no.1 downwards and line no. 2 to the right.

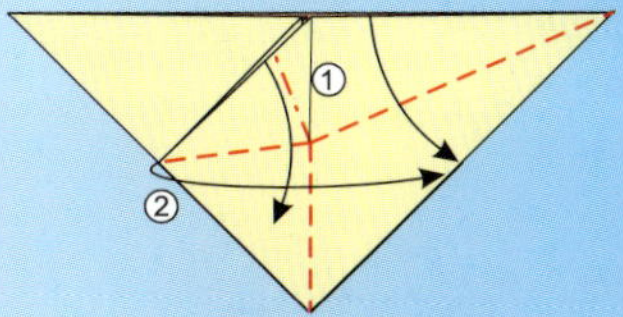

10. Schritt Nr.6-9 an der linken Seite wiederholen.
Repeat steps no. 6-9 on left side.

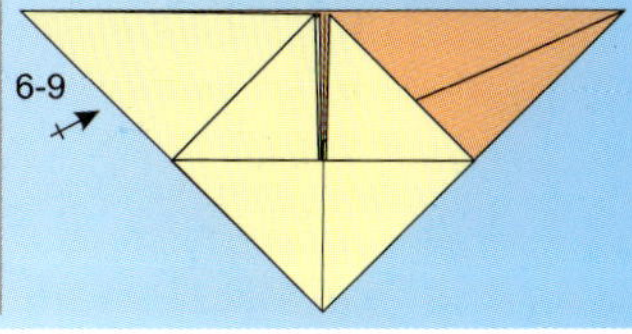

11. Siehe Pfeil, im Zickzack nach unten legen, liegen lassen.
See arrow, put downwards in zigzag line and leave.

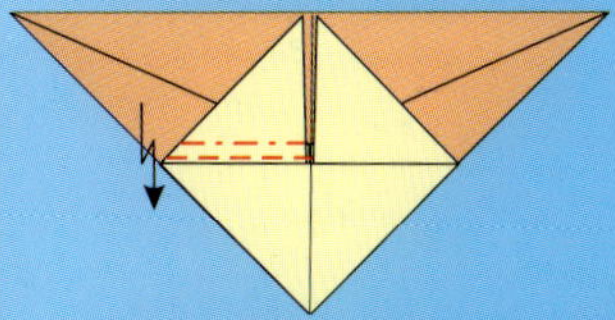

12. Siehe Pfeil, unter die obere Papierlage schieben.
See arrow, push under the top layer of paper.

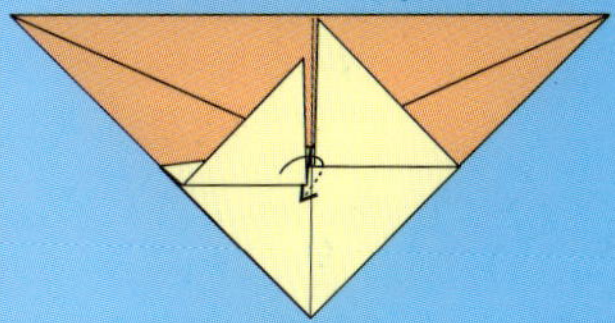

13. Brief in den Eckenhalter schieben.
Push letter in corner-holder.

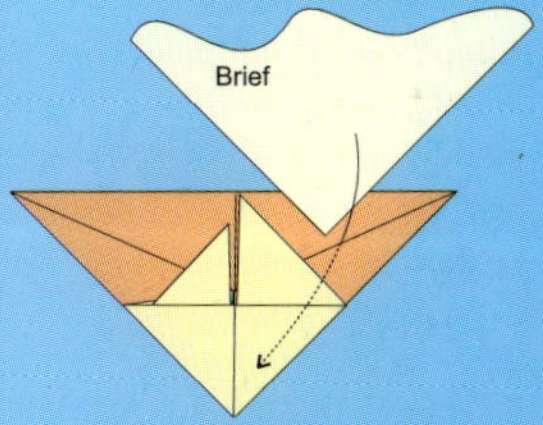

14. Spitze zur Rückseite falten, fertig.
Fold point to the back, ready.

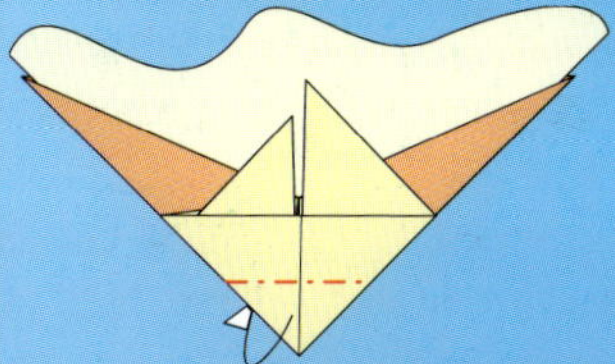

15. Fertiges Modell.
Finished model.

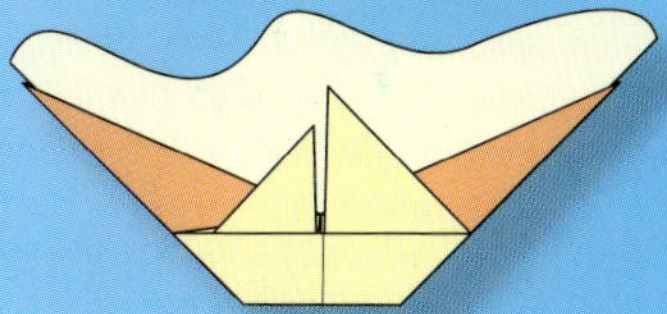

Bücher vom Q-Verlag Berlin

Paper Diamond
Ohrringe aus Papier in Origami Technik

Schöner Schmuck selbst gemacht! Mit dem Buch „Paper Diamond – Ohrringe aus Papier in Origami Technik“, haben Sie die Möglichkeit sich Ohrringe aus edlem Papier selber herzustellen. Insgesamt werden 16 verschiedene Modelle mittels farbigen Zeichnungen, Arbeitsfotos und Texten Schritt-für-Schritt vorgestellt. Zuerst wird das Papier gefaltet, dann das Zubehör angebracht und zuletzt die fertigen Ohrringe mit Hilfe von Lack dauerhaft haltbar gemacht.

Schwierigkeitsgrad: Anfänger.

Technik: Papier falten (Origami), Zubehör anbringen, lacken, fertig.

ISBN 3-938127-02-3 Preis: 7,95 EUR (D)

Colliers & Co.
Schmuck aus Papier

Schmuck mal ganz anders! Mit dem Buch - Colliers & Co. - , haben Sie die Möglichkeit sich verschiedene Ketten, Halsbänder, Haarspangen, Broschen oder einen Ring selber herzustellen. Die Papiere werden so kombiniert oder eingesetzt, dass jeweils eine neue Kreation entsteht. So erhalten Sie Schmuck genau passend zu Ihrer Garderobe. Insgesamt werden 14 verschiedene Modelle mittels farbigen Zeichnungen, Arbeitsfotos und Texten Schritt-für-Schritt vorgestellt.

Schwierigkeitsgrad: Anfänger

Technik: Papier falten oder rollen, Zubehör anbringen, lacken, fertig.

ISBN 3-938127-05-8 Preis: 8,95 EUR (D)

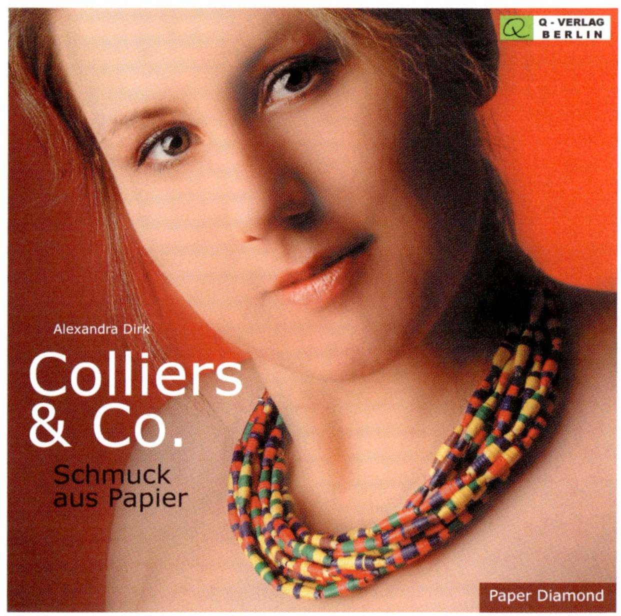

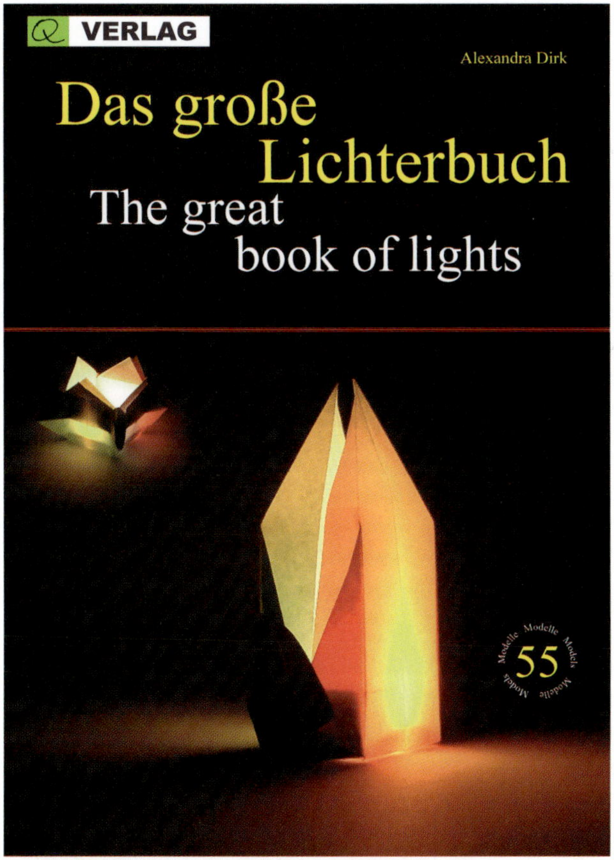

Das grosse Lichterbuch
The great book of lights
Lichter aus Papier in Origami Technik

Lieben Sie auch die tolle Ausstrahlung von Papierlichtern? Dann ist „Das große Lichterbuch“ genau das richtige für Sie. Insgesamt 55 Modelle, davon 34 exklusive Neuheiten, werden Sie begeistern. Für ein romantisches Abendessen, ein neues Wohnambiente, eine Party, das Weihnachtsfest, oder als Geschenk gibt es tolle Lichtobjekte und Lichterketten. Durch die ausführlichen Schritt-für-Schritt Faltanleitungen mit farbigen Diagrammen und dazugehörigen Texten kommen Sie sicher zum Erfolg.

Sprache: Deutsch (schwarzer Text), zusätzlich auch Englisch (blauer Text).

Schwierigkeitsgrad: Anfänger und Fortgeschrittene.

Technik: Papier falten (Origami), Glas mit Teelicht einsetzen, fertig.

ISBN 3-938127-03-1 Preis: 14,90 EUR (D)

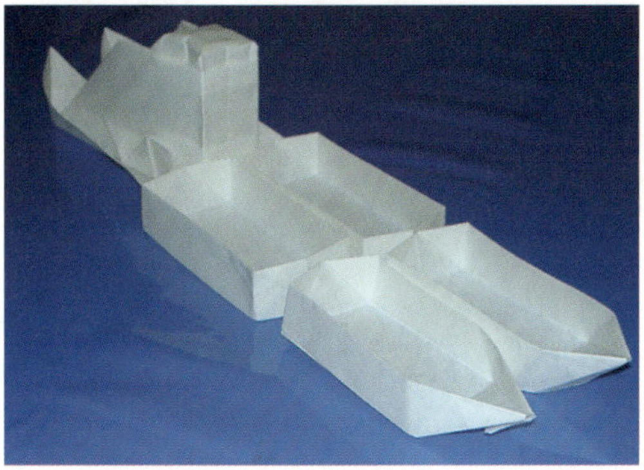

In Planung für 2007:

Ein weiteres Origami Buch mit Schiffen und Booten, siehe Model-Foto links ”Schubverband”.

Internetadressen:

www.paperfrog.de

www.nicepapers.com

www.q-verlag-berlin.de

Impressum + Quellennachweis

Imprint + Proof of Source

Die Deutsche Bibliothek verzeichnet diese Publikation in der Deutschen Nationalbibliografie;
detaillierte bibliografische Daten sind im Internet über http://dnb.ddb.de abrufbar.
Origami Schiffe, Vom Ruderboot zum Flugzeugträger / Jannie van Schuylenburg. – Berlin: Q-Verlag Berlin, 2006

ISBN 3-938127-04-X

ISBN 3-938127-04-X

Autorin: Jannie van Schuylenburg
Diagramme: Jannie van Schuylenburg
Übersetzung: Hannelore Emmerich
Herstellung: Q-Verlag Berlin
Layout: Q-Verlag Berlin
Fotos: www.prokopy.de
Umschlaggestaltung: Yves Roger Weber
Gedruckt in Deutschland

Quellennachweis:

Die Autorin bedankt sich auf diesem Wege bei der Firma nice papers für die Bereitstellung des gut zu faltenden und schwimmfähigen AQUAPAPIER.
Das verwendete AQUAPAPIER, sowie LAMPENPAPIERE, Origamipapiere und Bücher vom Q-Verlag Berlin können im Internet Shop: www.paperfrog.de bestellt werden.